4/24/00

MW00914559

CONSERVATIVE CAPITALISM

Conservative Capitalism

The Social Economy

David Reisman

First published in Great Britain 1999 by
MACMILLAN PRESS LTD
Houndmills, Basingstoke, Hampshire RG21 6XS and London
Companies and representatives throughout the world

A catalogue record for this book is available from the British Library.

ISBN 0–333–77282–2

 First published in the United States of America 1999 by
ST. MARTIN'S PRESS, INC.,
Scholarly and Reference Division,
175 Fifth Avenue, New York, N.Y. 10010

ISBN 0–312–22315–3

Library of Congress Cataloging-in-Publication Data
Reisman, David A.
Conservative capitalism : the social economy / David Reisman.
p.   cm.
Includes bibliographical references and index.
ISBN 0–312–22315–3 (cloth)
1. Capitalism—Moral and ethical aspects.   2. Conservatism.
3. Free enterprise.   4. Social interaction.   I. Title.
HB501.R3958   1999
330.12'2—dc21   99–11254
                                                         CIP

This book is printed on paper suitable for recycling and made from fully managed and sustained forest sources.

10   9   8   7   6   5   4   3   2   1
08   07   06   05   04   03   02   01   00   99

Printed and bound in Great Britain by
Antony Rowe Ltd, Chippenham, Wiltshire

Contents

1 Introduction

Capitalism looks forward: restless, dynamic, innovative, it treats permanent revolution as the norm and sleepy *stasis* as a problem to be solved. Conservatism looks backward: socialised, legitimised, embedded, it relies on established patterns for the specification of the self, on consensual standards for the rules of the game. Conservative capitalism is a mixed economic system which at one and the same time looks forward to the future and backward to the past. The duality is not a contradiction. It is a *sine qua non*. The conservative integument once burst asunder, stakeholders in the capitalist dream would be well advised to liquidate their assets and buy a gun.

The subject of this book is the duality and the mix. Its theme is the breaking of the mould in partnership with the preservation of the mould. Its thesis is the fundamental complementarity of choice and non-choice, refusal and acceptance, achievement and prescription. Its argument is that bygones must forever be cherished and respected in order that bygones may forever be written off as sunk costs. We start from here. We start from there. We start from here *because* we start from there. Opposites pair up. We like it that way: 'Our reasons for wanting things come down in astonishingly large measure to the desire to be like other people, and the desire to be different; we wish to do things because we can, or because we cannot; we crave companionship, of the right kind, but the requirement of privacy, even solitude, is equally imperative; we like the familiar, also the novel, security but likewise adventure.' (Knight, 1922:30). God was taking a real risk when he put his faith in Adam and Eve. History might have been spared its polarisations and its ups and downs if he had opted for the snake instead.

The third part of this Introduction explains what is meant by the two-headed ethos that lends its name to this book. The first and the second parts reconstruct the Ideal Types which have so much potential when they collaborate and combine. Not every feature of each of the Types will be found in the full range of real-world empiricisms. Without, however, some definitional indication of what is most essential to the nature of Capitalism *in abstracto*, of Conservatism *per se*, no consideration of the mixed ideology which is a blend of the two can be expected to advance very far.

1

1.1 CAPITALISM

Capitalism is a network of property-rights. Private individuals hold defined titles of ownership in respect of outputs such as consumables and non-human inputs such as land and capital. Private individuals also hold a property in themselves. In contrast to slavery or feudal serfdom, free labour is emancipated from station, rank or birth such as substitute status for contract and frustrate the non-precommited negotiation of advantage.

The right to own is amplified by the right to acquire and to alienate: whereas pre-capitalist property can be encumbered with constraints such as the conventions of primogeniture and entailing, commerce is a liberating regime which is predicated upon the primacy of the bargained exchange. The market mechanism enables the supply-and-demand price (not physical units, not historic labour embodied, not time-out-of-mind ratios) to serve as the basis for comparison. Its contribution to economic precision owes much to the use of money as a third-party lubricant. A unit of account, money makes possible a quantitative measurement of value-in-exchange which is a world away from the qualitative discrimination proposed by the normative thinker. A store of value, money is the precondition for that inter-temporal speculation in things and claims that is the rational response to an unknowable future. A means of exchange, money enables the transfer of equivalents to proceed more smoothly than could ever be the case in a system of barter transaction. Using money and the market value, an aggregated sum of titles exchanged can then meaningfully be constructed. Guns for the first time in history can be added up with butter to constitute a single index of quintessential heterogeneities.

The hegemony of the market presupposes a respect for persons without which the preferences revealed would enjoy no moral legitimacy. In that sense the capitalist system may be said to be expressing its confidence that the sovereign individual will as much serve as the best judge of his own self-interest when selecting a job or shopping for a consumable as he is believed to be doing when casting his vote or putting Eth above June. The capitalist system relies upon the factored-down to rank alternatives and to make non-random choices. It is by virtue of the trust invested in the isolated and the atomised that the system is able to reduce needs to wants and to take market price as a proxy for subjective welfare. It must be noted, however, that the respect and the sovereignty are the attributes of effective demand alone. The market assigns no legitimate claims to the homeless and the starving who are not in a position to pay. Nor does it question the huge differentials in the claims of the film-star as compared to the factory-worker. Respect for persons means supply and demand. Accepting the procedure, there is an inconsistency in disputing the verdict.

Capitalism treats the autonomous decision-taker not just as self-conscious and self-aware but also as goal-orientated, purposive and economical of scarce resources. The pure capitalist, in other words, is the economic man in the sense of Mill, the one-dimensional being 'who invariably does that by which he may obtain the greatest amount of necessaries, conveniences, and luxuries, with the smallest quantity of labour and physical self-denial with which they can be obtained in the existing state of knowledge' (Mill, 1844:144). It is as a direct consequence of this determined single-mindedness that the norm of instrumental rationality emerges as the means–ends standard in a gain-seeking, loss-avoiding environment which values efficiency and stigmatises waste. Capitalism is inseparable from choice. Importantly, it is also characterised by an orderly, practical, pragmatic, problem-solving approach to the evaluation of costs and benefits. The poet can build his self-image around spontaneous reaction and the impulse of the moment. The economic man or woman lives in a harsher climate. The consumer who wants maximum utility for money, the producer who wants maximum exploitation of opportunities to earn, simply cannot afford to neglect empirical evidence, to fall victim to sentiment, to relapse into other-worldly resignation. Particularly where competition is intense in the market, the consumer or producer who revolts against reason is especially at risk of returning home empty-handed. That is why an equilibrium will have the logic of an optimum as well.

Capitalism, however, is considerably more than the comparative-statics spot. The capitalist firm is orientated towards the impersonal goal of profit; and the profit-seeking imperative necessitates a *continuous* quest. The market competitor is aware that even higher rewards can be the prize for entrepreneurial alertness, targeted search, deferred gratification – and that the bankruptcy courts lie in wait for the captain of industry whose disciplined self-denial, imaginative initiative, intelligent inventiveness have failed to match the dividends of a rival. Capitalism, in short, is a profit *and loss* system, concerned not with the simple replication of an established way of life but with the constant change in products, processes and modes of organisation that is the *sine qua non* for going forward as a hedge against being left behind. Frugality and prudence mean savings for reinvestment. Accumulation of capital and rising productivity mean economic growth. Labour paid the subsistence wage in the Marxian tradition generates the surplus value that is ploughed back to produce the expansion in supply. Consumer acquisitiveness in all *including* the Marxian tradition validates that limitless increase by means of the concomitant expansion in demand without which the rise in affluence would soon level off into stagnation. Consumer demand is the precondition for sustainable growth. It is also the reason why a material improvement will so often be regarded as a moral victory. Christians eulogise the Bible, and the Renaissance found a Golden Age in Greece and Rome. Capitalism encourages people to look forward and not backward for the progress which it takes to be the continuous rise in the standard of living.

Capitalism is property: the contract having set out the rights and duties, no further obligations are expected or required. Capitalism is the market: price signals communicate information, flexible incentives are a stimulus to mobility, decisions are invisibly reconciled without recourse to a monolithic plan. Capitalism is the individual: sometimes a gambling risk-lover, sometimes a cautious consolidationist, the fragmented unit in the decentralised system is assigned the responsibility for paying the piper and choosing the tune. Capitalism is rationality: factual evidence and problem-solving accounts fulfil a systemic function that is too important to be left to the next-best technologies of traditional acceptance, trust in fate, religious invocation or the antinomian random act. Capitalism is expansion: businesses strive to increase their profits, consumers expect an uninterrupted rise in the satisfaction of appetite, and public opinion in general is positive indeed towards the ongoing growth in the nation's wealth. Property, the market, the individual, rationality, expansion – these five characteristics delimit what capitalism in essence *is*.

A single image must always be at risk from the variance in space and time. Different cultures produce their own unique strains within the *genus*: thus labour is less price-responsive in a society which channels ambition through the internal labour-market than it is in a nation that welcomes sequential disloyalties as an indicator of good performance, while individualism is *de facto* householdism or even extended-familism in most of Asia and much of the West as well. The same culture throws up different strains at different times in its historical development: the aggressive egoism of devil-take-the-hindmost competitiveness may, for example, soften into a less frenzied, less ruthless approach to profit-seeking once economies of scale have made salaried managers and not owner-enterprisers the ultimate decision-makers in the giant corporation. Cultures differ. Cultures change. In terms of its five core characteristics, however, capitalism *qua* capitalism is a dictionary quasi-constant, recognisably the same.

It is tempting to conflate capitalism with modernisation – to argue that there is an inevitable progression from traditionalism into capitalism; to treat as the adoption of the capitalist system the transition from peasant agriculture into sophisticated manufacturing. The temptation must be resisted. Industrial and technological upgrading are, admittedly, frequently situated within the capitalist parameters. Even so, it must not be assumed that growth is synonymous with capitalism, or that capitalism is to be held responsible for much that is the direct consequence of modernisation itself.

The subdivision of labour may be a cause of alienation and depersonalisation, of self-realisation stunted at work and labour routinised to the rhythm of the machine. Yet the same specialisation would be a functional imperative even in a socialist society industrialising with a plan. Impersonality, anonymity, loneliness, distance, separation may be the by-products of monetisation, urbanisation, pluralism, upheaval, bureaucracy. Yet the same expulsion from community could occur in any economic order that ranked the throughput of concentrated production above the solidarity of village-based interaction. Capitalism is often intertwined with modernisation; and perhaps the two together are jointly responsible for the best and the worst of the take-off into the industrial and the service mode. Intertwined though they often are, still the two constructs are distinct. Capitalism is incompatible with the pre-modern. Modernisation, however, is possible even without the five core characteristics that signpost the capitalist way.

Modernisation is possible even without the coordination of the capitalist choice. What is not possible is the adoption of the capitalist system without at the same time guaranteeing it the full protection of the rule of law. The minimal State, the *laissez-faire* response, may or may not be implicit in the factoring down, the flexible exchanging, the subjective calculus that distinguishes economic decentralisation from leaderly direction. What is clear is that the reliable enforcement of contract is not only explicit but also a precondition on which there can be no compromise – and that the State itself must be bound by a constitution strong enough to protect the wealth of nations from the self-interested particularism of the politicians and the civil servants. Modernisation may or may not mean the constable and little intervention else. What it must mean is the impartiality of the arbiter without which the *quid pro quo* would all too easily slip into the conflict and the chaos of the Hobbesian *bellum*.

1.2 CONSERVATISM

Conservatives wish to conserve. Attached to the *status quo* because it satisfies their needs, resistant to change because 'a known good is not lightly to be surrendered for an unknown better', they are strongly disposed 'to use and to enjoy what is available rather than to wish for or to look for something else': 'To be conservative, then, is to prefer the familiar to the unknown, to prefer the tried to the untried, fact to mystery, the actual to the possible, the limited to the unbounded, the near to the distant, the sufficient to the superabundant, the convenient to the perfect, present laughter to utopian bliss.' (Oakeshott, 1962: 168–9, 172). The conservative, Oakeshott says, delights in the present rather than in the dream of what might be gained; values continuity precisely because existing institutions are something around which a firm identity has been built; fears innovation unless and until the anticipated improvement in the opportunity-set is enough to compensate for the certain loss of the recognisable, the expected, the cared-for, the esteemed, the loved. Both by virtue of contentment and of anxiety, it is clear, the conservative in the sense of Oakeshott will seldom have the temperament appropriate to the gambler, the risk-lover, the adventurer – or the efficiency-chasing capitalist entrepreneur: 'All activities, then, where what is sought is enjoyment springing, not from the success of the enterprise but from the familiarity of the engagement, are emblems of the disposition to be conservative.' (Oakeshott, 1962: 178).

Conservatives wish to conserve. Their ideal is the end-in-itself, their nightmare the uncharted course. Translated into the language of economic sociology, their world-view recalls the contention of Karl Polanyi that economic activity is by nature a part of the *Gestalt*, that market automaticity is always and everywhere a threat to the social fabric: 'The more comprehensive the market system became, the more it revealed its incapacity to satisfy the requirements of a stable society.' (Polanyi, 1977:1). Conservatives would therefore advise that capitalists should study carefully the case for the customary lest an ill-conceived libertarianism revolutionise the society and the economy alike into a dystopia that was no part of the free marketeer's design.

Conservatism begins with shared conventions and builds on common experience. Its unit of analysis is not the individual but the collectivity, its discourse that of macro-sociology and not of micro-economics. In place of liberty and independence, the conservative speaks of integration and belonging. In place of privacy and inclination, the conservative speaks of conformity and role. Conservatism is about community – geographical like the locality, occupational like the professional association or guild, encompassing like the nation or race or people, subjective most of all in the sense of a family or a tribe that affirms its self-definition by means of banding together. Conservatism is about membership, loyalty, allegiance, situation. It is not about hedonism, transferability, utility or the isolated atom's insatiable quest for maximum pleasure. Restore the bonds, the conservative will say, and the consumer will not need to compensate with commodities for the emptiness within.

Conservatism is a world-view that takes the whole and not the part, the organism and not the cell, as the irreducible entity in its sociological economics. Yet there is more: not only does the conservative appeal to the 'We' when the capitalist assigns pride of place to the 'I', the conservative also feels obliged to take the advice of past participants and not just of present-day players. After all, as John Gray observes, it is precisely the time-dominated 'traditions that we inherit from our forebears' that, neither fetters on our self-realisation nor shackles on our self-development, are in truth the 'necessary conditions of having selves to express': 'We are not like the butterfly, whose generations are unknown to each other; we are a familial and historical species, for whom the past must have authority (that of memory) if we are to have identity, and whose lives are in part self-created narratives, woven from the received text of the common life.' (Gray, 1993:125, 136). The truth is the whole. The whole includes the past. The conservative takes the view that the institutional order can only be understood as a frozen still taken from a still-moving picture. Believing that human society cannot easily be engineered into the manipulator's favourite image, the conservative therefore enlists the assistance of custom, routine, prejudice, precedent and habit in order to ensure that the embodied wisdom of the folk-memory will pass on to the team-members yet to come the inter-generational gift of a continuing culture.

The traditions handed on will have stood the test of time. Simple survival in that sense gives rise to the inference that they must be fulfilling some social function, however dimly glimpsed, in order to have resisted the potential tribulations of competitive trial and error. Unknowledge being the ultimate barrier to calculation, the reliance upon the evolution of social facts through the iterations of repeated encounters may actually be said to constitute the most rational procedure in an imperfect world where even the scientists are lacking in overview and comprehension. Acceptance in such circumstances can evidently be more expedient than design. To a conservative, however, it will be the acceptance *per se* and not the practical pay-off that will command the stronger attachment. Socialisation circumscribes the freedom of each citizen with a non-individual standard of comparison and evaluation. Broadly contented with the matrix, and unaccustomed in any case to any other, the social agent as the conservative sees him will come to think of social repression as cherished prescription which it is the non-rational, non-conscious response of each to replicate and to reproduce. Conservatism is the realm of emotive commitment and of self-disciplining duty. It is not the realm of the shopkeeper's *quid pro quo* that substitutes sprouts for spinach along a disembodied curve that is driven by greed to become indifferent to the common code.

The conservative assigns particular value to the shared, the continuing and the accepted. Conservatism is thus a philosophy of overlap, fidelity and obligation, not of novelty, variety and the right to be left alone. The emphasis on the patterned way of life extends to the social structure as well. Conservatives (whose uncompromising absolute can be as immutable as kith and kin) tend to be suspicious of social mobility where it disturbs the stable web of relationship. Resistant to over-rapid change brought on by an immature impatience for gratification and advancement, conservatives look to seasoned leadership to defend the unique collective core against the recklessness of the impetuous. Conservatives are strongly in favour of authority and hierarchy. They are deeply concerned about unanchored meritocrats without an apprenticeship in the going concern, without a training in its rituals and ceremonies – and without an established base in the existing social structure that might hold experimenters back from going too far.

Conservatives embed the market in the whole. Their vision of political involvement is no less a strand in a skein. One consequence of their methodological synthesis is a pragmatic openness in their political economy. Libertarians are led by their methodological reductionism to express a bias in favour of nightwatchman-like restraint. Conservatives, sympathetic to subordination and subjection as they are, recognise the nation-building potential of the State even as they share with the libertarians the fear that Leviathan will crush the civil society into an amorphous mass.

Conservatives clearly have mixed feelings about concentrated State control. On the one hand the totalitarian State might do no more than reinforce the organic articulation of the totality's culture. Thus the government might insist on the unity of the nation State with its monopoly Church; it might resist the emancipation of women from their domestic role in the citizen-making of children; it might restrict the importation of newspapers that sow discontent while subsidising broadcasters who diffuse mainstream opinions. On the other hand, however, the powerful State might take for its own a reforming function every bit as disruptive as the mad dogs of *laissez-faire*. This might be the case where inheritance tax is deployed to break the historic link with the family property of the past; where school prayers and national service give way to liberalised abortion and divorce on demand; where the relaxation of border controls leads to an influx of other-acculturated immigrants with no intention of converting to the host-country's customs. Attracted by the power to reinforce but repelled by the power to destroy, conservatives clearly have mixed feelings about the licence to print dominance that is granted to the State.

Some conservatives will take the risk and sign away their discretion to the guide. Other conservatives, less confident and less optimistic, will opt instead for damage-limitation and cautious minimax. Nervous conservatives often call for the checks and balances of the separation of executive, legislative and judiciary; for the bicameral legislature and the electoral college; for the 75 per cent majority and the 30-plus voting age; for the constitutional clause that prescribes the money supply and proscribes the budget deficit. Nervous conservatives often welcome the devolution of power (to the region and the locality) and its pluralisation (the polity sharing its authority with the unions, the churches, the professional bodies and the other intermediate associations of the corporate society). Confident conservatives, needless to say, will be less concerned about what might go wrong should the State become a destroying Leviathan and not a conserving Leviathan, embedded and embedding.

1.3 CONSERVATIVE CAPITALISM

Capitalism is property, the market, the individual, rationality, expansion. Conservatism is the shared, the continuing, the accepted, social structure and political embeddedness. In many respects the two orientations are different. In some respects the two perspectives are incompatible. And they are frequently found in combination. Efficient or inefficient, loved or hated, the truth is that the mix of conservatism with capitalism is not a philosophical conceit but a simple fact of social life. That simple fact of social life is the subject of this book.

Chapter 2 on 'Choice' and Chapter 3 on 'Inductive Conservatism' document the extent to which the past, epistemologically speaking, supplies a frame of reference and an intellectual map. Able admittedly to distort or mislead where the orientation provided has been outdated by events, still it is the great attraction of the non-ego cosmology that it situates phenomena in a context. Isolated observations have little meaning without a schema that makes sense of the world. The lenses of the inherited outlook are preexistent structures that facilitate the selection of data and the solution of the puzzle. The past in that way shapes the future through the focusing of search.

Deserted without a compass in a universe of unexplained observations, the homeless mind falls victim to anxiety, confusion and an instinctual fear of the unknown. Rational choice is one instrument at the disposal of the insecure and the unrelated when they seek to blaze their trail through the newness of the uncontrolled and the unfamiliar. The custom, the routine, is another. The heuristic or learned response inhibits the wide-ranging scan that at its worst could lead to despair, at its best to *ab initio* discovery. Conservatism, epistemologically speaking, offers the option of a tried-and-tested rule with a reasonable track-record. The choice seems somehow pipe-and-slippers when compared to the open flood-gates, the unbounded maximisation, of the fresh in-period adaptation. The human mind, however, is what it is; and familiarity too can pay rich dividends in utility.

The human mind, Schlicht observes, has an emotive attachment to existing endowments and established benchmarks which impose upon each new departure the reference-points and the ratchets of the comfortable and the confirmed. Any revision in that sense must always involve a cost, expressed as the loss in 'the utility of maintaining the *status quo* as such. Moving from a bad alternative to a good one involves the "objective" gain minus the costs from departing from the *status quo*. Moving from a good to a bad alternative involves the "objective" loss plus the loss of departing from the *status quo*'. (Schlicht, 1998:114). Habituated to focal points, defensive of reassuring regularities, dependent on ('other-directed' by) the validating reinforcement of others' approval, the respectful student of 'the ancestor within and the friend without' (Riesman, 1954:23), ashamed to admit to (and write off) an embodied error of judgement, the sheer conservatism of the psychological inclination constitutes a real problem for the capitalist economy which powers its market flexibility with the *what ought to be* of instrumental rationality. Perhaps it does – but we start from here, and from there, and not from where we ought to be.

Chapters 4 on 'Economy and Society', 5 on 'Convention', 6 on 'Evolution and Economy', 7 on 'Individual and Interest', emphasise the embeddedness of the wealth of nations in a shared social home that is at once a beehive of present-day relationships and a repeated acting-out of an old, respected script. Röpke, a strong advocate of the *social* market economy who watched the Nazis' perversion of rootedness from the safe haven of Geneva, has this to say about the inter-personal structures with which market-priced exchange enjoys the close links of organic symbiosis that are only to be expected from the fact that the social and the economic actors are not different faces in the mirror but rather the same ones: 'It was indeed the cardinal fault of the old liberal capitalistic thought to regard the market economy as a *self dependent* process whirring away automatically. It was overlooked that the Market represents but one narrow sphere of social life, a sphere which is surrounded and kept going by a more comprehensive one; a wider field in which mankind are not merely competitors, producers, men of business, members of unions, shareholders, savers and investors, but are simply human beings who do not live on bread alone, men as members of their family, as neighbours, as members of their churches, as colleagues, as citizens of the community, men as creatures of life and blood with their sentiments, passions and ideals.' (Röpke, 1944:31–2). The economy is life and blood, Röpke is saying. It can never be sprouts and spinach, abstracted from human life and traded in the frictionless fiction of an asocial vacuum.

The economy is people – not desert-island autarkists whose capital is own time and energy, not self-contained negotiators who meet only sporadically for the maximisation of mutual benefits but socialised individuals who internalise received conventions and reproduce existing standards. The rules coordinate interaction; they contribute salience to expectations; they resolve conflicts of interest which might otherwise make human strivings red in tooth and claw. Social shaping ensures that the members of the group (fearful both of ostracism and of a spoiled self-image) will take other players into account even when their personal acquisitiveness is in that way narrowed by the commonalities that were the effect and cause of consensus when their trainers were being taught. Normative order is clearly a significant consequence of the limitation of choice. Even the methodological individualist who collects up revealed preferences may be said to be identifying the pre-programmed tokens of the bandwagon culture and not just the self-originated wants of the Adam who is thirsty, the Eve who needs food. Yet there is a further consequence of the shaping and the overlap; and it has to do with the perceived value of the membership *per se*. Polanyi took the community to be the basis of brotherhood and belonging, cohesion and solidarity, without which there could at best be a flat, fragmented and impoverished *I*. Polanyi attributed to society *sui generis* a liberating force which seems in the limit to take on a quasi-mystical significance: 'The discovery of the person *is* the discovery that society is the relationship of persons. ... The discovery of the individual soul *is* the discovery of community.... Personality is not real outside community.' (Polanyi, 1935:370). *I* am *I* because *We* are *We*. There is no way in the circumstances that my capitalism, that *our* capitalism, can be anything other than conservative.

The whole is supra-individual, the standards handed on. In that sense the capitalist economy would seem to have the character of a residual claimant, the unintended outcome of social institutions which constrain maximisation while themselves lacking a maximising character. The inference is a capitalism of non-endeavour and non-rationality; and thus a past-photographing present which is clearly at variance with the kaleidoscope of reality. An active element, custom undoubtedly channels the economy and protects an incentive-structure which need not be that of the free and competitive market. Yet custom is also passive, the malleable product of an on-going evolution which has a momentum of its own. In that evolution the capitalist economy will itself have a significant causal contribution to make. As Marshall writes (his deterministic tendencies recalling the basis/superstructure nexus in the work of social economists like Smith and Marx): 'Even in such a country as India no custom retains its hold long after the relative positions of the motives of demand and supply have so changed that the values, which would bring them into stable equilibrium, are far removed from those which the custom sanctions.' (Marshall, 1885:170). If Marshall was right about reciprocal causality, and especially about the capitalist contribution, then today's conservatism might not be incompatible with capitalist economics so much as the lagged – but functional – result of yesterday's profit-seeking materialism.

Chapter 8, 'The Ethical Constraint' and Chapter 9, 'Structure as Capital', take up the inter-related issues of attitudinal capital and social capital. They do so in the light of Röpke's diagnosis that norms and networks are not just components of but the precondition for any viable capitalist process: 'Market economy requires a firm framework which to be brief we will call the anthropo-sociological. If this frame were to break then market economy would cease to be possible.' (Röpke, 1944:32). *Would cease to be possible* – Röpke's assessment that freedom is a chimera in the absence of its opposite recalls the contention of Edmund Burke that tradition is a complement to the Age of Reason and not its intellectual antithesis. Edmund Burke, blaming the 'sophisters, oeconomists, and calculators' for the 1776 that had unchained the 1789, warned that liberty become all-permissive must by its uncontrollable licence dissolve the bounded society into 'an unsocial, uncivil, unconnected chaos of elementary principles' (Burke, 1790:170, 175) that no responsible emancipator could ever regard as good: 'Society cannot exist unless a controlling power upon will and appetite be placed somewhere. . . . Men are qualified for civil liberty in exact proportion to their disposition to put moral chains upon their own appetites.' (Burke, 1791:389). *In exact proportion* – Burke's insistence on a social contract of order and virtue recalls the later fears of the post-Leninist liberals, unconvinced that the casino capitalism of post-1989 Russia was the Pareto Optimum they had heard about late at night on the Voice of America. Perhaps the inter-personal obligation, the inter-generational partnership, of Chapters 8 and 9 constitutes the conservative response that, Röpke-like, Burke-like, can make their unembedded market economy into a more cordial, more cooperative public good.

Ethics and *ought-to-bes* are always a support to the market economy – if only because, as John Gray points out, 'like other variations on the Enlightenment project, liberal theory runs aground on the impossibility of formulating a rational morality' (Gray, 1995:ix). At its most basic, it is the expressive symbolism of the shared value-system that makes legitimate the social facts of contract, choice, competition, merit, expediency without which self-interested gain-seeking would be inseparable from exclusion and guilt. In so far as it approves of entrepreneurship and experimentation, in so far as it stigmatises the timidity of the conditioned reflex and the wastefulness of inertia, the common culture may be said to be not the antagonist of market individualism but rather the launch-pad for risk-led change. The *ought-to-be* of self-indulgence can be an input in the capitalistic production-function. So can the ought-to-be of self-denial. The norm of altruism leads to a stream of stranger-services like aid to the mugger's victim which in the absence of the gift-relationship would not have been supplied at all. The norm of truth-telling improves the efficiency of non-local trade, of verbal undertakings, of deferred payment. In ways such as these, inherited standards hallowed into generalised expectations may be said to correct a market failure by means of a conservatism that is entirely at home with the capitalism that moves on.

As with the consensual *ought-to-bes*, so with the face-to-face interactions. Social networks situate the buyers and the sellers and rescue them from the short-termism of anonymity. The family, the locality, the long-standing customer, the customer's customer – stable contacts such as these provide collective support for moral values such as personal loyalty and the keeping of promises. Encouraging as they do the re-adoption of familiar channels, they also reduce the transaction-costs of doing business. Reputation becomes a commercial asset. Acquaintances facilitate job-search. Trust is built up over time. Debts of honour are not disregarded. Other people, in other words, become a capital investment with a rate of return. The perfect competitor is powerless, faceless and unattached. The social capitalist is identified, embedded, and historical. And conservative.

2 Choice

The norm is instrumental rationality: 'It is one of the fundamental characteristics of an individualistic capitalistic economy that it is rationalized on the basis of rigorous calculation, directed with foresight and caution toward the economic success which is sought.' (Weber, 1904–5:76). Decision-makers living out the imperatives of a non-capitalist ethos will see no incongruity and incur no penalties when they act 'in terms of affectual orientation, especially emotional'; or where their choice is 'traditionally oriented, through the habituation of long practice'; or where their action, *wertrational*, is the emanation of 'a conscious belief in the absolute value of some ethical, aesthetic, religious, or other form of behaviour, entirely for its own sake and independently of any prospects of external success' (Weber, 1947:115). Actors living in the individualistic capitalistic economy will have to judge themselves by the strict standard of the cost-effective pay-off.

The capitalist way, Max Weber posited, was the *zweckrational* way, concerned as the purposeful economiser must inevitably be with the attainment of 'discrete individual ends', with 'expectations as to the behaviour of objects in the external situation and of other human individuals', with 'making use of these expectations as "conditions" or "means" for the successful attainment of the actor's own rationally chosen ends' (Weber, 1947:115). Romeo and Juliet act on the basis of impulse and love. The Chinese perpetuate the patriarchal institutions of the convention-bound mandarinate. The Hindus devote themselves to absolute values without regard to outcome or advancement. The capitalist *qua* capitalist employs the norm of instrumental rationality. No other selective standard will suit his needs as well.

The subject of this chapter is the making of the choice. Section 2.1, 'Instrumental Rationality', says what it means to suit the inputs to the outcomes with the aid of the optimising analytic. Its theme is a variation on a *homo economicus* of Becker: the rational man is one who 'would read in bed at night only if the value of reading exceeded the value (to him) of the loss in sleep suffered by his wife' (Becker, 1976:268). Section 2.2, 'Ignorance and Uncertainty', casts doubt upon the predictive power of means–ends efficacy. Its text is taken from Shackle, unafraid to own up to his own unknowledge: 'In economic theory, conduct is a rational coping with circumstances; in real life it is a leaf blown in the wind.' (Shackle, 1967:215). Section 2.3, 'Cognition', demonstrates that the mind can let the thinker down and that perception might not be all that it seems. The clergyman Wicksteed was only one utilitarian among many to accept that the computer within could have a will of its own: 'A great part of our conduct is impulsive and a great part unreflecting; and when we reflect our choice is often irrational.' (Wicksteed, 1910:28).

Anxious about evidence and confused about psychology, the reader may be excused if he seeks solace in conservative capitalism. The reassurance that he seeks will have much in common with Hayek on the economic benefits conferred by the invisible hand: 'All of this is possible because we stand in a great framework of institutions and traditions – economic, legal, and moral – into which we fit ourselves by obeying certain rules of conduct that we never made, and which we have never understood.' (Hayek, 1988:14). We never made them. We have never understood them. Thus does the past provide a context for the future and repression make possible the problem-solving of choice.

2.1   INSTRUMENTAL RATIONALITY

Economists whose study is market enterprise are in no doubt about the norm: 'An economist by training thinks of himself as the guardian of rationality, the ascriber of rationality to others, and the prescriber of rationality to the social world.' (Arrow, 1974:16). On the one hand there is the intuitive, the inert, the momentary, the qualitative, the spontaneous, the sluggish, the erratic whim, the flash of insight. On the other hand there is the economist by training, convinced that the social actor can reasonably be modelled as a careful quantifier of means and ends. Economists whose study is market enterprise have confidence in the value of a theory built around self-conscious reflexion and a prudent, deliberative approach to life. Some would even say that their vision of man as a computing agent sensitised to probable outcomes is nothing less than a fundamental truth of universal relevance: 'Human action is necessarily always rational. ... The ultimate end of action is always the satisfaction of some desires of the acting man.' (Mises, 1949:19).

Mises made much of the ubiquity of thought: 'Choosing determines all human decisions.' (Mises, 1949:3). The very ranking of survival above suicide is evidence of a felt desire and an act of mind: 'To live is for man the outcome of a choice, of a judgement of value.' (Mises, 1949:20). The outcome of a choice – and of a *rational* choice at that: 'Acting man chooses, determines, and tries to reach an end. Of two things both of which he cannot have together he selects one and gives up the other.' (Mises, 1949:12). The scarcity of time, of energy, of other resources imposes a material constraint which then focuses the mind on choice. Man is free to choose laziness instead of productiveness, hit-and-miss instead of efficiency. What he cannot do is to choose *not* to choose. Even the choice of inertia, Mises would say, is the decision to buy lethargy at the margin, to pay for it the opportunity cost of the next-best forgone. Mises believed that it was in man's nature to become involved in 'conscious adjustment to the state of the universe that determines his life': 'What distinguishes man from beasts is precisely that he adjusts his behavior deliberatively.' (Mises, 1949:11, 17). Mises made much of goal-orientated choice: 'Human action is purposeful behavior.' (Mises, 1949:11). It was because he saw human action as purposeful action that Mises was able to deduce from his *a priori* the conclusion that 'modern subjectivist economics' had 'converted the theory of market prices into a general theory of human choice' (Mises, 1949:3). The core of economic action was not the striving for material wealth but rather choice, choosing and the survival-standard of instrumental rationality. The core of social action was precisely the same.

The logic is the post-Benthamite emphasis upon the maximisation of pleasures (the benefits), the minimisation of pains (the costs). Initially, the rational actor will seek to rank the ends selected and to define the cardinal distance that separates the alternative options. The rational actor will then attempt to isolate the least-cost means, combining them in a non-random manner in order to minimise the sacrifice and maximise the return. The rational actor will plan and programme, monitor and scan, in an attempt to make the best-feasible use of limited possibilities. Secondary consequences will be evaluated, future choices will be weighed alongside present-day opportunities, and a determined effort will be made to collect all relevant facts that are needed for a full assessment. Choices made, the preferences revealed may be expected to manifest the properties of transitivity and consistency that confirm *ex post* the robustness of the patterns intended.

The urgency of the end can never be established using an economiser's model: always a reflection of absolute values, emotion or tradition, the one thing the goal can never be is *zweckrational*. The choice of the means, conceptually speaking, is more open. The choice of the means, conceptually speaking, can fall into any one of the four Weberian categories – the economiser's shortest distance between two points, certainly, but also the influence of unconditional values (the taboo, the religious calling), emotive affiliations (service to charismatic authority, blood ties that breed preferment), traditional structures (the custom, the social obligation). The same choice (as in the case of the Puritan absolute values that lent their support to the *zweckrational* and the mechanistic) can even be justified with reference to more than a single selective standard: 'It would be very unusual to find concrete cases of action, especially of social action, which were oriented *only* in one or another of these ways.' (Weber, 1947:117). That said, capitalism is not an intellectual game but rather an economic system with its own momentum and imperatives. The pure-vacuum abstractions of the hypothetical ideal type rapidly give way to the binding *ought-to-be* of instrumental rationality when challenged in the real world by market competition and self-seeking gain. Businesses that value profits, households that value consumables, have only limited freedom to love their Samaritan as themselves or to follow a gerontocrat who stubbornly computes with no more than an abacus. The choice of the means, conceptually speaking, is an open one. Given capitalism, however, the choice has a tendency to focus on a norm so persuasive as to acquire the attributes of a description and a prescription. Money-making is symbiotically linked to instrumental rationality. The system breeds the norm that it requires most.

Instrumental rationality is the core economising orientation both of market capitalism and of textbook economics. Gary Becker has gone so far as to make the maximising mindset the centrepiece of non-market social theory as well: 'The economic approach provides a valuable unified framework for understanding *all* human behavior.' (Becker, 1976:14). Like Mises, Becker believes the cost-benefit nexus to have a comprehensive explanatory value in respect of a wide range of social phenomena not normally associated with prices and shadow-prices payable at the margin.

Consider the case of crime: 'The approach taken here follows the economists' usual analysis of choice and assumes that a person commits an offence if the expected utility to him exceeds the utility he could get by using his time and other resources at other activities. Some people become "criminals", therefore, not because their basic motivation differs from that of other persons, but because their benefits and costs differ.' (Becker, 1976:46). Obedience to the law is not taken for granted and not made a civic duty. Instead, it is treated as an economic tradeable like any other. From the point of view of the criminal the task is to weigh the prize against the price: he takes into account the expected win but also the probability of detection, the severity of the punishment, the subjective disutility of a fine or a prison sentence, the subjective trade-off between risk and gain. From the point of view of society as a whole, the choice involves the specification of the optimal quantity of crimes committed: the community must determine the proper balance between apprehended offenders on the one hand, resources sunk in policemen, courts, prisons, fingerprinting, wiretapping on the other. To increase the charge to the consumer of crime is to diminish the supply of broken laws demanded. To put up the price to the criminal is, however, to put up the cost to the nation. The criminal calculates the pay-off. The nation calculates the spend. In that way does the equilibrium number of manslaughters and break-ins emerge.

The market for marriage-partners provides a second illustration of the entrepreneurial mindset: 'According to the economic approach, a person decides to marry when the utility expected from marriage exceeds that expected from remaining single or from additional search for a more suitable mate.' (Becker, 1976:10). One choice involves the *whether*: here the consumer will compare the costs (search for a mate, legal fees incurred, the wedding overheads) with the benefits (most distinctively children since cooking, cleaning, sex and companionship can be bought in without a stable union) and will then opt for the higher-ranked alternative. A separable choice involves the *whom*: competing products will be sorted by characteristics (wealth, intelligence, education, ethnicity, height, religion, attractiveness, age), the consumer (and/or his parents) will enter the market with preferences and utility-functions, and the shopper will extend his sampling and scan up to the economic cut-off when 'the value to him of any expected improvement in the mate he can find is no greater than the cost of his time and other inputs into additional search' (Becker, 1976:243). Optimality in the sense of Pareto will be said to have been established when no person can feel better off in his own estimation either by shifting to a different candidate or by committing to the single state.

A third illustration of the rational choice mindset is the size of the family. Children are consumer durables producing a multi-period stream of psychic (and, especially in less-developed economies, pecuniary) income for their parents. It is Becker's contention that, the lower the price per child, the greater the number of children that will be demanded and supplied. Contraception endogenises fertility: voluntarism then takes over from biology, making quantity and spacing into variables to be decided. The elasticity of the asset further reinforces the freedom to choose: 'There are no good substitutes for children, but there may be many poor ones.' (Becker, 1976:177). The evidence from the United States suggests to Becker that the facts do indeed lend support to his welfare-maximising calculus. Legislation restricts child labour. School-years have multiplied. Private education has come into fashion. The cost per child, in other words, has gone up. The size of the family, simultaneously, has gone down. The inverse relationship suggests to Becker that a prediction derived through the assumption of rational choice can even in non-market social situations be an accurate one.

Becker believes that economics, distinguished from the other social sciences less by its subject-matter than by its analytical approach, possesses in rational choice an instrumental orientation of considerable generality: 'I contend that the economic approach is uniquely powerful because it can integrate a wide range of human behavior.' (Becker, 1976:8). Competitors suffer psychic costs if they give employment to blacks but make financial losses if racial discrimination deprives them of the most productive inputs. Smokers sacrifice life-years to slow suicide but gain in utility where the extra satisfaction is worth more to them than the potential healthiness given freely in exchange. Citizens, in Anthony Downs's economic theory of democracy, spend votes in order to purchase policies: 'Each citizen casts his vote for the party he believes will provide him with more benefits than any other.' (Downs, 1957:36). Students, in James Coleman's economic theory of assessments, spend conscientiousness in order to purchase recognition: 'At equilibrium, control of students' time and effort and of grades is observed as the time and effort that students have given up to the teacher and the grades that students have received from the teacher.' (Coleman, 1990: 136). Exchange is all around, the budget-restraint a fact of life – Lionel Robbins found all of this 'so much the stuff of our everyday experience' that it had 'only to be stated to be recognized as obvious' (Robbins, 1933: 79). Confident that people will not willingly squander those limited endowments that they do possess, Becker is able to put his faith in the explanatory power of rational choice.

Becker unifies the theory of action. Max Weber posits a spectrum consisting of four selective standards – the instrumental, the value-driven, the affectual, the traditional. Becker compresses the four into the orientation of the one. Occam's razor simplifies the analysis. Economic imperialism, however, fails to capture the complexities.

Thus, in respect of *value-driven action*, Becker puts right and wrong on the same footing as tastes and preferences. Honesty is not a moral duty with a Kantian imperative but the purchase of a clear conscience, the sale of an exploitable opportunity. Theft is not an absolute infraction of a social norm but a lightning calculator's estimation of a cost–benefit nexus. Becker is not commenting on the moral status of duties, the social cement of norms. What he is saying is that these pressures may usefully be interpreted as simple utility-counters in the homogenising framework of the maximising trade-off. Others deny, however, that the binding can ever be made commensurate with the marginal; or that constants can be called constant if they can be made subject to compromise. Pointing to a qualitative distinction, a difference in kind, value-driven thinkers insist that there is a crucial break between actions that are evaluated by outcomes and successes that are defined by intent: 'Deontology uses as the criterion for judging the morality of an act, not the ends it aspires to achieve, nor the consequences, but the moral duty it discharges or disregards.' (Etzioni, 1988:13). The utilitarian looks to the means–end posture and the intellectualism of adjustment. The deontologist eulogises conformity to a non-ego principle or obligation. The two orientations are alternatives, different windows on the world. They are not the same.

Again, the case of action in response to *affects*, Becker would treat emotive attributes as characteristics of the output-bundle that the maximiser will at the margin demand: 'Love and other emotional attachments, such as sexual activity or frequent close contact with a particular person, can be considered particular nonmarketable household commodities, and nothing much need be added to the analysis.' (Becker, 1976:233). It is clear that emotive attributes *can* be approximated to economic tradeables: this happens, say, where A loves B but chooses C because of non-emotive properties that in A's eyes make C the better buy. What is less clear is whether the generality of decision-makers actually situate the generality of their impulses in the specific, delimited context of the comparative and the substitutable. A brother donates a kidney to save a sibling's life. The Good Samaritan empathises spontaneously with the absolutely deprived. The battered commit murder out of hatred and obsession. The compulsive over-eat out of self-loathing and addiction. It is simple enough to calculate the marginal cost of the doctor's professional pride or the craftsman's delight in beauty and finish. The crucial point is that the doctor or the craftsman will not necessarily have made their choices in – or *as if* in – the non-instinctual, non-intuitive, non-sentimental manner so scrupulously being reconstructed.

More than that, people will often find morally repugnant the very suggestion that the passions ought to be pared down to their logical core. Sophistry can make partner-selection no more than a market transaction, the wife a private prostitute depreciating to scrap at 8.5 per cent. Yet people will often find morally abhorrent the very idea that the acquisition of a spouse could be modelled with an apparatus better suited to the purchase of a car. Just as sacred experiences have a feel that is different from the profane, so, arguably, might the non-rational be perceived as something other than simple goal-attainment, hidden and misinterpreted: 'Clearly, a mature social science will have to accommodate both intellect and affect' (Simon, 1957:200).

Action, finally, is susceptible to mass production through the time-honoured mould of *tradition*. Tradition-stamped action is action intended to perpetuate the agreed and the acceptable. It is by definition *not* adventure-seeking action such as could so easily upset the conventional way of life. The rules being the identity, it is merely playing with words to suggest, as Becker would, that the social actor rationally contemplates the exchange of procedure for outcome: possible perhaps in a traditional society that is modernising rapidly, the duality of ethos is by definition excluded in a traditional society that makes cultural replication a paramount objective. If cohesion and stability are what we want, we will not welcome the calculation that we are selling the equivalent of two fishes when we purchase the norm that ritual armbands are not to become economic tradeables. The accountant will be right to insist that a statistical sacrifice has indeed been made. We ourselves, however, will see no meaning in the inference that we could somehow live better if we sold off the family symbols. We are not over-developed businessmen, we will say, but uncompromisingly what we are. *We* start from *here*. *Here* is our map, our bonding and our self-image. Instrumental rationality, valuable in those areas where we are allowed a discretionary freedom, simply fails to account for the inflexible constancy that is at once the means and the end in the presence of our tradition-stamped commitment.

To homogenise the heterogeneous into a single rational standard is to understate the explanatory power of values, affects and traditions. This is not to deny the obvious attractiveness of an orientation associated so closely with rising material affluence. Nor is it to paper over the oppressive tribalism that is so frequently the alternative to problem-solving science. The rational standard is not difficult to defend or justify on normative grounds. The real world is, however, a source of endless frustration to the moral philosopher.

A positive step would be, eschewing logical deduction from an axiom that is an *explicandum*, to reason bottom-up from the raw data of experience. Proceeding empirically, the observer would both collect factual data on particular associations and explain those sequences in terms of motivational states. The problem would be the imputation that links the objective to the subjective. Is a failure to exploit an opportunity the result of error, inertia, a conscious choice not to break a taboo or an emotive impulse not to bankrupt a brother? Is a decision to select A before B on Monday but B before A on Tuesday a violation of the consistency condition or a simple mutation in the rank-orderings of the tastes? Preferences revealed through actions do not provide the answer to questions such as these. Thus it is that the observer must employ the empathetic methodology of Weberian *Verstehen* in order to enter into the actors' minds, to think as the actors' think, to discover the meanings that the actors themselves attach to their interventions.

The use of the interpretative methodology in place of the economist's *a priori* has the advantage that departures from the instrumental standard, no longer inconvenient deviations from the rational norm, are made explicable in terms of the non-random patterns expected by the actors themselves. Even if the standard were no more than instrumental, however, still there would be a further obstacle in the way of successful maximisation. That obstacle is limited information – the most common reason why even the most single-disciplinary of optimisers will so frequently be waiting at the wrong station for a train that never comes.

2.2   IGNORANCE AND UNCERTAINTY

Actors suiting the means to the ends are seldom in possession of all the relevant information: they shop for goods and agree to prices but their knowledge of the present-day parameters is nevertheless incomplete and imperfect. Actors when they plan for the future cannot anticipate the unintended outcomes, the unpredictable skeins, that the invisible hand will produce out of the microcosm's blinkered strivings: history-to-come being a discovery process, economic men and women will only find out what they have chosen when it is already too late for them to recontract their moves. Actors making decisions build on a personal psychology that makes them something more than simple pleasure-maximising machines: biased, frightened, hopeful, uncertain, the preferences they reveal may be consistent with the whole of their mental make-up but still be at variance with the normative instrumentality of rational capitalism.

On the one hand there is Muth, who writes as follows about *ex post* results made equal to rational expectations: 'I should like to suggest that expectations, since they are informed predictions of future events, are essentially the same as the predictions of the relevant economic theory.' (Muth, 1961:316). On the other hand there is the reluctant scepticism that is the message of this section.

(a)   Ignorance

Let us assume a theoretical prism that concentrates search on the evidence that is required. Let us assume a data-set that is conveniently complete and costlessly accessible. Let us assume a predictive model that inputs current choices and outputs future consequences. Given the assumptions, the logical inference is then a darkness become as bright as day. The facts are accurately identified and correctly processed. The conclusions are the product of sound reasoning and careful interpretation. The decision made is every bit as rational as would have been that of an impartial analyst, unlimited in capability and fully informed.

The world of the assumption is a world of availability and automaticity, collection and deliberation. The world of the anxious everyday is less accommodating to the captain of fate. Purposive decision-makers always intend that their actions should lead rationally to the realisation of some future state. Their hopes are high but their ignorance can let them down. Wishing to travel to Bognor and finding themselves in Scunthorpe, they will not need the services of an objective expert to tell them that their allocation of scarce resources was an inefficient one.

Economists schooled in the Walrasian theory of the auctioneer, the *tâtonnement* and the general equilibrium will brand any departure from instantaneous maximising and bilateral omniscience as a failing in the allocative mechanism. As sympathetic as the traveller in Scunthorpe will be to their assessment, there are reasons nonetheless for thinking that some ignorance may actually be the functional precondition for the success of market capitalism.

Thus Lamberton has pointed out that, absent the auctioneer and present the differentiated rivals, it is ignorance itself that keeps the competition process in business: 'In the real world, fraught with uncertainty, firms attempt to increase profits by searching for those things which satisfy the want which is just emerging.... For when wants are known and either stable or controllable, uncertainty disappears and monopoly power is possible.... Competition then only exists in a world of incomplete information.' (Lamberton, 1971:10). Lack of ignorance is lack of markets. It is a lesson which supporters of rational capitalism must take to heart.

Just as there is a search benefit, so there is a protective purpose: 'In a free enterprise economy, inventive activity is supported by using the invention to create property rights; precisely to the extent that it is successful, there is an under-utilization of the information.' (Arrow, 1962:149). Risk-averting profit-seekers would rationally under-invest in research and development were the information about their new products and technologies immediately to be diffused to other firms in the industry. The incentive to invent is in effect the appropriability of the title. Economic welfare would be higher if the information were to be made available at no more than the cost (an overhead comparable to that of the auctioneer and of the *tâtonnement* themselves) of its general transmission. Higher – except for one thing: 'In a free enterprise economy the profitability of invention requires a nonoptimal allocation of resources.' (Arrow, 1962:150). Invention once made public becomes a public good. Public goods in the private sector tend to be under-supplied. Sometimes they are not supplied at all.

Search and competition, indivisibilities and spillovers, are all reasons for a catallactic community to purchase some ignorance as a hedge against market under-performance. Nor should it be forgotten that information itself is an economic tradeable. Even if the ignorant decision-maker feels frustrated by his lack of knowledge, there too, it would appear, can the exchange orientation assist him to make an upward move in the direction of his best-attainable bundle.

Consider Stigler on the variance in price: 'Price dispersion is a manifestation – and, indeed, it is the measure – of ignorance in the market.' (Stigler, 1961:62). Stigler accepts that an identical product will go for an identical price in a marketplace where the buyers and sellers are all aware of how each is transacting. Stigler notes, however, that to sample and canvass is in itself to incur an economic cost – a cost, indeed, which (as where the percentage of the household's income devoted to a particular commodity is extremely low or where the opportunity cost of a high-earner's search-time is exceptionally high) might actually be in excess of the price-improvement expected. Employing the exchange orientation, Stigler therefore advises the commercially rational not to plunge on principle either into ignorance or into knowledge. Instead, he suggests, they would do well to mix their portfolio by means of proportioning marginal cost to marginal benefit as if the purchase were that of any other return-bearing asset.

The recommendation is a simple one. The optimum is unlikely to be the maximum where there is a cost. Rational choice means the substitution of information for other resources up to the point where additional increments become uneconomic to acquire. Even in the equilibrium state it is likely to be a rational choice to buy in some ignorance, to turn down some knowledge because it does not pay its way.

Information is an economic tradeable. Yet it is a tradeable with a difference – since, bought and sold as it can be, there is no standard unit (a good name, Boulding suggests, would be the 'wit') in which it can be quantified and compared: 'It is a little hard to put a price on it because of the difficulties of measuring the quantity of the commodity itself. We can put prices on the printed page, the hour's lecture, the newspaper.... The absence of any unit of knowledge itself, however, and perhaps the intrinsic heterogeneity of its substance, makes it very difficult to think of a price of knowledge as such.' (Boulding, 1966:23). Even where the titles are clear, private and exclusive, it is not easy to quantify the standard knowledge embodied in a trade secret or a patent. Unless the traders can agree on the metric, they are unlikely to be able to agree on the price.

Knowledge is differentiated by quality and not just by amount. Given the opaque imperfection of monopolistic competition, of oligopolies in intelligence, the rational shopper will have to invest time, effort and even money in an attempt to identify the most reliable supplier. Sometimes a professional adviser (the doctor or lawyer is a common agent) will be employed (technically, 'consulted') in order to give focus to the search. Sometimes a second or further opinion will be sought, the advance into infinite self-protection serving here as a paid-for insurance policy against the exploitation of asymmetrically distributed information, of 'information impactedness' (Williamson, 1975:14). At the end of the day the consumer will still not be certain that he has bought the right information about the right information: 'The value of information is frequently not known in any meaningful sense to the buyer; if, indeed, he knew enough to measure the value of information, he would know the information itself.' (Arrow, 1963:18). Theory teaches that the consumer will equate the marginal cost to the marginal benefit. Reality teaches that very often the information-seeker won't know which way to turn for a clue.

Market reality is in any case not the equilibrium state but the dynamic process. What this means is that the learning curve is continually being put on the defensive where economic change is continually throwing up new parameters. The threat to inertia or entropy is in capitalist conditions not a once-for-all exogeneity but a permanent shock. Knowledge is at once the outcome and the cause of the sequence: there is a Heisenberg principle at work in any model of instrumentality that legitimates the purchase of information in terms of the expected return from its use. Importantly, however, the knowledge held will be quintessentially date-stamped and intrinsically perishable, susceptible to mutation both because of Ego's conjectures and of Alter's innovativeness. In the natural sciences it may make sense to treat 'the facts' as somehow 'out there', as inert empiricisms waiting passively for the detached observer to discover them where they lie hidden. In the economics of capitalism the constancy and the predictability cannot so easily be taken for granted. The rational actor in the marketplace for a clue will have to pay the material cost of acquiring the data, the psychic cost of incorporating the new, the adaptational cost of acting on what he has learned – and may do all of this only to discover that market reality has subsequently decamped to a different address. Adjustment to feedback, in other words, is not a fixed point like Stigler's maximising conditions. Rather, it is disequilibrium and surprise such as make involuntary ignorance a fact of business life.

The final topic to be addressed in respect of ignorance relates to the falsifiability of the norm. It relates, specifically, to the real-world testing of the hypothesis that it is rational to be under-informed.

Calculative A purchases 10 units of ignorance because he believes this to be the cost-effective maximum. Ethical B purchases 10 units of ignorance because he is loyal to an absolute value which leaves no room for an alternative. Emotive C, sentimental and engaged, purchases 10 units of ignorance because this is the quantity on which the heart and soul converge. Traditional D, in a routine and in a rut, purchases 10 units of ignorance because of a lagged adaptiveness which he may or may not have made up his mind to correct. Intuitive E, volatile and impulsive, purchases 10 units of ignorance because of an unconditioned reflex that favours snap-decisions at random. Even, clearly, if the impartial observer had access to a standard unit, it would still be a difficult task to homogenise the motivation. A is instrumentally rational. B is value-rational. C and D are non-rational. E is irrational. Yet their revealed preferences as picked up by the standard 'witless' were seen to be absolutely the same.

The record of the actions only restates the blur. If two or more impartial scientists were to agree on the return-maximising scenario, it would in theory be possible to use the baseline to detect the deviant. The problem is that science will only identify actors less economical than the instrumental ideal where all actors are known to be modelling from the same information-set. There is no reason to think that this will be the case, that all observed players will necessarily be drawn from a common game. Thus Jack will be as rational as a management consultant when he refuses to desecrate a sacred glen with a high-speed railway while Jill will be as rational as a Pentagon analyst when she declines to declare war after consulting the entrails of a fowl. The data-base selected by Jack or Jill will no doubt be described as sub-efficient by two or more impartial scientists. The facts themselves, however, must not be confused with the juice that is squeezed from them. It is rational for Jack to defend a sacred glen – but not rational for him to defend a non-sacred glen which he mistakes for it. It is rational for Jill to consult the entrails of a chicken – but not rational for her to hazard her army on the entrails of a hawk. Jack and Jill act on the basis of the information at *their* command. It is only on the basis of *their* information that their choices, evaluated, can be categorised as purposive or spurious. The record of their actions only restates the blur.

It is rational for Tom to buy inaction as the proper means to a quiet life. It is not rational for him to buy the speculative excitement of the futures market. It is rational for Dick to prolong a transitional order. It is not rational for him so rapidly to correct a disequilibrium state as to put his personal balance at risk. It is rational for Harry to choose red today but blue tomorrow. It is not rational for him to cling to consistency when in fact his preferences will have altered. In order to test any hypothesis involving rationality, it will clearly make sense to mobilise the empathetic methodology of *Verstehen* in order to anatomise each deviation, to decompose each *ceteris paribus*. Without understanding the knowledge at the disposal of Jack and Jill, without understanding what it is that makes Tom, Dick and Harry each so different, the danger is real that instrumental rationality will become a meaningless tautology – and that the stock of ignorance held will always and everywhere be the optimal one.

(b) Uncertainty

However imperfect man's overview of the real, existing present-day, his grasp of non-empirical future sequences must be that much more imperfect still. It is precisely because of that veil of uncertainty (thicker even than the veil of ignorance which blankets out so much of *what is* in the here-and-now) that decision-makers are able to preserve their freedom of choice: 'If knowledge is perfect, and the logic of choice complete and compelling, then choice disappears; nothing is left but stimulus and response. . . . If choice is real, the future cannot be certain; if the future is certain, there can be no choice.' (Loasby, 1976:5). *There can be no choice* – Loasby argues strongly that there is simply no way to reconcile the spontaneous creativity of market capitalism with the situational determinism that is the inevitable consequence of perfect foresight: 'The rational choices that economists attribute to economic agents exhibit no signs of purposeful reasoning; they are programmed responses to the circumstances in which those agents are placed.' (Loasby, 1991:1). Unknowledge frees the imagination. Predictability pulls the shutters down.

The present is obscure in the absence of the auctioneer but at least it *is*. The future is more of a problem – since 'tomorrow is yet uncreated': 'The history-to-come which will flow from men's decisions is non-existent until those decisions themselves are made. What does not yet exist cannot now be known.' (Shackle, 1972:xi, 3). Rational choices are made in response to reliable information: 'It is only in the timeless fiction of general equilibrium that reason can prevail alone.' (Shackle, 1972:96). Entrepreneurial choices are made in a spirit of enterprise and vision, 'of break-away, of origination, of poetic creation or innovation': 'We cannot claim Knowledge, so long as we acknowledge Novelty.' (Shackle, 1972:23, 26). It was precisely because of his perception of changing circumstances as an expectational kaleidoscope, 'a skein of *potentiae*', 'a skein of numberless ideas', that George Shackle was able to conclude that human action is so frequently questing *ex ante*, unsuccessful *ex post*: 'The mind is always exploring, experimenting, guessing and gambling, and is constantly misled.' (Shackle, 1972:76, 107, 125). The mind is not to blame for its failure to compute the unforeseeable. Simply, it is the essence of human action that people are more than passive price-takers, swept along by currents that they cannot control: 'Human affairs consist in *making* history' – and 'we cannot know the history we make before we make it' (Shackle, 1967:vi).

New products, new processes, new entrants, new opportunities, all make it difficult to plan for future regularities without the unwanted risk of waste or loss. Non-conformity rather than adaptive acceptance will often be the gateway to the windfall gain: 'Competitive success depends on guessing better than one's rivals.' (Loasby, 1976:192). Oligopolistic interdependence, product differentiation, business strategy, games-based bargaining, intra-organisational negotiation, all mean that the pre-programmed solution must give way to perpetual indeterminacy. Searching and marketing become central to the new behaviouralism of buying based on learning, selling by means of persuading. So therefore do the new overheads of want-exposure and customer-creation in a business environment where the future is a manufacture and not a constant: 'The distinction between production and selling costs is strictly valid only in a world of perfect information. In this alternative view, selling costs are search costs.... Product differentiation is an attempt to discover, as well as to modify, consumer preferences; and this is a two-way process, because consumers often need to discover what the relevant part of their own preference function is.' (Loasby, 1976:185). The consumer does not know he has a latent want for a machine that writes until he sees an advertisement for a typewriter in the press. The producer does not know his project will pay off until he has invested his money both in contriving the object and in unlocking the desire. Both the consumer and the producer know that the future dwells nowhere so frequently as in the mind: 'Valuation is expectation and expectation is imagination.' (Shackle, 1972:8). Both the consumer and the producer know that the future will only be knowable once the *will be*, immobilised as the *is*, has lost its bite: 'For our knowledge is knowledge about the *present*, but choice is choice of what we hope for. We cannot *choose* the present: it is too late.' (Shackle, 1972:122). We cannot choose the present – it is too late. We cannot choose the future – 'What is the future but the void?' (Shackle, 1972:122). Trapped between the irrelevant and the unknowable, it is a wonder that the consumer and the producer can have any confidence at all in the choices that they make.

Sequence and sequel complicate still further the anticipation of the outcome. In some cases an initial error can actually trigger off a self-amplifying series of deviations from an agreed-upon ideal. Thus the cure for unemployment might be wage-cuts; but still the lower wage might not be recognised as the market-clearing signal. In the short run, workers might prefer quits to cuts (a quantity-adjustment rather than a price-adjustment) and might regard the income forgone as an invest-ment in search. What one can do, however, all cannot: the initial fall in income (assuming a Keynesian-type consumption-function) is translated into an initial fall in consumption, the consequent fall in other people's incomes is amplified by the multiplier into further-round falls in total demand, and the workers who decide after a lag to settle for the ori-ginal cut might therefore find that only an even greater cut would be successful in pricing them back into jobs. Communication is deficient and expectations are inelastic: it is explicitly in terms of market signals effective only when they are understood that Axel Leijonhufvud, reject-ing the administered rigidities of market failure, treats unemployment in Keynesian theory as a micro-dynamic doing the best that it can. Leijonhufvud advises that 'we should look for descriptions of *processes*, rather than of states, in *The General Theory*' (Leijonhufvud, 1971:29). He no doubt believes that the micro-economy would function with less slack if only the market would stay long enough in one place for per-ception to catch it up. The market is, however, by nature a creature of sequence and sequel. The infinite progression is the cause of mutually inconsistent conceptions but also of improving material affluence. It is impossible to secure the benefit from the process without coming to terms with the uncertainty that is the precondition and the con-sequence.

Leijonhufvud models his interpretation of voluntary idleness in the market for labour on Keynes's theory of liquidity preference in the market for money. In the one case as in the other the decision-maker has a reservation price. In the one case as in the other it might be the wrong one.

Idle balances would not be held if the future were fully foreseen. Idle balances (not spent, not lent) are held precisely because there is thick fog ahead: 'Money is a *medium of search*.... Money is the means by which a seller gains *time* in which to acquire *knowledge*.' (Shackle, 1972:207). Money is an asset which has the attraction that it puts off the *quid pro quo*. It is an asset like insurance, an asset which delivers con-fidence at the cost of return: 'The premium which we require to make us part with money is the measure of the degree of our disquietude.'

(Keynes, 1937:116). The rate of interest is the measure of the marginal valuation we assign to our non-rational expectations: 'Our desire to hold money as a store of wealth is a barometer of the degree of our distrust of our own calculations and conventions concerning the future.' (Keynes, 1937:116). We pay an opportunity-cost in order to purchase an interest-free hoard. We are right to do so in a second-best situation where money at least keeps our options open.

Keynes identifies two ways in which actors' unknowledge generates a conscious desire for idle balances in excess of transactions requirements. One is the precautionary motive, 'to provide for contingencies requiring sudden expenditure and for unforeseen opportunities for advantageous purchases' (Keynes, 1936:196). The other is the speculative motive, 'the object of securing profit from knowing better than the market what the future will bring forth' (Keynes, 1936:170). In the former case the decision-maker doesn't have a clue. In the latter case he has an expectation but not a certainty. The one denied all access to the frequency distribution, the other told the probability but not the outturn; both have this in common, that they go for cash because they live in a cave: 'We have, as a rule, only the vaguest idea of any but the most direct consequences of our acts....We know very little about the future.' (Keynes, 1937:113, 115).

Speculation is the more active of the two reasons for liquidity. It must not be anticipated, however, that the prospective conjecture will have anything like the track-record of the backward glance. Keynes infers that there is much convergence, that individuals are 'much more similar than they are dissimilar in their reaction to news' (Keynes, 1936:199). Even so, he continues, there is bound to be some dispersion, partly because different people will make different guesses – 'The rate of interest is a highly psychological phenomenon' (Keynes, 1936:202) – and partly because the gambler's real win comes from eccentric arbitrage such as outwits the crowd. In Shackle's words: 'The speculator holds particular assets because he *disagrees* with the market's valuation of them.' (Shackle, 1972:111). The Keynesian cash-holder speculating on an early fall in the price of bonds is taking a calculated risk that the postponement will yield the expected pay-off. Perhaps it will – or perhaps his intuition will simply let him down. Either way, the epistemological position lends little support to the imputation of rationality: '*Knowledge of the future* is a contradiction in terms.' (Shackle, 1972:47).

The more remote, needless to say, is even more difficult to anticipate than is the nearer consequence. Speaking of the return to a railway, a copper mine or a textile factory, Keynes expresses the opinion 'that our basis of knowledge for estimating the yield ten years hence ... amounts to little and sometimes to nothing': 'Human decisions affecting the future, whether personal or political or economic, cannot depend on strict mathematical expectation, since the basis for making such calculations does not exist.' (Keynes, 1936:149–50, 162–3). The marginal efficiency of capital is 'determined ... by the uncontrollable and disobedient psychology of the business world' (Keynes, 1936:317). Long-term expectations are 'liable to sudden revision' (Keynes, 1936:31). The rate of interest two decades down the road is unknown and unknowable: 'There is no scientific basis on which to form any calculable probability whatever. We simply do not know.' (Keynes, 1937:114). Business decisions are more frequently the result of 'animal spirits' ('a spontaneous urge to action rather than inaction') than they are 'the outcome of a weighted average of quantifiable benefits multiplied by quantifiable probabilities': 'It is our innate urge to activity which makes the wheels go round, our rational selves choosing between the alternatives as best we can, calculating where we can, but often falling back for our motive on whim or sentiment or chance.' (Keynes, 1936:161, 163). Enterprise is not passive extrapolation but pioneering initiative, 'the outflanking of imagination by superior imagination': 'The greatest secret of victory is *surprise*.' (Shackle, 1972:92, 422). The kaleidoscope shaken, the mould shattered, the unthinkable thought, it was Keynes's view that the succession of endstates would best be conceived as unintended outcomes, unforeseeable in advance of entry into the competitive process. He did not believe that the succession of endstates could usefully be plotted on the textbook assumption of the well-behaved means–ends nexus, transparent and mechanistic, that led ineluctably to a unique and ineluctable equilibrium: 'The hypothesis of a calculable future leads to a wrong interpretation of the principles of behaviour which the need for action compels us to adopt, and to an under-estimation of the concealed factors of utter doubt, precariousness, hope and fear.' (Keynes, 1937:122). Of uncertainty, in other words, which makes so much of rationality into a wishful rationalisation and a stab in the dark.

Hayek, like Keynes, Shackle and Loasby, was unprepared to model the marginal utilities and the marginal rates of substitution as if proportionality were automatically the free gift of an efficiency-maximising foresight. Unknowledge, Hayek said, was too important to be hidden away as an embarrassing *ceteris paribus*. The core and not the periphery,

Hayek insisted, the discovery problem of dispersed and uncreated information, was the fundamental issue that the useful economist was obliged to address: 'The economic problem of society is thus not merely a problem of how to allocate "given" resources – if "given" is taken to mean given to a single mind which deliberately solves the problem set by these "data". It is rather a problem of how to secure the best use of resources known to any of the members of society, for ends whose relative importance only these individuals know. Or, to put it briefly, it is a problem of the utilization of knowledge which is not given to anyone in its totality.' (Hayek, 1949:77–8).

Economics is built around the central constitutional limitation that no discrete individual can ever command more than a tiny part of social information. The single mind is unlikely to know enough to equate the ratio of the marginal utility and the price for all the goods and services in the choice set. It is even less likely to be able to guess the fragments of intelligence at the disposal of the multiple anonymous others; to predict the plans which their unique stocks of facts and assumptions will be inducing them to make; to anticipate the impact which their choices will have on the choices of their fellows in an interdependent real world where all are simultaneously engaged in generating the data that will define the parameters for each. Given the division of knowledge (an economic phenomenon on a par with the division of labour), it must be the task of the economist to explain how people learn (how they make use of logic and intuition in order to make sense of social signals) and how they communicate (how they react to advertisements in the press, how they interpret the patterns of intercourse in the collectivity to which they relate). Above all, it must be the task of the economist to explain how (in the absence of omniscient coordinators, infallible educators, reliable fact-gatherers) the decentralised reasoning of the atomised and the isolated produces a reasonable measure of mutual compatibility despite the constraint that the person on the spot sees little of the economic system beyond his own immediate horizon. Hayek is attracted by the exchange mechanism because only the catallactic process can ensure the prompt reconciliation of the partial and the particular: 'Nobody can know *who* knows best.... The only way by which we can find out is through a social process in which everybody is allowed to try and see what he can do.' (Hayek, 1949:15). Thus does the libertarian's commitment to voluntary, uncoerced interest-seeking merge with the economist's quest for synthesised information manufactured through the same free process that enriches and upgrades.

The market combines the disparate. It also stimulates the new: 'The solution of the economic problem of society is in this respect always a voyage of exploration into the unknown, an attempt to discover new ways of doing things better than they have been done before. This must always remain so as long as there are any economic problems to be solved at all, because all economic problems are created by unforeseen changes which require adaptation.' (Hayek, 1949:101). Economic problems arise as a consequence of unexpected developments, of evolutionary disturbances, of unsurveyable adjustments that uncover new possibilities even as they experiment with existing conditions. Inventions, environmental accidents, product differentiation, personal relationships, the reactions of rivals – unpredictabilities such as these ensure that competitive capitalism will be 'a succession of events' (Hayek, 1949:102) and not a static equilibrium state where things will continue precisely as they are. The requisite knowledge is simply not available in advance of play. The requisite knowledge must continually be created by the spontaneous procedures of entrepreneurship and contract. Will the consumer buy a new product and at what price? What strategy will a competitor employ in answer to a marketing campaign? Will the arrogant take-over bidder genuinely have estimated the true value of a company better than the market would have done? As desperately as the risk-taker would like to engineer his future in the light of this data, the dilemma is that there is no way for him to do so until he himself has played his part in the production of the information. The choice is now. The facts are yet to come.

Knowledge is disparate. Capitalism means change. The outcome is coordinated action without governmental plan. Attracted by the 'extended order of human interaction' and by the way in which the market is capable of unifying the dispersed and integrating the emergent, Hayek writes as follows in defence of the invisible hand: 'Adam Smith was the first to perceive that we have stumbled upon methods of ordering human economic cooperation that exceed the limits of our knowledge and perception. ... We are led – for example by the pricing system in market exchange – to do things by circumstances of which we are largely unaware and which produce results that we do not intend.' (Hayek, 1988:14). The process, Hayek is saying, has sweep and vision that improves upon the provincialism of the individual's design. Perhaps it does; but the emphasis upon the accidental and the unexpected can for all the upgrading be a cause of some anxiety to the theorist of purposive choice. Man puts forward ideals: he makes use of instrumental rationality in order, overcoming his dependence, to predict and control. Market adjudicates and ranks: free enterprise sews the calculated into the incalculable and remunerates the gain-seeker with 'an end which was no part of his intention' (Smith, 1776:I, 477). Purposive choice in competitive capitalism evidently means acting as rationally as one can, but also accepting that the price of the market is eternal surprise.

Hayek is critical of neoclassical over-confidence: 'The character of the fundamental problem has ... been obscured rather than illuminated by many of the recent refinements of economic theory, particularly by many of the uses made of mathematics.' (Hayek, 1949:78). So is Keynes: 'The fact that our knowledge of the future is fluctuating, vague and uncertain, renders wealth a peculiarly unsuitable subject for the methods of the classical economic theory.' (Keynes, 1937:113). So is Shackle: 'Economics cannot be a precise science of calculable effects. Its nature is to be the subject-matter of critical imagination, a subject-matter suited to an essentially literary expression, like history itself.' (Shackle, 1967:vi). So is Loasby: 'Actual competition is a process, not a state.... Competition is a proper response to ignorance.' (Loasby, 1976:190, 192). Not one of these four theorists of uncertainty is nihilist enough to recommend the suppression of economics as an academic discipline. All four of these radical subjectivists are, however, persuaded that the mainstream conceptualisation must be brought into a closer alignment with what little is actually known about the realities of business life.

Especially misleading in their view is the general equilibrium orientation. The picture conveyed is one of prereconciled choices, simultaneous determination, universal timelessness, the stationary state. Tidy, amenable to mathematical symbols, the problem is that there is no choice and no change – no entrepreneurship and no entrepreneurial profit – in the model. Initiative, indeed, would actually be dysfunctional to the permafrost of the matrix, a threat to the determinacy of the equilibrium state itself. Businesses in such a scenario adapt passively to price signals proclaimed *ex machina*. Businesses in the real world tend to have a different mentality: deviants where the model calls them robots, they are less involved in the efficient allocation of a fixed endowment of scarce means than they are in strategy and hubris such as expand welfare potential explicitly because they dislocate and disrupt.

Products in the real world tend to be non-standardised: reactions of rivals take the place of perfect competition, bargaining for advantage becomes the successor to the unique solution, and optimisation loses the mechanistic automaticity that so early on attracted the economists to the laws of the physical sciences. The maximand is as problematic as it is multiple: only a definition of utility so broad as to be tautologous will allow the differential calculus to be used to describe the consumer's choices, and the same must be said of profits and producers in the large-firm sector of managerialism and technocratic objectives. Rationality is at best bounded where the parameters are not known at the moment of choice: today's marginal cost cannot be compared with tomorrow's marginal revenue, *ceteris paribus* cannot realistically be assumed over the long life-span of an investment good, decisions are always conjectures where future realities are dynamic processes. Given the ignorance, given the uncertainty, there is a certain attraction in setting the *a priori* deductivism of the economics textbook to one side in favour of a more cautious, more empirical methodology that scans widely without an expectation that instrumental rationality will necessarily be found to be the norm.

2.3 COGNITION

The facts at hand, rational individuals may be assumed to respond as if piloted by an unbiased computer: 'Everyone more or less agrees that rational behavior simply implies consistent maximization of a well-ordered function, such as a utility or profit function.' (Becker, 1976: 153). The problem is that not all individuals in the real world are seen to be squeezing the maximum pay-off from the information at their disposal. Rational choice presupposes rational agents. Human psychology is, however, somewhat more complex than consistent maximisation in a formalistic vacuum. Perception and interpretation are always and everywhere among the greatest obstacles to the instrumental efficiency of the capitalist economy. If only the raw data were to be supplied pre-ordered, pre-selected and pre-packaged, the slippage due to cognitive distortion would be considerably reduced. As things stand in the market economy, the raw data is instead supplied, untreated, in bulk; and human psychology is left with the task of converting the inert potential into a basis for action. It is not a task which the human mind is likely to

perform with the detached objectivity that is modelled through mathematical abstraction. It is an intellectual effort which must nonetheless
be properly understood by the social scientist who wants to grasp how
the economic system actually operates in a mixed real world which
owes no greater loyalty to instrumental rationality than it does to any
other orientation suggested by the multi-dimensional complexities of
the human mind.

Consider what happens when an inconsistency is observed between
expectation and outcome. The contradiction (the dissonance) is a cause
of psychological discomfort and in that way an irritation which the
afflicted will attempt to reduce: 'Dissonance acts in the same way as a
state of drive or need or tension. The presence of dissonance leads to
action to reduce it just as, for example, the presence of hunger leads to
action to reduce the hunger.' (Festinger, 1957:18). Some people have a
low tolerance for disparity while others are prepared to accept a considerable measure of disequilibrium. Particularly, however, where the
choices are seen by the actors as significant ones – where, say, a car is
being purchased and not a bar of soap – it is the thesis of psychologists
such as Festinger that a move is very likely to be made to bring belief
and outturn more closely into alignment.

One scenario would involve the modification of action in such a way
as to damp down the offending feedback. Thus the smoker who sees
smoking as a threat to his health can give up his addiction while the
home-owner whose self-image is at variance with the character of his
street can transfer to a more congenial neighbourhood. The other scenario would involve the modification of opinion until some new set of
perceptions and values had come to validate behaviour-patterns that
could in consequence be left unchanged. The smoker rationalises his
choice by reasoning that to give up would lead to an increase in weight,
equally bad for his health. The fox without the grapes convinces himself
that he never much liked sour grapes, expelled from his utility-set. The
racist seeks out newspapers that reinforce his views and associates with
peers who lend mutual support to his prejudices. Recourse to new arguments and to new evidence would not be required if people were prepared, persuaded by their existing frame of reference, to reform their
conduct in keeping with the facts. The point is that they are not. Conservative at the level of deeds where actors in the first scenario were
conservative with respect to ideas, they react to cognitive dissonance by
seeking to defend a constant.

The two scenarios both build non-rational inflexibilities into the
capitalist system. In the first case an investor who clings to the low-

probability contingency of an imminent earthquake moves his assets out of property despite the return. In the second case a resident in an acknowledged flood-plain refuses to buy insurance because he has convinced himself that the statistical life will not be his own. Both the investor and the resident are deviating from the model of rational man as a calculator of costs and benefits that dominates the world-view of Mises and Becker. Their intention is not to maximise their return so much as to minimise their inconvenience. Desperately, one could say that the conservatives' approach to facts and frequencies, partial, selective and unscientific, is in truth the fully rational purchase of traditions and fictions such as are in themselves a source of utility to the consumer. In that sense people are not misinformed by accident so much as misinformed by design: 'If they believe something other than the truth, they do so by their own choice.' (Akerlof and Dickens, 1982:143). Even so, the economic outcome of the refusal to adapt to changing circumstances or to revise an 'incorrect' belief is the same as it would have been had the choice been made in unplanned ignorance and random error: upgrading is retarded and efficiency braked.

People derive utility from not having to admit they had made a mistake. People lose utility, however, when they discover *ex post* that their expectations are at variance with predictable reality. The criminal who discounts probable apprehension through the wishful thinking of 'it'll never happen to me' ends up in prison. The zealot who anticipates that God will provide is let down by his faith when, dancing with snakes, he is bitten. In neither case can it be said that the rejection of instrumental rationality produces the state of affairs that the decision-maker had intended when he opted for the non-logical filter. Buying psychic reassurance, the decision-maker is also buying a real-world destination different from that which he would have preferred.

The criminal and the zealot end up with a package which they know to be a wrong one. In other cases, however, the decision-maker in Bognor never finds out what it would have meant to be in Scunthorpe instead. One example of an 'incorrect' belief never identified as such is the case of the consumer who only reads advertisements for his favourite product. Successfully shutting out the disharmony of cognitive dissonance, such a conservative fails in consequence to meet the alternative brand that would better satisfy his requirements. Another example of an 'incorrect' belief never identified as such is a coffee-shop which, as Elster describes it, initially charges a higher price for a better product and then, retaining the high price, surreptitiously lets the quality slip:

'The twist to the story is that because of cognitive dissonance reduction, nobody experiences any subjective loss. Since they are paying more for the coffee, it must be better, they tell themselves.' (Elster, 1989:27). It was better *once*. It is not better *now*. In their resistance to noticing a difference in the taste of the coffee there lies the germ of 'a Pareto improvement: the shopkeeper gains more and the customers are happy' (Elster, 1989:27). The criminal and the zealot discover *ex post* that their perception has let them down. Pangloss, on the other hand, was the victim of a cognitive dissonance which he managed consistently to hide, to ignore, to explain away.

Akerlof and Dickens give the example of workers in a well-paid but dangerous occupation who select information in such a way as to confirm that the job is safe. On the one hand the anticipated consistency, on the other hand the realised dissonance – Akerlof and Dickens use economic reasoning to show that beyond some threshold level the self-deceiving risk-takers will come to accept that their illusion is imposing an unacceptable threat to life and limb: 'The cost of believing that work is safe is the possibility of making a mistake in the choice of safety practice. The worker chooses his beliefs according to whether the benefit exceeds the cost, or vice versa. If the psychological benefit of suppressing one's fear in a particular activity exceeds the cost due to increased chances of accident, the worker will believe the activity to be safe. Otherwise he will believe it to be unsafe.' (Akerlof and Dickens, 1982:125). Once the experience of accident rises above the threshold of inaction the workers, becoming more flexible, will purchase new beliefs that better accord with the observable state of affairs. Below the critical cut-off, however, the workers will continue to reveal preferences deliberately formulated without recourse to the full data-set to which potentially they all had adequate access. Their ostrich-like optimism (analogous, perhaps, to the Marxian interpretation of religion as a self-inflicted opiate) must, of course, be met with the same tolerance that is accorded any other life-style choice without significant spillovers. Less clear, however, is whether rational policy-makers should found democratic interventionism on deliberate errors revealed in defence of a misperceived *status quo*. Citizens non-rationally disregard the risk of crossing against the lights. Should the democratic State legitimate the number of pedestrian subways on the wishful thinking of those citizens or should it rely instead on the statistical evidence of detached assessors? The philosophical status of the non-rational cognition is clearly one of the central problems that must be resolved by a democratic individualism that takes people as they are.

Psychological experiments confirm that, in making predictions behind a veil of unknowledge, subjects do not necessarily converge on the calculated probabilities. Psychological evidence suggests that manifested assessment, no mirror-image reflection of non-ego reality, is in truth a locus of distortion and misapprehension, of 'severe and systematic errors' (Kahneman and Tversky, 1973:48). Bias is common in the course of cognition. One inference from the studies must be that to assume the universality of rational choice is to jump to a conclusion that is unlikely to be fully warranted.

A first source of bias involves the judgemental heuristic of *representativeness*. In deciding if object A factually belongs in category B, people evaluate the likelihood that A is a part of B on the basis of perceived similarity. The search is for connotative distance; but still it might be cut short by intuition before a sufficient number of salient characteristics have responsibly been scanned. The term 'Frenchwoman' calls up an image of a young, elegant Parisian. The statistical Frenchwoman is middle-aged and provincial.

Predicting by representativeness, people tend to stereotype while neglecting the full range of variables which impact upon the classification. Subjects told in one study that 'Steve' was meek, tidy, helpful, passionate about order, guessed his occupation as 'librarian': in fact, in a rural community, the probability would be high that he would be a farmer. (Tversky and Kahneman, 1974:5). Subjects informed in another study that 'Tom W.' was good with numbers at school inferred that he was more likely to undertake postgraduate training in computing than in humanities: they forgot that Tom might have changed since school, that the personality-sketch might have been incomplete even then, that the higher absolute numbers in the humanities have a statistical linkage to Tom's own destination (Kahneman and Tversky, 1973:49–51). People tend to be insensitive to nature and size of sample. People tend to generalise on the basis of a sub-set of characteristics. Sometimes people will be right but at other times their subjective judgement will lead them astray. The problem is not (or not only) the informational deficiency. The problem is the lens, the prism and the rule of thumb.

The disparity between perceived location and statistical probability is well illustrated by the empirical studies (mainly of university students) that were conducted by N.D. Weinstein. Confronted with a sample of negative outcomes (alcoholism, divorce, crime, disease, unemployment) and a sub-set of positive occurrences (enjoying good health, owning one's own home, travelling abroad, living past 80), the subjects were asked to estimate their own chances relative to the mean of the pool.

The results pointed strongly to cognitive bias and unrealistic expectations: 'Students tend to believe that they are more likely than their peers to experience positive events and less likely to experience negative events.' (Weinstein, 1980:818). The more unpleasant the outcome, the greater the propensity (a cause of risk in itself where the subject in consequence ignores standard safety precautions) to believe in one's own invulnerability. The more attractive the occurrence, the stronger the tendency (despite the mathematical impossibility that each and every participant will succeed in jumping one and the same queue) to believe that one's own chances are greater than the average. The exaggerated optimism, the repressed pessimism, are the result of factors at once motivational and perceptual: fearing the worst, hoping for the best, people employ the representativeness heuristic in such a way as to place themselves in a status more desirable than that which detached induction would have deemed appropriate. People in effect over-estimate salient features which work to their advantage while selectively censoring risk-factors which would threaten their confidence. There is logic in their illogicality. Not, however, instrumental rationality: failing to have cancer screens, to write a will, to wear a seat-belt, to wear a hockey-helmet, they are revealing preferences which are in effect founded in a representativeness which they have no right to claim as their own.

A further source of systematic error is the assessment that is inspired by *availability*. Associative distance, it would appear, is not the same as measured frequency. Perceived likelihood, it would appear, is strongly correlated with ease of recall: 'It is a common experience that the subjective probability of traffic accidents rises temporarily when one sees a car overturned by the side of the road.' (Tversky and Kahneman, 1974: 11). A recent heart-attack of a middle-aged colleague causes a personal acquaintance to down-scale his life expectancy. A spectacular stock-market collapse or a well-publicised business failure drives savers back to the banks. A television documentary on an airplane disaster makes the experience of catastrophe instantly imaginable. In all three cases the contingencies, vividly retrievable, end up over-weighted in the mind. The result is action which is non-rational if not contra-rational when examined from afar. The middle-aged man buys more life-assurance than the actuary would recommend. The minimax investor forgoes capital returns in favour of an interest-rate pittance. The frightened flyer goes back to the roads where the risk of death exceeds that in the sky. Each one of these social actors ends up with a product different from that which he would have preferred had the brain impelled him to the dispassionate norm of instrumental rationality. Instead, however, the brain impelled him to strength of association as the heuristic of frequency – and a judgemental slip becomes then the inevitable result.

The image is in the past. The action is in the present. In that sense availability, like representativeness, is a conservative filter. Most words beginning with consonants, most subjects in a study systematically disremembered the discovery that the consonants K, L, N, R and V could be found in other positions as well: 'Each of the five letters was judged by a majority of subjects to be more frequent in the first than in the third position. . . . Among the 152 subjects, 105 judged the first position to be more likely for a majority of the letters. . . . The results were obtained despite the fact that all letters were more frequent in the third position.' (Tversky and Kahneman, 1973:167). New information may, of course, shock the mind out of its rut. This is the argument for the propaganda war against tobacco, say, or for the battery of publicity that accompanies a product launch, or for the multiple repetitions which manipulate the listener into acceptance: 'The more a person has been exposed to a particular view, the easier its retrieval from memory and, hence, the higher its perceived validity.' (Kuran, 1995:166). Overall, however, the possibility is real that the mind will feel most at home with the familiar – and that the consonants will systematically be assigned to a position in which they do not predominate.

Tversky and Kahneman write as follows about availability as a conservative heuristic: 'The production of a compelling scenario is likely to constrain future thinking. There is much evidence showing that, once an uncertain situation has been perceived or interpreted in a particular fashion, it is quite difficult to view it in any other way. . . . Thus, the generation of a specific scenario may inhibit the emergence of other scenarios, particularly those that lead to different outcomes.' (Tversky and Kahneman, 1973:178). One could argue that specialist buyers for competing retailers would enjoy a much-abridged career in business if their cognitive procedures were as sub-optimal as those of the misguided respondents who recalled a 50–50 sample as disproportionately female because the women in the sample were disproportionately well-known. Even so, the conservative bias of the intellectual screen must clearly raise a question about the assumption of rationality in an economic system where it is people who make the choices.

A similar conservatism may be identified in the gravitational pull of *anchoring*. First impressions are hard to dislodge. That being the case, the order, the sequence, the agenda become in themselves causes of cognitive bias.

The product of digits 1 to 8 is 40320. The guesses articulated in a study ranged from 512 to 2250. (Tversky and Kahneman, 1973:170–1). The mental bias revealed by the study lends support to the premise that first impressions count. Thus the profoundly incorrect results may be taken to mean that the subjects were disproportionately influenced by the low value (1, 2, or even, backwards, 8, 7) of the numbers involved: they in that way forgot that multiplication is factorial, the product growing at an ever-increasing rate. Also, the direction of the bias was directly correlated with the initial number that was given to the candidates. Subjects asked to guess at the product where the starting point was 1 consistently recorded lower values than did subjects told that the sequence went in reverse from 8. Logically speaking, subjects should have realised that the product of digits 1 to 8 must be the same as the product of digits 8 to 1. Judging the sequence disproportionately by the value of the digits that they earliest encountered, they did not. A job-applicant, learning from their errors, would be well-advised to wear his best suit when he is first invited for an interview.

A non-rational approach to external reality may be identified as well in the manifest asymmetry of the *certainty effect*. Mathematically speaking, a medical programme certain to save 200 lives has the same expected value as a one-third probability that 600 lives will be saved accompanied by a two-thirds probability that 600 lives will be lost. Mathematically speaking, the two hypothetical programmes may be said to save the same number of lives. Subjectively speaking, however, the data from the experiments suggests that they are far from equivalent in the eyes of the sample: 'The prospect of certainly saving 200 lives is more attractive than a risky prospect of equal expected value, that is, a one-in-three chance of saving 600 lives.' (Tversky and Kahneman, 1981:453). Tversky and Kahneman found in their study that 72 per cent of the respondents opted for the guaranteed gain while only 28 per cent selected the possibility of the 600-life gain jointly packaged with the possibility of the 600-life loss. The sample respondents, overwhelmingly risk-averse, were signalling the view that 200 sure lives should not be put under threat even if a further 400 lives – probable lives – would be saved in the event that the gamble paid off. A sub-set of risk-lovers would, of course, have articulated the reverse ranking. Mathematically speaking, the two bundles of lives are numerically the same. In terms of felt satisfaction, however, they apparently are not.

The ranking of the certain value above the probable outcome is a utility-seeking choice. The choice in one sense is unambiguously a rational one: individuals lining up the alternative packages are trying to pick out the specific bundle that would leave them best-off in their own perception. The choice, on the other hand, is strongly non-rational to the extent that it is bound up with personal philosophy. Just as there is no hard evidence on the scientific superiority of the bird in the hand, so there is no convincing proof that the rescue of the 200 at the expense of the 400 is anything other than a value-laden *de gustibus*. The rank-ordering, indeed, may be seen to change where the certain outcome is believed to be a bad and not a good. The same respondents who condemned the 400 in favour of the 200 also said that they would have put the probable above the certain had the certain been deaths and not survivals. The result is a manifest asymmetry: the respondents showed that they preferred the sure gain to the higher prize of the same mathematical expectation – but that they were quite prepared to switch from an insurance strategy to a gambling strategy where a sure loss was involved. There is no way that the theorist of rational choice can postulate consistency and transitivity when confronted with a population of decision-makers who, fully informed about the consequences, reveal different preferences when the same choice is presented in different ways. The framing of the choice, the editing of the facts, leads to a reappraisal of the prospects. The perception changes. The risks do not.

Kahneman and Tversky write as follows about the ratchet of acquisition: 'A salient characteristic of attitudes to changes in welfare is that losses loom larger than gains. The aggravation that one experiences in losing a sum of money appears to be greater than the pleasure associated with gaining the same amount.' (Kahneman and Tversky, 1979:279). Their statement provides the bridge between the certainty effect (which relates to the primacy of the guaranteed above the speculative) and the *endowment effect* (which relates to the non-rational commitment to the perpetuation of the *status quo*). To obtain, psychologically speaking, is not the same as to give up. To buy is to secure a psychological gratification. To sell is to experience a psychological wrench. The complementary activities are evidently not equal-but-opposite in the utility-function of the economic person who negotiates the price. Opposite certainly, but certainly not equal; a judge awarding damages in respect of economic loss would therefore do well to set the value of compensation above the corresponding purchase price in order to ensure that there should be no unfair diminution in the level of psychic well-being.

The willingness to be paid to pass on shows a consistent tendency to lie above the willingness to pay to acquire. Surveys 'have consistently found that people say they would require a far larger sum to forgo their rights of use or access to a resource than they would pay to keep the same entitlement' (Knetsch and Sinden, 1984:508). An example of the disparity (in this case, 4:1) would be the figures proposed by a sample of North American duck-hunters: they told the investigators that they could pay a maximum of $247 each to maintain a wetland but would expect a minimum of $1044 to agree to its demise. (Knetsch and Sinden, ibid.). Sometimes probing for hypothetical valuations, sometimes tracking real-world negotiations, the evidence suggests that there is indeed a psychological proclivity to weight more highly than an accretion any encroachment into a *status quo* allocation. Indifference curves *can* intersect. The market-clearing price need not be the same when the same sentimental soul switches his status from demand to supply.

The disproportionality might reflect a neurotic insecurity that fears any severance of attachment. It might be indicative of a Freud-type obstinacy that finds its biological expression in constipation, its economic expression in miserliness. A risk-averse reluctance to part with assets might be a deliberate hedge against subsequent regret. It might also be a self-protective instinct that buttresses the mind against unproductive exertion until such a time as the need for effort and calculation has proved itself. Subjectivists like Bernoulli, Marshall, Friedman and Savage would say that the diminishing marginal utility of money must always make the satisfaction from a win less than the dissatisfaction of an equivalent loss. Whatever the reasons, the experiments confirm a conservative bias. This bias then compels a reappraisal of market theory in the light of a prevalent inertia which is effectively non-rational.

Consumers offered a money-back guarantee are seen to be reluctant to surrender the commodities at the end of the trial period: to return what they already have (and this independently of the transaction costs of packing and transporting) is perceived by them as a loss of property and an admission of error. Ticket-holders attend events for which they have paid even if in the interim they have reappraised their desires: not wishing to waste their sunk costs, they refuse to heed the rational maxim that bygones are forever bygone, that good money should not be thrown after bad, by failing to concentrate their assessment exclusively on the incremental costs that remain within their control. Purchasers (even where the price difference is precisely the same) spend more if asked to forgo a cash discount than they do if required to add on a credit surcharge: the surcharge being perceived as an out-of-pocket drain, the simple labelling of the price-difference has a subjective effect on the position of the reference point. Recipients having chosen between two gifts in a study actually rated the chosen gift more highly (and the rejected gift less highly) *after* they had made their selection: the same inflated commitment to a decision already made (a phenomenon which some will call self-hypnosis as insulation against mental conflict) is replicated in the behaviour of lottery-participants who demand a price-supplement to sell on a ticket in which they have invested their trust. University students are more sensitive to the paid-out costs of their education than they are to the opportunity costs of not earning a salary: the fees and charges deter because they are a loss, the next-bests forgone are brushed aside as a gain that never was. Money back not demanded, sunk costs not disregarded, card surcharges not understood, snowball momentum not resisted, opportunity costs not incorporated – findings such as these from the experiments and the questionnaires demonstrate the prevalence of the endowment effect and with it the strength of cognitive conservatism. Capitalism is a dynamic system which starts from here. The human mind, however, is a time-bound thing, disposed forever to lag behind.

3 Inductive Conservatism

Capitalism is a gain-seeking discovery process. Its enterprise is an ambitious one. Conservatives collect historical information about *what once was*. Deceived by cognitive bias, let down by gaps in the data, frustrated by the overload of interpretative schemata, at least they can centre their quest on a destination where the train is acknowledged to have stopped. Capitalists, on the other hand, are in the market for dependable guidance on *what is to come*. Their search is the greater challenge. Not sure if a disequilibrium is a trend or a fluctuation, in the dark about what the competition knows and plans, exposed at all times to surprises, windfalls and catastrophes, capitalists are confident of one thing alone – that they are advancing towards a station that does not yet exist, that no one has ever seen, that no one can accurately describe. The conservative economy yields a good indication of the routines and sequences that a past-driven future is more than likely to repeat. The capitalist economy does not. Some capitalists will make profits. Some will make losses. Some will go bankrupt. Capitalism may go hand in hand with the *norm* of instrumental rationality but conservatism is possibly more amenable to its real-world application.

There is a long tradition in the sociology of capitalism which argues in defence of the *zweckrational* standard. Parsons and Smelser (their assessment reflective, no doubt, of the melting-pot American culture in which the high social valuation of achievement, success and efficiency does so much through socialisation and sanctions to breed and form the *desire* to be rational) are very much a part of that tradition: 'From the point of view of economic theory, economic rationality is a postulate.... But from the point of view of the economy as a social system, economic rationality is not a postulate, but a primary empirical feature of the system itself.' (Parsons and Smelser, 1956:175). A 'primary empirical feature' and not a simplifying ideal type; Parsons and Smelser would clearly not reject the logic of the deductive neoclassicism which would take instrumental rationality as a strong and reliable assumption.

Some critics have called into question the empirical status, the explanatory power, of the familiar *a priori*. Thus Hargreaves Heap, emphasising 'its limitations as a model of human action', has expressed the opinion that economists will make a singularly impoverished contribution to public-policy debate so long as they do not reappraise the relevance of their axiom: 'Mainstream economics is ill-served by its exclusive,

48

formal reliance on the instrumental sense of rationality.' (Hargreaves Heap, 1989:1). Other critics have expressed doubts about the use which the 'esoteric irrelevance' of academic economics ('Economists often seek to mystify rather than enlighten the public') has made of the unrealistic abstractions upon which it founds its analytics: 'Conventional economics offers a very misleading view of how the world actually operates. . . . It needs to be replaced.' (Ormerod, 1995:vii, 20, 27). Lester Thurow is one commentator who has drawn attention to the misleading predictions which result in a model built restrictively upon rational maximisation: 'Economics is in a state of turmoil. . . . The mathematical sophistication intensifies as an understanding of the real world diminishes.' (Thurow, 1983:236). Keynes is another critic who has commented adversely on the substitution of mathematical deduction for a sensitivity to the business life: 'Too large a proportion of recent "mathematical" economics are mere concoctions, as imprecise as the initial assumptions they rest on, which allow the author to lose sight of the complexities and interdependencies of the real world in a maze of pretentious and unhelpful symbols.' (Keynes, 1936:298). Not one of these critics would deny the importance of informed selection and goal-orientated economising in any theory of the capitalist market. What all would say is that the extent and impact of the *zweckrational* standard simply cannot be determined without an open-minded inspection of the particular circumstances. To call economic rationality a 'primary empirical feature' is to jump to a conclusion which may or may not be justified.

The same intellectual cautiousness is recommended in the present chapter. Stressing that every economic system is an inter-breed of the rational choice and the non-rational chosen, the chapter concentrates on temporal sequencing to suggest that present-day computations are inextricably embedded in patterns and rules of thumb which are the imprint of the past. In that sense the to-be-chosen is influenced, even pre-determined, by the once-was-decided, by the already-on-board. We start from here. We *also* start from there. Our normative mixed economy is thoroughly mixed up. That, however, may be a reason why the capitalist system is able to function with tolerable success.

The present chapter recommends open-minded empiricism in time and space. It does not endorse a single bundle or mix. Its thesis is no more than this, that mixedness is the normal state and that current choices tend to have a conservative dimension. The argument proceeds in three stages. Section 3.1, 'Extrapolation from Experience', builds on the previous chapter by invoking a mould that was here before the present day arrived. Section 3.2, 'Mind and Prediction', shows that established heuristics, economical or idiotic, can be used to purchase consistency even at the cost of sensitive adaptation. Section 3.3, 'Bounded Rationality', examines the contention that a limited scan might be the only scan that is cost-effective in a capitalist kaleidoscope forever rich in new departures.

3.1 EXTRAPOLATION FROM EXPERIENCE

In general equilibrium there is nothing to be discovered or learnt, no further need for the calculus of the single-valued optimum. In the state of search and change, groping and experimenting, there is instead of certainty the desperate clutching at straws that makes the most of existing knowledge and established procedures: 'Uncertainty exists because agents cannot decipher all of the complexity of the decision problems they face, which literally prevents them from selecting most preferred alternatives. Consequently, the flexibility of behavior to react to information is constrained to smaller behavioral repertoires that can be reliably administered.' (Heiner, 1983:585). Uncertainty is not the residual error but the essence of the economic process. Normative conservatism is a yellowing map that is employed for guidance in the void. Less rational than the global maximisation which inconveniently is not an option, the question to be asked in this section is whether extrapolation and the heuristic make the past of any value at all to the blindfolded and the disoriented when they stumble confused towards a future that no bookkeeper has ever catalogued.

Trapped between the fiction of omniscience and the black hole of cluelessness, the mapless will no doubt hope that the historical second-best will at least move them some way in the direction of Bognor and not leave them stranded somewhere in the vicinity of Scunthorpe. The conclusion reached in this section is that a limited confidence is probably not misplaced. Mathematics is more elegant and physics more precise. Even so, it would be a mistake to write off normative conservatism in favour of simultaneous equations which give to the model world an optimistic predictability that the real world can never hope to match.

Economic choices relate to a future that is not yet a fact. Economic choices influence the processes to which they also seek to adapt. It is not easy to aim at the 'best' when the novelty that maximises long-run gains has yet to be invented and the doctrine of unintended outcomes serves as a perpetual reminder of the unanticipated *ex post*. No one can foresee the size of next year's wheat harvest or the surprise of a random external shock such as a war abroad. Profit-seekers cannot know how many other opportunists will rush in to exploit a high-return imbalance: in their darkness dwells the fallacy of composition and the microeconomic cobweb. Entrepreneurs cannot know which single speculation will deliver the greatest pay-off: it is precisely in the dispersion of their conjectures that the differential to luck or judgement will be founded. There is much that cannot be foreseen. There is much that cannot be known. A good historian can assemble the evidence on 1066. 2066, however, is yet to come.

Alfred Marshall recognised that continuous flux is more difficult to model than would be the stationary state: 'Time ... is the centre of the chief difficulty of almost every economic problem.' (Marshall, 1890:vii). Yet he also believed that economic change has a tendency to be slow and gradual, not sudden and revolutionary. It was his vision of impermanence channelled through stability that led him, following Darwin, to situate what Schumpeter would call 'creative destruction' (Schumpeter, 1942:Ch. VII) within the broad evolutionary perspective, more organic than mechanistic, of *natura non facit saltum*. The embeddedness of progress in constancy has an important implication for the instrumental conservative. The conceptualisation of *the different* circumscribed by *the same* makes it reasonable to estimate the probability of future out-turns on the basis of a frequency distribution derived from the past. Bread may be expected to be transported by train next winter – although the loaves have not been baked and the locomotives not even ordered. Primary schools will probably be staffed with primary school-teachers in 20 years' time – although the masters and the mistresses are currently in receipt of primary education themselves. Inferences such as these may not be 100 per cent accurate but nor are they the mere guesses they would be if the past were deemed to throw no light at all on the future of the sequence.

Extrapolation from experience, Keynes observes, is a prominent part of the predictive strategy: 'It would be foolish, in forming our expectations, to attach great weight to matters which are very uncertain. . . . For this reason the facts of the existing situation enter, in a sense disproportionately, into the formation of our long-term expectations.' (Keynes, 1936:148). The very fact that people project long-term on the basis of what they know and see can – the self-fulfilling prophecy – be a source of stability, the cause of a far greater rationality in expectations than would be the case if each idiosyncratic adventurer made up his mind not to look back. Given the stability, and experimenting with the different weightings that might have been applied for the recent relative to the more distant past, statisticians are then in a position to quantify a number of macrosocial aggregates. Discovering constancy in the marginal propensity to save, for example, it becomes possible to work out the cumulative impact on total demand of households' abstinence, the multiplier effect of firms' investment on the growth-rate of the national product. The fact that the future data will originate in the reaction-process need evidently be no insuperable barrier to prediction based on perception of the past. Again, the Marxian contention that the capitalist class, by accumulating capital, manages both to reduce the rate of profit and (producing its own gravediggers) to destroy the capitalist system can be made the focus for an empirical investigation very much like those into trends in the not-dissimilar externalities of environmental pollution or moral decay. The microsocial inferences from the extrapolations are often less precise than the encompassing aggregates: as far as the individual saver, investor or capitalist is concerned, it can clearly be a rational choice to note what the others are expected to do and then (consider free-ridership on public transport or the Keynesian paradox of thrift) to seek a personal and private gain through swimming against the tide. Extrapolation from experience cannot be expected to identify for each the optimal strategy for checkmating all. Nor will it reassure the prudent economiser that there is anything intrinsically rational in predictable choices made on the basis of past practices that may never have been chosen and may never have been rational. Extrapolation from experience has for all that a moderately optimistic message to communicate about the possibility of rational expectation in a society in which people take as their baseline the experience of the *status quo*.

Individuals shop for future apples with the intelligence gleaned from remembered fruit. Nations pattern macroeconomic down-turns in consultation with tried-and-tested indicators. Market researchers anticipate the average male life-span and the probable weather in August on the basis of what has gone before. In ways such as these the community is signalling its confidence in time-honoured mental equipment and indicating its belief that history may be expected to resemble itself. Obviously, a prediction made in the light of a regularly repeated past can be blown off course by unexpected disturbances such as sudden-death obsolescence or barricades and revolutions in Bognor. Yet it would be a mistake to concentrate on the worst-possible scenario while neglecting the extent to which serviceable information is generated through inter-temporal images and widely shared models. Most people are tolerably content with an intellectual conservatism that, building on structures, reserves the *ab initio* for special occasions. Businesspeople are likely in this respect to be as conservative as the mean.

Shackle has perceptively identified within the business community 'the desire of ambitious men to transform only a part of the scene, their own standing, against a background of stability in the rest. For only within a stable environment can success have a clear meaning and measure. The man whose frame of reference is rotating, whose world is adopting new valuations, cannot establish his claim to success.... Ambition and conservation have a large interest in common.' (Shackle, 1972:78). Shackle is here postulating a paradox of ambition – each wants to move ahead, each wants the n–1 to frame with constancy his advancement and his progress – which is in effect an intellectual contradiction that rational capitalism cannot resolve. Conservative capitalism is more reassuring. Conservative capitalism cannot assist each ambitious person to leapfrog every neighbour or provide a guarantee against unwelcome new entrants. What it can do, however, is to ensure that economic change takes place within the context of an economic environment that does not alter at an unmanageable pace. Sometimes accurate, sometimes mistaken, the fact is that expectation is more likely to be validated by experience where *natura non facit saltum*. The conservative nature of much of real-world capitalism is a cause of that stability which contributes so greatly to the ability to predict.

Much of real-world capitalism is at once divided by differentiation and unified by interdependence. In the case of textbook perfect competition there is the *as if* auction (the fiction that makes equilibrium prices a simple matter of logic) but no account of the adjustment process through which households and firms actually arrive at the endstate price-vector. Such a theory of price-setting is in truth no theory of price-setting at all. Searching for paths and being fobbed off with solutions instead, Loasby (following G.B. Richardson) has therefore expressed the opinion that non-perfect theorising at least adds behavioural content to a model that would otherwise be under-explained: 'Formal perfect competition provides no plausible basis for expectations, whereas oligopoly does at least define the apparently relevant set of competitors, and may well promote the exchange of information which gives firms the confidence to make commitments. It is perfect competition which is indeterminate. The imperfections are what make the system work.' (Loasby, 1976:187).

One dimension of competition among the influential is product heterogeneity. To the extent that each recognisable supplier holds the discrete quasi-monopoly in his own unique brand or service, he is clearly trading along a private as well as a generic demand curve. The fact that he is powerful in his own sub-market means that he is in a position to exercise some control over the price–quantity relationships which house-specific experience has effectively schooled him to anticipate. The local shopkeeper will seldom be distinctive enough to prevent his customers from scanning next-best alternatives nor the friendly boss be able to impede all mobility and fluidity on the part of his labour-force. What the quasi-monopolist may expect, however, is that his trading partners will put up with a slightly exploitative, moderately unfair economic relationship (as estimated in terms of identified opportunity-costs) because of the non-replicable advantages of location, personality, quality or speed which he is able to offer.

The attraction of the unique is complemented by the disincentive of the search. The goodwill in place, the patronage up and running, the differentiated know that their customers and their suppliers are to some extent locked in by the sunk costs of past decisions and the marginal costs of reopened sampling. A wants his investment in training and qualifications to pay him a return and B is deterred by the prospect of kissing an indeterminate sequence of frogs. Wasteful re-certification, the admission of failure, the sense of regret, the fear of the unknown are all reasons for the disaffected to stay where they are. Often there will be an age-related ratchet effect as well, in the sense that sector-specific decisions made at a crucial stage in the life-cycle can later prove difficult or impossible to reverse. Imperfections such as these reinforce the conservatism of *stasis* and retard the maximising efficiency of the capitalist market. Open competition would arguably be more rational if the economic agents were opting and reacting for the first time, if the flow of fresh choosers were high relative to the stock of old contractors, inflexibly sealed in.

Non-rational in one sense, however, it is a paradox of prediction that the repeat purchase and the economic rut can also prove highly rational in another. Seen from the perspective of the customer or supplier, the long-lasting tie economises on the transaction overheads of information and agreement. Seen from the perspective of the heterogeneous producer, the implicit contract of inter-temporal purchase lends support to the rationality of expectation. Each party, presumably, could force the other to reconsider and switch – the sellers by demanding a price above the maximum the buyers will pay, the buyers by offering a price below the minimum the sellers will accept. Repeat business makes it possible for the parties (precisely because they are not strangers or new entrants) to know the bargaining range within which the indeterminacy of meaningful negotiation will have to be situated. Wishing to see the continuation of their mutual support, the players will find it in their interest not to overstep the mark. Product heterogeneity increases the deadweight of searching out the new. The buyers and sellers may in the circumstances regard it as reassuringly economic that so much of real-world capitalism happens also to be conservative.

Product heterogeneity is one dimension of imperfect competition that is favourable to lasting correlations and rational extrapolation. Oligopolistic interdependence is a further dimension that once again is conducive to the accuracy of expectation. Oligopolists are rivals, tempted to invade profits and protective of market share. Oligopolists are also allies, aware that trade is war and determined not to be the inferior in strategy. The zero-sum option is like a game of chess about which few firm predictions can ever be made. The co-insurance choice is different. Sometimes overt (the cartel), sometimes tacit (price leadership), oligopolists in the mutual aid case are observed to collude and coordinate in order to give each other the parameters needed for the business plan.

A common procedure where reactions are uncertain is to keep prices constant while leaving quantities to the gravitation of the market. Where the price loses its status as the focus for competition, at least the competitors are able to approach the process with the knowledge that nothing other than the past price, the going price, is the price they should expect. Firms would actually risk a loss of goodwill if they tried to resolve a market imbalance by means of that rationing by price that most non-economists would expect from them in the free enterprise system. The theory of the 'kinked' demand curve codifies the functionality of the frozen fixprice. It does so in terms of the choice-calculus of business rivals for whom others' reaction-functions will forever be a closed book: 'In pricing they try to apply a rule of thumb which we shall call "full cost".... Maximum profits, if they result at all from the application of this rule, do so as an accidental (or possibly evolutionary) by-product.' (Hall and Hitch, 1939:113).

Starting from here and not from there, the theory does not (and, indeed, cannot) explain the adjustment process that ground out the reference-point or say why history opted for *that* unique position in preference to the infinity of others. All that the theory can do is to predict self-perpetuating stability on the basis of a past price that is adopted by a nervous present for use in an uncertain future. The gain is the beacon and the map. The loss is enforced queuing in the case of excess demand, involuntary unemployment in the case of excess supply. Without price signalling there can be no homeostatic gravitation to a precise and determinate balance of demand and supply. The waits of aspiring shoppers, the demand-deficient reserve army, would automatically be eliminated at a stroke were the economy in a position to rely upon profit-maximisation to restore it to perfect-information general equilibrium.

No doubt they would – but MC = MR is not a choice. It is always a mistake to juxtapose the real to the ideal when a more useful comparison would pit one fall from grace against another. Flexprice allocates but unknowledge blurs and blocks. Fixprice is history but extrapolation becomes robust. Each economic second-best has both its bad side and its good. The conservative option clearly condemns real-world capitalism to trade with out-of-date fallacies. On the other hand, it is an insurance scheme in which potential performs below capacity but enhanced foresight improves performance. Insurance is a valid choice in a capitalist economy. It seems unkind to deny to real-world capitalism any form of economic insurance that can be shown to satisfy the wider objectives of the consumers and of the voters.

Insurance, like knowledge, will never be comprehensive: 'The taking of desirable economic risks is inhibited by the inability to insure against business failure'. (Arrow, 1974:34). Explicit cover for capitalists is a problem because of the costs of negotiating and enforcing the contracts; and also because of the moral hazard that boosts the risks as a direct consequence of the contingencies being insured. Yet explicit cover does exist; and so, even more commonly, does implicit protection. One illustration of the protection is the futures market (alongside the spot that remains the rule when the consumer buys petrol from the pump or does the household shopping) that offers predictability in a dynamic world in exchange for a premium that compensates the risk-sharer for smoothing out the fluctuations. Another illustration of *de facto* insurance protection is price-inflexibility in the less-than-perfect economics of the agricultural marketing cooperative. Extrapolation from experience makes real-world capitalism more rational than it would have been were all businesses obliged each morning to start from here. The possibility cannot therefore be ruled out that real-world capitalism brings the market economy closer to the Walrasian price auction and the static Paretian optimum than it would have been had the pricing been left to the invisible hand.

It is imperfect rather than perfect competition that lies at the heart of White's conception of the market as mimicry. White sees markets as people, 'tangible cliques of producers observing each other' (White, 1981:543). Not disembodied abstractions but sociological entities, White says, businesses make decisions on the basis not so much of conjectures anticipating consumers as of the observed positions taken by inter-related producers. It is this mutual awareness, this confirmation of expectation that, overcoming uncertainty and conflict, is the primary reason for the interlocking of the disparate into an integrated matrix: 'Markets are self-reproducing social structures among specific cliques of firms and other actors who evolve roles from observations of each other's behavior.... The key fact is that producers watch each other within a market. Within weeks after Roger Bannister broke the four-minute mile, others were doing so because they defined realities and rewards by watching what other "producers" did, not by guessing and speculating on what the crowds wanted or the judges said. Markets are not defined by a set of buyers, as some of our habits of speech suggest, nor are the producers obsessed with speculations on an amorphous demand. I insist that what a firm does in a market is to watch the competition in terms of observables.' (White, 1981:518).

Building a market, White is arguing, can usefully be modelled in terms of social roles, social location and self-reproducing linkages. Absent the auctioneer but present the embeddedness, there is a tendency for the uncertain to learn from the observation of their peers, to follow the guidance of their competitors in the herd. White's interpretation of the market as a locus of conspicuous production brings to mind Marshall, much influenced by Bagehot's socio-psychological explanation of 'Why Lombard Street is Often Very Dull, and Sometimes Extremely Agitated' (Bagehot, 1873:Ch. 6), on the return of the bulls once the lower turning-point is believed to have been reached: 'Confidence by growing would cause itself to grow.... There is of course no formal agreement between the different trades to begin again to work full times.' (Marshall, 1879:155). In Marshall's case as in that of White, there is no prediction in terms of supply and demand for the point or equilibrium that is the product of the interaction of mind. White effectively says this when he makes producing units the primary building-blocks, quantity and price the economic variables that have to fit in: 'Markets are defined by self-reproducing cliques of firms, and not the other way round.' (White, 1981:520).

White may be criticised for a one-sided approach which under-estimates the importance both of consumer demand and of market balance. To that extent his theory ought perhaps to be seen as a theory of production-decisions and not an account of the market as a whole. White's theory is unable to explain observed price/quantity relationships or to comment on the allocative implications of the levels that emerge. What it does do is nonetheless of considerable value. It shows that communication by means of copying improves the predictive power of extrapolation from experience. Other people assist us to predict. A stable society is a support to rational choice.

Other people assist us to predict. So too does the State. Galbraith in particular has emphasised the constructive lead that can be taken by the polity – via regulation, support and selective ownership – in a market economy where long gestation periods and heavy capital overheads threaten the future with under-performance and failure: 'One rewarding result of these necessities has been the discovery of how much government initiative is welcomed in a capitalist economy once it is discovered that capitalism cannot do the job.' (Galbraith, 1965:63). Unknowledge means that similarities and patterns cannot realistically be anticipated. The State gives capitalism the fixed points it requires to plan ahead.

Thus macroeconomic stabilisation policies (accompanied by income-related unemployment benefits) are often said to smooth out the amplitude of cyclical fluctuations; while indicative economic planning (not excluding the pre-publication of the public sector's own medium-term spending targets) represents to some a usefully-centralised forecasting mechanism. Coercion imposes coordination where without the law a 'prisoner's dilemma' would have veiled the reactions. Patents provide the security that is needed for the risks of research and development. Rigidity in some areas – fixed exchange rates, import tariffs, pay directives, rent controls – may be the informational bedrock for flexibility in others. What all of this suggests is that perhaps the capitalist orchestra plays more effectively with a conductor than where each instrument is expected to strike up on its own.

Conservatism enables capitalism to project. Politics can reinforce the past so as to make the transition informed. Seen in that light, the leadership of the State, like social interdependence and vicarious experimentation, has the attractive property that it makes the market economy function more effectively by means of disciplining it into predictable matrices. The opposite view is, of course, that the mixed economy at the disposal of the mixed ethos has the effect of buying certainty at the expense of want-satisfaction. Precisely *because* the future is hidden from sight, it may make better sense to opt for differentiation, search and speculation – 'The argument for competition rests on the belief that people are likely to be wrong' (Loasby, 1976:192) – than to rely on consistency and uniformity imposed by means of authority and directive. Authors sympathetic to the 'catallactic' or exchange-prioritising perspective do not say that decentralisation and price-signalling are in every respect ideal. All that these theorists of *laissez-faire* would contend is that, no single agency having an overview of dispersed knowledge (and the particular goal-function of politicians and bureaucrats threatening itself a further distortion in the public interest), the market in the real world is the best-*possible* means of discovering and communicating, harmonising and systematising, integrating and coordinating. Perhaps it is – but uncertainty remains. Conservative capitalism given structure through coercion and proclamation at least improves the effectiveness of extrapolation from the known.

Natura non facit saltum. Gradualism, like mimicry and polity, makes a contribution of its own to the rationality of choice. Some commitments, expensive and irreversible, are quintessentially vulnerable to the tyranny of the unforeseen: a giant dam cannot be dismantled if the river dries up and a maverick reactor cannot economically be converted into a student residence. Even more choices, however, are small, marginal and susceptible to recontract: thus a Chinese restaurant faced with a change in tastes can invest in Italian recipe-books while a saver noticing an upward pressure on interest-rates can shift from equities to bank-accounts before shares fall further. Not all assets are sector-specific and non-adaptable. Not all mutation is discrete, sudden and once-for-all. Where the commitments have a high degree of malleability, where the changes are relatively slow, there the long-run can reasonably be conceptualised as a series of short-runs, each context only a small step on from the context that went before.

Gradualism, it will be clear, has a double meaning. The term, first of all, refers to the incremental micro-progression that incorporates the opportunity to re-think as the situation develops. Then, secondly, the term picks up the non-revolutionary macro-changes that make forecasting possible despite the evolving environment. Both the plasticity and the transparency make a contribution of their own to the rationality of choice.

Sometimes, indeed, that contribution will be explicitly institution-alised at the planning stage of a sequence. One variant of embodied gradualism will be contingent contracting of the form 'If A decides to supply X, B undertakes to purchase it'. This conditionality, acknow-ledging incomplete foreknowledge and leaving the options open, ensures that not all choices will have to be made at the same time. Another variant will be scenario planning, selected in preference to the one-off calculation in order to allow enhanced flexibility of response. In the case of the intellective tree the agent proceeds on a live-and-learn basis from the trunk to the branch, from the supporting branch to the dependent growth. Where no good map is available at the outset, the continuous reaction might be the most effective way of reaching the destination. Each turning has a probability-distribu-tion inferred from the past. Rational choice means the best-possible thoroughfare selected at *each* junction on the journey. The norm of rationality refers to each *each* in isolation. The agent will hope, natur-ally enough, that the rationality of each *each* will add up to the ration-ality of the skein. As with the one-off choice, so with scenario planning, the inconvenient fact is that the use of a norm gives no guar-antee.

A further variant of institutionalised gradualism will be the precau-tionary buffer. Consider the case of a politician who, expecting to be asked questions but not knowing in advance which ones, equips him-self with the answers he will need to explore a range of avenues. It is true that his less-than-perfect foresight commits him to wasteful over-preparation that would not have been necessary had the questions been made public before. On the other hand, his supplementary information-seeking builds on the non-refundable overheads of his background knowledge, allowing him at relatively low marginal cost to rise to a disproportionate spread of challenges. His behaviour is non-maximising (in the sense that he returns home with unused capacity) but it is gain-seeking nonetheless (in the sense that he is able to be as rational as he can). The gain-seeking element in the knowledge buffer is closely related to the conservative nature of institutionalised gradu-alism. Gradualism enables the decision-maker both to predict the limits of the unvisited playing-field and to take his precautions with-out prohibitive incremental investment. To the extent that he is so cushioned and sheltered, he is able to go forward without the costly computational exercise that would have been set in motion had the long-term complex not been decomposable into a series of smaller risks and contingencies.

A final variant of institutionalised gradualism is the speculative hedge. Chosen on the maximin principle of damage-limitation, the hedge protects against future regret to the extent that it encourages the cautious to opt for a mixed portfolio. To hedge against the 'wrong' choice might also be to block out the 'right' one; and it must also be remembered that differentiation (witness Keynesian liquidity preference that could have been plunged at interest) is not without a cost. Even so, as Peter Earl explains, it can be a reassuring strategy to avoid the maximal exposure that would be the consequence of all eggs concentrated in a single basket: 'A British family might normally take a holiday in Spain in a single fortnight and stay at a hotel they know well. But if taking their holidays in Britain "for a change", they may choose to have two separate weeks to insure themselves against the vagaries of British weather, even though this will mean two lots of packing and travelling.' (Earl, 1986:75). The British family knows that extrapolation leaves them open to error. To contain possible losses, they therefore opt for small advances along two separate roads in preference to a single giant step that might mean two weeks in the rain. Conservatism allows them to extrapolate. The hedge allows them to diversify – but at a cost.

Institutionally embodied in the hedge and the buffer, scenario planning and contingent contracting, gradualism has the attraction that it leaves room for the in-period change of mind. People do not cease to learn from experience once they have made their choices and set off on their journey. Rather, they continue to filter new stimuli through existing models and correct their initial conjectures in the light of unexpected feedback. Rational choice in such circumstances means not a point but a succession of points, not a once-for-all but a process. The revisions could, of course, aggravate a disparity that they were intended to reduce; while changing conditions could be blamed for a predictive error that was actually the product of an outdated paradigm. Yet much is lost by simplifying instrumental rationality into the status of an on/off norm. Decisions seldom are entirely rational or entirely non-rational but tend to be situated somewhere between the two polar types. The error-correction mechanism is unlikely to smooth systematic errors into fully predictable patterns. All that can be contended is that flexibility *en route* will be the cause of a greater convergence of expectation with outcome than would be the case were rational choice to be modelled in terms of mathematical statics rather than the psychological dynamics that guides and informs on the disequilibrium path.

3.2   MIND AND PREDICTION

Mises saw no great value in the statistician's pursuit of empirical evidence: 'As a method of economic analysis econometrics is a childish
play with figures that does not contribute anything to the elucidation of
the problems of economic reality.' (Mises, 1962:63). A praxeologist,
a deductivist, a believer in the sound *a priori*, Mises defined the realm
of economics to be the realm not of non-ego reality but of the human
mind: 'The economist ... deals with matters that are present and operative in every man. ... The economist need not displace himself; he can,
in spite of all the sneers, like the logician and the mathematician,
accomplish his job in an armchair.' (Mises, 1962:78). The realm of the
economist, Mises insisted, was to be found in the psychological make-
up of the individual decision-maker. It was not to be sought in comparative sociology or a knowledge of the material constraint.

Mises was at once logical and psychological. The link between the
deductions and the reductions in his work was his belief in the purposive behaviour of the representative agent: 'The specific goals that
people aim at in action are very different and continually change. But
all acting is invariably induced by one motive only, viz., to substitute a
state that suits the individual better for the state that would prevail in
the absence of his action.' (Mises, 1962:77). *Homo economicus* is not
per se a possessive wealth-accumulator, single-minded about consumption, investment and value for money. What he is, however, is a prudent
maximiser who lives his life by the norm of instrumental rationality.
Homo sociologicus, Mises would suggest, cannot be modelled as being
very different. In the words of Gary Becker: 'The combined assumptions of maximizing behavior, market equilibrium, and stable preferences, used relentlessly and unflinchingly, form the heart of the
economic approach as I see it. ... The economic approach provides a
valuable unified framework for understanding *all* human behavior'.
(Becker, 1976:5, 14). Action is optimising action, intervention to produce a more satisfying state. Action is not random action, effort
expended without intention or aim.

Few people would say that they act at random, or that they waste
scarce resources on free-floating transformations for which they hold
no brief. *Homo sapiens* is a proud creature, reluctant to state that he
orders his life with the informed calculativeness of the chicken that
crosses the road. Self-image is flattered by the expectation of purposive
choice – but the mind, for all that, remains absolutely its own master.
Stereotyping and misclassification engender unfounded inferences.

Selective recall favours the recent past. The acquired is ranked above the new. Loves and loyalties drive people into non-calculative choices. Much of human action, as was shown in the previous chapter, appears to have a remarkably non-maximising character. What the evidence suggests, in short, is that human action is mixed action, sometimes rational and sometimes not. Mises and Becker were arguably too quick to universalise a selective standard which can account for cheapness preferred to costliness but not for amortised costs overweighted or opportunity costs ignored. Rational choice might be taken to be a theory of how people *would* act or *should* act. Whether it is also a theory of how people *can* act or *do* act is considerably more problematic. The mind is what it is. There is no point in imposing on the mind an idealised unidimensionality that can neither explain nor predict.

There is slippage from the *zweckrational* norm. That slippage is of considerable importance for an understanding of the capitalist system. Mass unemployment at an impressionable age can lead to non-probabilistic exaggeration long after recession has given way to over-heating. The sub-conscious can drive shoppers to colour and shape when they believe their choices to be governed by prices and qualities. The fear of the unknown can lie behind an anxiety-discount that makes best-possible projects into unattractive gambles. In terms of the economic market, the state of affairs that is the emanation of the economic mind stands here in some contrast to the allocative optimality that is modelled in the economics text. It is playing with words to say that people are here making a rational choice to buy the memory, the image, the reassurance at the cost of undesired inflation, under-performing consumables and missed opportunities. Looking at the economic system as a whole, people who as a rule make a purchase of non-rationalities such as these are in effect depriving capitalism of its core dynamic. The economics of capitalism only makes sense if most people rationally opt – and if most people opt rationally for the *zweckrational* norm.

Olson defines (market) economics not in terms of the end of wealth so much as the norm of purpose: 'Economic (or more precisely microeconomic) theory is in a fundamental sense more nearly a theory of rational behavior than a theory of material goods.' (Olson, 1969:142). Becker, interpreting crime, suicide and divorce with reference to the economist's standard, takes the view that the maximising orientation is, socially speaking, the general one. The evidence from the experiments, admittedly small-scale rather than aggregative, suggests a more cautious approach. As the studies are multiplied which call into question the ubiquity of goal-orientated conduct, so authors like Russell and Thaler reach the conclusion that psychological bias is not a footnote exception, anomalies not randomly distributed or likely to cancel out in large numbers. The departure from the economist's norm, Russell and Thaler observe, is not *obiter dictum* but central to the account. The very idea that 'competition will render irrationality irrelevant is apt only in very special cases, probably rarely observed in the real world' (Russell and Thaler, 1985:1071). The contention that irrationality is all around casts a considerable shadow over the use of the means–ends, input–output model.

Even where human action is less than perfectly rational, however, the departure from the economist's norm need not mean that the sequence is intrinsically non-predictable. Detached and objective assessment is not the precondition for the anticipation of a future choice. All that is required for patterning is method in the madness in the sense of stability in the bias. The bias understood, the actors and the observers will be in a position to estimate one another's moves and reactions without recourse to scientific facts but simply in the light of known perceptions. The actor's felt frequencies can be unfounded and distorted. To the extent that they are out of touch, they are unlikely to do much for the efficiency of the economy as a whole. In respect of prediction, however, the position is more encouraging. Felt frequencies, however misperceived, can form the basis for revealed preferences that are as susceptible to prediction as they are unsubstantiated outside the mind.

Economics by its very nature must always be a science of subjectivity. Concerned with thoughts, satisfactions, guesses, conjectures, perceptions, it must always be closer to the psychology of cognition than to the physics of mechanism, object and thing: 'In natural science, what is thought is built upon what is seen: but in economics, what is seen is built upon what is thought.' (Shackle, 1972:66). The thought is the trigger for the process. For that reason all prediction in economics must depend on a sound understanding of the state of mind. The economist may identify wastefulness in a sequence or even assert that the means is inappropriate to the end. No doubt this advice will be as much appreciated by the *zweckrational* actor who has made a straightforward mistake as it will be resented by the *wertrational* actor who is competing in a different sport. In terms of prediction, however, the economist is able to spare himself the labour of normative judgement. Taking the state of mind as his initial focus, his task is not to evaluate possible bias but to establish expected consistencies. Some behaviour, genuinely random, will always escape his patterning: inspiration, intuition, flashes of insight, entrepreneurial imagination can be almost as difficult to forecast as divine revelation. What is important is that many stimulus–reaction relationships can be brought within the ambit of anticipation that would have been lost had the economist concentrated his search too narrowly on rational choice and efficiency criteria. Extrapolation can and must reflect real-world systematisation. If it is a fool's assessment that imposes the logic, then the economist must make himself the student of fools and their intellectual frameworks.

Cognitive bias is a part of economic choice. Three illustrations will serve to show the implications of predicting the future with the biases and illusions that worked like reflexes in the past.

The first illustration concerns the value of life. People tending to believe that they are less likely than the average to get lung-cancer or be attacked in the street, a national policy to build new hospitals and expand the police-services would fall short of the consensual optimum if based upon the revealed risk-taking of cigarettes smoked and dark alleys visited. The problem is not the statistical risk (about which people have the option to become well informed) but rather the personal risk (which the mind loves to discount and downgrade). The position, in Bruno Frey's terminology, is the following: 'The possibility set which a *particular* person takes to be relevant *for himself or herself* – it will be called the ipsative possibility set – differs from the objective possibility set.' (Frey, 1992:198). *Ex ante* a nation of optimists discards small probabilities of large losses on the grounds that 'it can't happen to me'. *Ex post* a nation of victims complains that the hospitals are under-bedded and the streets are under-policed. To act on the basis of the objective possibility set is to alienate the taxpayers. To act on the basis of the ipsative possibility set is to disappoint the victims. A government that wishes to maximise felt welfare in the nation will evidently not find it easy to do so where it depends for its value of life on the expected utilities of citizens with a skew.

The second illustration concerns the language of framing. Quattrone and Tversky conducted a study on attitudes to price-rises and labour-markets. The study was conducted twice. The first set of respondents were asked if they could approve of a 12 per cent inflation-rate where 10 per cent of the labour-force would be unemployed: only 35 per cent of the respondents felt able to do so. The second set of respondents were asked about 12 per cent inflation where 90 per cent of the labour-force would be in work: 54 per cent found this to be acceptable (Quattrone and Tversky, 1988:2). The reactions differed. The information presented did not. People obviously reacted more strongly against the negative eventuality (loss of endowment) than they did in favour of the positive one (jobs) despite the numerical equivalence of the two packages. A government knowing from questionnaires the value of the asymmetry would in the circumstances do well to keep its macroeconomics constant but to alter its linguistic formulations. In doing this, it would only be falling in line with the prediction from bias that is the logic of the supermarket display positioned for impulse-buying or the advertising strategy that sells a life-style and not a product. Medical professionals can alter the rankings of treatments by converting the benefits from death-rates into survival-ratios. As in the case of unemployment, so in the case of mortality, the prediction is not hindered by non-rationality and the frame can be re-structured to suit.

The third illustration concerns the tacit knowledge of the habituated mind, able like a Pavlovian dog to produce a reaction such as a golf-swing without being in a position to supply a theoretical justification. Unconscious repetition makes learnt routines 'second nature'. Michael Polanyi, convinced that 'we can know more than we can tell' (Polanyi, 1967:4), has this to say about them: 'Though I cannot say clearly how I ride a bicycle nor how I recognize my macintosh (for I don't know it clearly), yet this will not prevent me from saying that I know how to ride a bicycle and how to recognize my macintosh. . . . I know these matters even though I cannot tell clearly, or hardly at all, what it is that I know.' (Polanyi, 1958:88). Recourse to the time-out-of-mind frees the actor to think out the unexpected and the strategic with the confidence that unthinking drills in less challenging areas will deliver an acceptable result: 'They become familiar. He forgets that they were novel when he began. He is unable even to explain them to outsiders. They have become routine, taken for granted. His mind is no longer called upon to think about them.' (Commons, 1934:697–8). A gain in that sense, there is also a cost: the automatic pilot repeats but it does not optimise. Should adaptation be required, the cognitive bias that reproduces the standard response – Leibenstein's 'ratchet rationality' (Leibenstein, 1976:88) – can once again lead to an outcome which is deficient in problem-solving rational choice. In the words of Howard Margolis: 'Once a pattern (whether of behavior or of thought) has become well-entrenched so that it is habitually prompted by some pattern of cues, it cannot be easy to turn it off. An act of will ("Turn off that habit") cannot put in place some standing order for that effect.' (Margolis, 1987:122). Yesterday's judgements can in that way become the basis for tomorrow's refusal to face the facts. Clearly they can; but at least they facilitate prediction.

Cognitive bias, as is shown by these illustrations, is a part of economic choice. It must not be confused with the unenlightened misapprehension (the simple mistake, say, of money illusion) – even though the effect, as it happens, can be equally as damaging for the efficiency of the capitalist order. Cognitive bias means a selective assessment of facts (the consequence of supra-scientific values and affects) and a rationalisation of the incompatible (the imputation of logic to the inconsistent in an attempt to resolve tension and end dissonance). Cognitive bias means restricted feedback, less learning from experience, less market self-correction than would be expected in the light of the financial incentives to adapt that figure so prominently in theories of economic rationality. Cognitive bias need not be welcomed to be acknowledged. The point is simply that it does exist; that the non-instrumental need not be the random; and that systematic error can therefore be patterned without the assumption that means–ends utility constitutes the uppermost concern.

Predictable or not, what is clear is that the mind *as it is* must be at the centre of any theory of economic knowledge and economic truth. A processor and not just a camera, a thinking filter that makes an active contribution, the mind assigns meaning to facts and chooses the ideas that will survive. It is easy to misunderstand just what reality is, Boulding writes – or to underestimate the impact of the 'image' upon the ordering of experience: 'We really have no convenient word to describe the content of the human mind without regard to the question as to whether this content corresponds to anything outside it. For this reason I have ... used the term "image" to mean this cognitive content of the human mind.' (Boulding, 1966:21).

External reality, Boulding stresses, is perceived through the selective vision of the personal past: 'The image is built up as a result of all past experience of the possessor of the image. Part of the image is the history of the image itself.' (Boulding, 1956:6). The image is by definition dated. The *is* in that sense must always be trapped in the context of the *was* that makes it recognisable. Nor should it be assumed that each discrete occurrence will be referred back on its own. Accompanying the image there is the surrounding value-scale which influences the impact that each new piece of information is likely to have: 'The message which comes through the senses is itself mediated through a value system. We do not perceive our sense data raw; they are mediated through a highly learned process of interpretation and acceptance.' (Boulding, 1956:13–14). On the one hand our personal past makes us look at today's events with the lenses of yesterday's news: 'Our image is in itself resistant to change.' (Boulding, 1956:8). On the other hand, new messages at variance with the entrenched orientation have a greatly increased chance of being ignored: 'What this means is that for any individual organism or organization, there are no such things as "facts". There are only messages filtered through a changeable value system.' (Boulding, 1956:14). Both because of the personal past and the surrounding value-hierarchy, the effect is that the mind becomes rooted in time and grounded in space. Approaching accuracy as if truth were the same as familiarity, sharing values within a mutually reinforcing cultural group, the mind becomes nervous about novelty that is at once destabilising and distancing. The mind, in short, becomes conservative. Without the fixed points the mind would not find it easy to function.

Even a dog can find his way home (he has the capacity for spatial orientation) or recognise his master (he has an understanding of stratification and dependence). The dog like the human is evidently a creature with an openness to image. Yet the human can do more than simply absorb and react. The human, unlike the dog, can use words, signs and symbols to communicate his preferences. He can enter via language into conversation, discourse and event-shaping negotiation. He can, above all else, take a view on the future that allows him to imagine a 'better' situation than that which currently exists: 'His image contains not only what is, but what might be. It is full of potentialities as yet unrealized.' (Boulding, 1956:26). Just as the image is learned structure and not only raw data, so, in Boulding's view, is it intervention and initiative as well as the simple transmission of inherited schemata. Sometimes accepting the rules and socio-cultural bonds that have been handed down by the elders, sometimes people act to restructure the convection of external reality, to create new disturbances even as they smooth out the existing distortions.

The consequence is a mix of pictures reproduced alongside surprises introjected: 'The image not only makes society, society continually remakes the image.' (Boulding, 1956:64). Past references are mixed with imagined departures. The personal subconscious is mixed with peer-group socialisation. And matter is mixed with mind: 'If we jump off a skyscraper, no matter how elevated our thoughts on the way down, they will hardly affect the rapidity of our descent or the consequences at the bottom.' (Boulding, 1956:116). Boulding is clearly not attracted to solipsism, to the denial that there can be reality outside the self. Nor, however, is he attracted to economic determinism, to mechanistic materialism as in the Marxian model: 'Once we see society as a process of modification of images through messages, it becomes clear that there is no mechanical process of overthrow of one class by the one below it.' (Boulding, 1956:107). Messages are situated – in the forgotten childhood, in socially acquired values, as well as in the biological and physical environment. Yet messages are also autonomous, small transformations but still not the parental precedent. Boulding looks to social science to elucidate the links between messages received and messages sent. Neither a supporter nor an opponent of rational choice, he says simply that no theory can have predictive power that does not seek to understand the recall and the scanning of the human mind.

3.3 BOUNDED RATIONALITY

Image in the sense of Boulding is not difficult to estimate in the textbook world of neoclassical economics: 'If we accept values as given and consistent, if we postulate an objective description of the world as it really is, and if we assume that the decision maker's computational powers are unlimited, then...we do not need to distinguish between the real world and the decision maker's perception of it: he or she perceives the world as it really is.' (Simon, 1986:26–7). If we assume that complete knowledge is costlessly available and that computational skill is in perfectly elastic supply, then rational choice becomes a single right answer on which the sensible may reliably be expected to converge: 'We can predict the choices that will be made by a rational decision maker entirely from our knowledge of the real world and without a knowledge of the decision maker's perceptions or modes of calculation.' (Simon, 1986:27). His or her preference-function fed in, the facts and relationships inputted without a margin for error, the sole and optimal option comes up automatically as if guided by an invisible programmer: 'The rational person of neoclassical economics always reaches the decision that is objectively, or substantively, best in terms of the given utility function.' (Simon, 1986:27). Thus does the science of choosing become marginalised into the theory of no choice at all.

Herbert Simon, attracted by the neoclassical expectation of goal-orientated maximising and sceptical about the explanatory power of passion, instinct and affect, is quick to describe human behaviour as

'intendedly rational' (Simon, 1957:200). Convinced that great importance must be attached to the *zweckrational* striving, his reservations
relate not to the ideal itself but simply to the unrealistic enterprise
which assumes 'virtual omniscience and unlimited computational
power' (Simon, 1957:202) in present-day 'situations of increasing cognitive complexity' (Simon, 1978:9): 'The capacity of the human mind
for formulating and solving complex problems is very small compared
with the size of the problems whose solution is required for objectively
rational behavior in the real world – or even for a reasonable approximation to such objective rationality.' (Simon, 1957:198). Foresight is
imperfect. Calculations fall short. Theorists of instrumental rationality
commit themselves to a standard of perfection that is as unattainable as
it is appealing. Followers of Herbert Simon acknowledge the primacy
of the second-best and start from here: 'Broadly stated, the task is to
replace the global rationality of economic man with a kind of rational
behavior that is compatible with the access to information and the
computational capacities that are actually processed by organisms,
including man, in the kinds of environments in which such organisms
exist.' (Simon, 1955:241).

Simon writes that it is 'precisely in the realm where human behavior
is *intendedly* rational, but only *limitedly* so, that there is room for a
genuine theory of organization and administration' (Simon, 1957:xxiv).
The field of investigation remains the purposive norm. The emphasis,
however, is shifted from maximisation to acceptability, from global
rationality to bounded rationality. Mathematical modelling loses its
power to convince: decision-makers cannot make the most of preferences constrained by budgets where they are unaware of the spread
of options and do not know how to calculate the best-possible payoffs.
As neoclassical economics is revealed to be 'seriously misleading', the
source of solutions 'that are without operational significance' (Simon,
1978:12), so psychology becomes the cutting edge in order to understand the beliefs, aspirations, ideologies, assumptions – the 'image' – that
the encumbered economiser brings to the choice-calculus in an uncertain
world where the subjective dimension simply cannot be inferred from
the objective 'facts' alone: 'When this distinction is made, we can no
longer predict his behavior – even if he behaves rationally – from the
characteristics of the objective environment; we also need to know
something about his perceptual and cognitive processes.' (Simon,
1959:256). We need, in other words, to pay a visit to the economiser's
mind in order to gain a purchase on the subjective frame of reference
that he employs when he interacts purposively with the phenomena

that lie beyond the perception: 'Decision processes, like all other aspects of economic institutions, exist inside human heads. They are subject to change with every change in what human beings know, and with every change in their means of calculation. For this reason the attempt to predict and prescribe human economic behavior by deductive inference from a small set of unchallengeable premises must fail and has failed.' (Simon, 1976:146).

The deductive approach must be dropped – but the expectation of purposiveness must be retained. Drawing on his knowledge of real-world economic psychology, Simon makes clear that it is not his intention 'to substitute the irrational for the rational in the explanation of human behavior but to reconstruct the theory of the rational, making of it a theory that can, with some pretense of reality, be applied to the behavior of human beings' (Simon, 1957:200). What this means in practice is that Simon would like to see a shift in emphasis from substantive or outcome-oriented rationality – 'We can expect substantive rationality only in situations that are sufficiently simple as to be transparent to [the] mind.' (Simon, 1976:144) – to procedural rationality that goes forward gradually, heuristically, governed by rules: 'Behavior is procedurally rational when it is the outcome of appropriate deliberation. Its procedural rationality depends on the process that generated it.' (Simon, 1976:131). Substantive rationality is concerned with data-collection and problem-solving. So is procedural rationality, but with the following difference: it is concerned with the present-day at one remove, through yesterday's predetermination of the best-attainable method of attack. We search today with the tools that yesterday has forged. Yesterday's rationality contributed the multi-period constitution. Today's rationality adopts the best-attainable processes in order to score good if not optimal results in a world of limits and constraints.

The past, clearly, is at the core of purposiveness as procedure. The past is the source of the habits and conventions upon which the present is able to draw when it reacts to the new with the rules of thumb that make possible the quick, intuitive response. The past supplies the schemata that enable the experienced to reconstruct familiar patterns using learned decision-making mechanisms stored up in the memory. The past, in sum, makes the economic market both culture-bound and history-driven. Economists wishing to understand how real-world individuals *actually* make their choices in the capitalist system effectively have no choice but to study the conservative guidelines that focus the fact-gathering and short-cut the computations. Statistical extrapolation is easily frustrated by the sheer complexity of economic life: 'Even with the help of the computer, man soon finds himself outside the area of computable substantive rationality.' (Simon, 1976:135). The good procedure is in that sense a *desideratum* even as it is a commonplace in a fallen world where the decision-making mind, speaking realistically, 'has neither the senses nor the wits to discover an "optimal" path – even assuming the concept of optimal to be clearly defined' (Simon, 1956: 270).

Partly the procedure from the past is the make-do consequence of the fact that calculative rationality is seldom a genuine option. Arguing in its defence, however, the established process is also the result of trial and error, a product of experience that has been seen to perform with tolerable efficiency. Man with his limited computational capacity is likely to benefit from the focus of a rule *per se*. *A fortiori* is he likely to benefit if the non-rational standard is believed to have been the frame for good outcomes in the past – and if competing conventions are taken to have been productive of less desirable states. The learning is ongoing, present experiences either confirming or challenging the expectations. The rules adapt, the procedure is rational. For all that, the decision-making unit is condemned not to optimising but to getting by, not to maximising but to 'finding a choice mechanism that will lead it to pursue a "satisficing" path' (Simon, 1956:271). The satisficing process identifies the 'good enough' but not the best. In the circumstances, however, the 'good enough' might be the best that can be attained.

Decisions are made not all at once but in a sequence. Recognising the serial nature of human choice – and abandoning the global maximisation which presupposes the conjunction of omniscience with omnicompetence – Simon relates satisficing to the hurdle of a satisfaction threshold: 'One could postulate that the decision maker had formed some *aspiration* as to how good an alternative he should find. As soon as he discovered an alternative for choice meeting his level of aspiration, he would terminate the search and choose that alternative. I [call] this mode of selection satisficing.' (Simon, 1979:503). The agent in such a sequence is not expected to be familiar with all the choices or to be in a position to calculate all the consequences. What is postulated is that he has in his mind an image of what he can accept. When he finds it he discontinues his search. Marginal cost and marginal revenue are of no direct relevance to the agent's choice. The reason is simple: he cannot know what they are.

Applied to the sale of a car or house, the bids are received sequentially and at some point the vendor must make up his mind: 'In a satisficing model, search terminates when the best offer exceeds an aspiration level that itself adjusts gradually to the value of the offers received so far.' (Simon, 1978:10). Applied to business behaviour, profit-seeking becomes a sub-topic in the theory of utility once it is conceded that 'firms would try to "satisfice" rather than to maximize' (Simon, 1959:263). Different firms are likely to have different aspiration-levels (to say nothing of different trade-offs between psychic income and money). If some firms want high returns while other firms have low thresholds, there is no reason to think that the less efficient will be competed out of business or that profit-rates will show convergent tendencies. It is difficult to make any *ex ante* prediction at all about the functioning of a market where economic success is evaluated by more than a single standard.

The satisficing business, clearly, does not satisfy the neoclassical conditions for allocative efficiency in (perfectly) competitive markets. The procedure is rational but not the substantive calculations. The rule is from the past, the application in-period. The equilibrium is a dynamic one, never a static state. Agents' aspirations being idiosyncratic and unique, the success of the macro-economy is all but impossible to establish. What all of this suggests is that bounded rationality makes it more difficult to be confident of the efficacy of capitalism than would be the case if the political economist could put his faith in the neoclassical explanation. Simon's reply would be, however, that his reinterpretation does no more than model the economic processes which are seen to have delivered a broadly acceptable standard of economic performance. His theory of cognition is not intended to create a capitalist economy, only to understand the information-processing mechanisms upon which it relies.

Simon does not, of course, say what determines the content of the procedural rules or the position of the aspirational thresholds. His theory does not explain why a particular heuristic emerges or why one process is adopted in preference to another. Bounded rationality is an account of how the past constrains the present but not a history of how the past emerged and became itself. In that sense the theory is under-determined, unable to say what is explicitly *rational* in procedural rationality as a compass or a chart.

The purposiveness in the proceduralism may be said to be the product of an intellectual circularity. Simon's rules, after all, are not open to the economist's evaluation but are accepted effectively because they are the normative *status quo*. Such a defence of today's heuristics because they failed to disappoint when last applied is not, however, a strong endorsement. We search in the present using less-than-maximising mechanisms. The less-than-perfect mechanisms were selected in the past using standards inferior to the ideal of full information, non-problematic calculability. Allowing for error-correction through feedback updating, acknowledging Simon's contention that complexity makes utopia an unhelpful comparison, the *status quo* legitimation still appears to be confusing the rule that is the 'best in the circumstances' with some other rule that is merely adequate. Even if maximisation must be abandoned, even if horrendous performance may be assumed to be identifiable and rejected, it is nonetheless not obvious that the economy will gravitate automatically to the best-attainable procedure. Where the third-best has become the 'done thing', where the fourth-best is satisfying bounded expectations, there seems to be no clear reason in Simon's theory why the second-best will somehow evolve as the dominant strategy.

Observers who fear that procedural rationality will be operationally indistinguishable from procedural inertia or even from procedural defeatism will point with interest to Einhorn's illustration of a waiter in a busy restaurant: 'Because he doesn't have time to give good service to all the customers at his station, he makes a prediction about which customers are likely to leave good or poor tips. Good or bad service is then given depending on the prediction. If the quality of service has a treatment effect on the size of tip, the outcomes "confirm" the original predictions.' (Einhorn, 1980:282). The waiter could, of course, experiment with alternative heuristics in order to enrich his intuitions with self-correcting intervention. He would, however, then be losing income (if he were initially right) in order to gain it (if he were initially wrong). His learning, clearly, is not without the risk of loss. So long as his current rule is not suboptimal enough to be rejected as horrendous, he might not see any need to reconsider his decision-making framework. The customers remain under-served. The waiter remains under-remunerated. The reason is not the expected return compared at the margin to the transaction cost – that would be the different standard of substantive rationality. The reason is the pre-specification of concepts and the pre-patterning of cognitions – a procedure which in the case of the present illustration satisfies the common-sense test of 'tolerably good' without engendering any real confidence that it will be among the best-attainable rules in the less-than-perfect circumstances.

The social context complicates further the specification of the best-attainable make-do. The waiter in isolation has considerable freedom to build personal experience and idiosyncratic predilection into his choice of a rule. The individual in society, on the other hand, is often obliged to satisfice at the pace of the reference group.

The shared aspiration-level is a social fact, upheld by suggestion, imitation and the inter-personal pressure to conform. It is a common thought-pattern, a common mode of classification, a common answer to the questions 'What is that thing like?' and 'Is an error-correction process required now?' Science presumably provides a better-calibrated metric – but we start from here: 'To the extent that objective, non-social means are not available, people evaluate their opinions and abilities by comparison respectively with the opinions and abilities of others.' (Festinger, 1954:124). Unknowledge brings out the worst in the frightened Hobbesian, unprepared even to believe himself. The shared aspiration-level at least has a head start that provides a model.

The familiar baggage fosters the confidence always associated with patterning oneself after the median that has been seen to stay afloat. A model in that sense has the patina of respectability that is so reassuring a feature of the ivy on the walls even of a newer Oxford college: 'Once formulated, the artifice acquires venerability.' (Douglas, 1987:120). No doubt the already-adopted is a source of psychic comfort in itself: far worse than wearing a toga would be, when in Rome, having no inkling at all of what it is that the Romans actually *do*. Yet this book is about conservative capitalism; and here it must be conceded that the collective legitimation can mean systematic error such as slows down the rate of economic growth. On the one hand we want the conservatism because it makes us confident. On the other hand we want the capitalism because it makes us rich. Young Back Choi correctly points out that the duality of our desires is very likely to build an inescapable margin of under-achievement into our economic performance: 'Social paradigms, that is, conventions, have been devised to reduce uncertainty, and do so only to the degree that they are stable. . . . Suboptimality is the price we pay for the conventional resolution of uncertainty.' (Choi, 1993:103).

The shared aspiration-level, Choi would say, is a mixed heuristic which economises on early adaptation in order to defend the stable if also the non-maximal. Collective legitimation is evidently not on the side of the globally efficient: 'Even when individuals are clearly aware of the follies of existing conventions, mutual checks may discourage change. Shared paradigms therefore tend to be even more inflexible than individual paradigms.' (Choi, 1993:105).

The heuristic can become self-reinforcing on the principle of 'famous for being famous', 'any port in a storm'. It can also become self-reinforcing because the members of the community genuinely like it for what it is. Social values transcending economic expediency, social satisficing could easily involve the endorsement of a group convention which in effect wastes scarce resources in order to attain a goal which the society puts above wealth. An example would be liberal democracy, preferred by the members of the community even where totalitarian planning is generally believed to be economically the stronger procedure. As a theory of economic psychology, in other words, procedural rationality does not come with a guarantee that socialised men and women will necessarily *want* to squeeze all the outputs they can from the endowments at their disposal. Their conservative capitalism in such a case would not be the *horror vacui* which ranks any rule above no rule at all but rather a well-defined social consensus which values social institutions not just for their productive potential alone.

Simon assigns considerable importance to the psychology of the choice: 'It is illusory to describe a decision as "situationally determined" when a part of the situation that determines it is in the mind of the decision-maker.' (Simon, 1976:147). A part is in the mind. Another part, however, is in the environment outside. The social context exercises the force of an external constraint. So, significantly, does the economic market. Firms which adopt low-productivity heuristics are exposed to under-bidding from firms which employ cost-conscious procedures. Firms which stop short of maximisation are often more competitive than firms which process more detail than can possibly pay off. Acknowledging the logic of the economic market, the reader is struck by the possibility that cognitive processes and objective states might be complements and not the alternative routes that they are taken to be in Simon's political economy. The fact that there might be much substantive rationality even in the use of the heuristic is of some reassurance in respect of aggregation. Without a theory of function as well as an emphasis on perception, there would be no expectation that partial equilibrium in the discrete micro-patterns should ever point in the direction of general equilibrium in the economy as a whole.

Simon's theory may usefully be regarded as a mix of two contentions. The first contention, reflecting the biases uncovered in the experimental studies, is that the theory of substantive rationality 'does not provide a good prediction – not even a good approximation – of actual behavior' (Simon, 1979:506). The second contention, accepting that the evidence is 'a direct refutation of the neoclassical assumptions' (Simon, 1979:507), is that procedural rationality provides a superior account of how real-world people actually approach complex decisions where information is a problem and computational capacity is limited. Simon is making both a negative point and a positive one. Neither point, however, can be taken on trust. What is needed in practice is an empirical investigation, probing at once into how decision-makers actually decide and into the different outcomes that the different approaches are seen actually to produce.

Perhaps a cautious pragmatism is the correct posture to adopt as between the alternative frameworks. Even this, however, is by no means certain. Just as the *a priorists* and the maximisers will insist that strict logic confirms the truth of their case, so the subjectivists and the doubters will say that Simon's quasi-rationality fails to acknowledge the reality of a future that can never be anticipated. Simon does not deny the existence of an objective probability distribution, suggesting only that fallen men and women are not in a position to know what it is. The friends of radical uncertainty will reply that Simon's appeal to the 'good enough' is rooted in the same optimism that deprived the neoclassical maximisation of its cutting edge. The neoclassicals, needless to say, will have a response of their own: 'Our hypothesis is based on exactly the opposite point of view: that dynamic economic models do not assume enough rationality. . . . Information is scarce, and the economic system generally does not waste it.' (Muth, 1961:316). Simon is on the middle ground that separates Shackle from Muth. On each side the full and open scan, at the centre the time-bound rule – the emphasis on conservatism in place of confusion is both the greatest advantage and the greatest disadvantage of the ready-made guideline that was believed to be 'good enough' in the past.

Decision-making rules may relate to conditions which have disappeared: consider the knee-jerk vote for a party which once was biased towards labour but subsequently re-thought its stand. Intellectual constitutionalism may breed a false sense of security due to the lag in the recognition of the novel: consider the interpretative prism of military intelligence which focuses on traditional enemies while failing to spot a new aggressor. The heuristic may perpetuate the sub-standard because 'good enough' is declared before alternative rules have been sampled for success: consider the repeat purchase from a tolerable supplier, a lazy person's excuse for not shopping around. Rules may be convenient and not really rational – the economy may be sacrificing rationality to the extent that it trusts to past experience. Rules may direct attention to a single dimension – choice has many dimensions, occasionally in conflict. Rules, on the other hand, undoubtedly economise on cognitive capacity and the resource costs of time and energy. If people sought to resolve all issues through case-by-case deliberation, no more than a few decisions would actually be made.

Established procedures may promote economic efficiency or they may on balance retard it. The rationality of the heuristic must remain a matter of debate. What is not in dispute, however, is the frequency with which decision-makers fall back upon the rule of thumb. Businesses do not calculate the profit maximum but replicate instead the habitual markup. Cartels price with a view to market share and traditional targets. Fashion-leaders are copied on the grounds that the giant knows best which patterns will sell. Gamblers approach the table with a pre-arranged view on when to quit the game. Bureaucrats employ organisational precedents to defuse potential disagreements. The heuristic, in short, is familiar and it is widely used. No account of normative conservatism can afford to neglect its relevance to the broader topic of economic choice.

4 Economy and Society

Insulation from other people provides no immunity from the inertia of the established. The Tabula Rasa, deserted without family, peers or the internalised categories of remembered socialisation that kept Crusoe an Englishman, can still be a conservative. Extrapolation from experience makes him conceptualise the future as if it were the past. His mind employs rules of thumb which channel new cognitions through existing biases. Aspiration-levels which have not disappointed are pressed into service in circumstances which have changed. The hypothetical isolate, never other than alone, can, it would appear, become trapped in a rut that is no less a rut for the fact that he himself laid it out. The hut under attack from a boar, the river about to flood, Wild Peter still clings to his tea at three. His tendency to use his biography as a crutch is indicative of that normative conservatism that was discussed in the preceding chapter.

Wild Peter's conservatism is to be traced back to the romantic uniqueness of the liberated one-off. It is the conservatism of the I and not the We, of Rousseau and not of Burke. It stands in sharp contrast, therefore, to the normative conservatism that is the product of social interaction, collective constraint, historical evolution and cumulative causation – pressures which, in Michael Novak's view, typically cocoon the pull of autonomy and initiative within the common inheritance of community and culture: 'Each of us first begins to experience and to reflect *within* lived social worlds.... Human beings experience themselves first as social animals, shaped by traditions and nourished by symbols, languages, and ideas acquired socially. Our individuality emerges only later. For much of our lives we are more shaped than shaping.' (Novak, 1982:61). The Tabula Rasa emerges from the state of nature to plough his own rut. The socialised citizen simply carries on the baton in a relay that he never chose.

The subject of this chapter is the social and the handed-down. Concentrating on that conservatism which is supra-individual, supra-rational and supra-evaluative, it argues that shared conventions absorbed from an early stage of overlapping experience have the effect of funnelling human behaviour and of channelling it. Choice in such circumstances is not the marginal choice of optimising moves so much as the validating acceptance of a continuing game. Economics becomes a sub-discipline within the broader science of social relations. The economy becomes a sub-topic in the general theory of patterned replication.

The first section of this chapter, 'The Social Perspective', shows that there is much to be gained from a multi-dimensional economics, resistant to the 'economistic fallacy' that the self-regulating price mechanism is all that there is to the explanation of production, consumption, distribution and exchange: 'The human economy...is embedded and enmeshed in institutions, economic and noneconomic. The inclusion of the noneconomic is vital. For religion or government may be as important for the structure and functioning of the economy as monetary institutions or the availability of tools and machines.' (Polanyi, 1957b:250). The second section, 'Habit and History', examines the specific contribution to economic action of those 'settled habits of thought common to the generality of men' (Veblen, 1919:239) which Veblen, like other institutionalists, regarded as the hard core of an economics of shared perceptions, common beliefs and collective routines: 'Institutions are the rules of the game in a society or, more formally, are the humanly devised constraints that shape human interaction. In consequence they structure incentives in human exchange, whether political, social, or economic.' (North, 1990:3). The section does not deny that money matters. What it does maintain is that social usages matter as well.

The third and final section is concerned with Karl Polanyi – whose alternative to the unemployment and the Fascism of the 1930s was a *social* economics that saw in making and selling no more than the society at work: 'We find ourselves stultified by the legacy of a market-economy which bequeathed us oversimplified views of the function and role of the economic system in society. If the crisis is to be overcome, we must capture a more realistic vision of the human world and shape our common purpose in the light of that recognition.' (Polanyi, 1947: 109). *We* must think and *We* must act. The homeless *I* of textbook exchange is simply not enough: 'Nothing obscures our social vision as effectively as the economistic prejudice.' (Polanyi, 1944:159).

4.1   THE SOCIAL PERSPECTIVE

Conservative capitalism dwells in the social economy. The reason is obvious: while Wild Peter can be a conservative in an unpeopled void, there is no way that he can be a capitalist without his suppliers, his collaborators and his clients. The capitalist economy is a social system.

This section, divided into three parts, shows the ways in which the economics of capitalism is about collective action and mutual support at the same time as it deals with that part of the social fabric which is most closely connected to the nation's wealth.

(a) The Definition of Economics

Economics is often defined as the scientific study of competing opportunities: 'Economics is the science which studies human behaviour as a relationship between ends and scarce means which have alternative uses.' (Robbins, 1933:16). Economics is in that sense the science of constrained choices. It is the science of Oedipus at the crossroads, of Romeo who put Juliet first.

There is much to be said for a science which studies decision-making in the East of Eden niggardliness where not all roads, all partners, all bundles of hay can simultaneously be selected. The difficulty in the definition is, however, that all of human life is there. Where it is economics to change the television-channel or to replace a used-up spouse, economics becomes nothing because nothing is not economics: 'In this sense economists have no subject matter.' (Coase, 1988:3).

Yet economists do have a subject-matter; and its borders may be inferred from the study of what economists actually do. Alfred Marshall, delimiting the discipline in terms of firms, industries, consumers, markets, money, employment, made clear that it was the generation and absorption of desired value-added, not uniquely the perceived scarcity of life-years and other resources, that gave to his branch of investigation its distinctive identity: 'Economics is a study of men as they live and move and think in the ordinary business of life.' (Marshall, 1890:12). Marshall understood the ordinary business of life to mean the ordinary life of business. So did Richard Ely, who had no doubt that economics is overwhelmingly the study of production and its distribution: 'Economics is the science which treats of those social phenomena that are due to the wealth-getting and wealth-using activities of man.' (Ely, 1893:2). Neither Marshall nor Ely believed that producers would continue to expand the supply of goods and services once the consumers had reached the ceiling of absolute satiety, self-defined. To that extent the condition of scarcity is implicit in the work of both. It is implicit in the work of both because it is explicit in human life as a whole. Implicit or explicit, the crucial point is that neither Marshall nor Ely made it the specific characteristic that set his subject-matter apart.

J.R. Commons, like Marshall and Ely, defined the discipline in a manner to which generations of materially minded undergraduates could easily relate: 'Economics deals with the problems of mankind as they go about trying to make a living or get rich.' (Commons, 1950:21). Scarcity is present, implicit and explicit, in the economics of Commons. Resulting from it is, however, the man-made constraint of the agreed-upon-rules: 'Out of scarcity derives not only conflict, but also the collective action that sets up order on account of mutual dependence.' (Commons, 1934:6). Out of material deprivation is born – the midwife is 'negotiational psychology' (Commons, 1934:7), the conciliatory bargaining of give and take – the working rules which then give a conservative structure to the pursuit of wealth. Without those standards, Commons was persuaded, there would simply not be enough harmony of interest to sustain the activities of appropriation and transfer. That is why he made clear that his economics was first and foremost the study of collective action in control, only secondarily the study of land, labour and capital fused: 'Institutional economics is the relation of man to man, but engineering economics is the relation of man to nature. The engineers' concept of wealth excludes all reference to the proprietary economy, which is the historical and institutional economy of the evolution of rights, duties, liberties, and exposures.' (Commons, 1934:256). Economics is the study of man and nature but *also* of man and man. The two together, and not the allocative imperative alone, define the domain that the economist rightly calls his own.

Herbert Simon writes as follows about the city and its boundaries: 'Broadly speaking, economics can be defined as the science that describes and predicts the behavior of several kinds of economic man – notably the consumer and the entrepreneur.' (Simon, 1959:253–4). Like Marshall, Ely and Commons, like Adam Smith and Karl Marx, Simon is here defining the discipline to be the study of the wealth of nations. The economist describes and predicts the creation of the national product, why household consumption rises with income, how the national income is divided up. The economist, 'notably', describes and predicts in what way the supply-and-demand dialogue addresses the coordination problem that is posed by the division of labour. Simon would be the last to question the inclusion of the trading relationship or to brand it as sterile. If the planting, the mining, the manufacturing are all of relevance to the wealth of nations, then so too must be the exchange process that makes possible the realisation of the production-plans through the orderly commutation of superfluities.

Kenneth Boulding goes so far as to treat the study of exchange as the distinguishing feature of the economist's realm. Defining economics as 'the study of the "econosphere" with a view to gaining knowledge about it', he defines the 'econosphere' quite specifically as 'that subset of the sociosphere, or the sphere of all human activity, relationships, and institutions, which is particularly characterized by the phenomenon of exchange' (Boulding, 1966:22). Purposive marketeering is inescapably on the agenda.

Mill made the market the core of the message: 'Only through the principle of competition has political economy any pretension to the character of a science.' (Mill, 1848:242). Buchanan saw free catallaxy as the mission as well: 'As a discipline or area of inquiry, economics has social value in offering an understanding of the principle of order emergent from decentralized processes, of spontaneous coordination.' (Buchanan, 1979:282). The market employs 'the measuring-rod of money' (Pigou, 1920:12) to quantify subjective intensities; and it recon-ciles divergences of interest by means of individually negotiated swaps. In ways such as these, Mill and Buchanan would say, the marketeering posture makes a contribution to social intercourse that is as civilised as it is productive. Be that as it may, ideological liberalism must not be confused with positive economics. Economics as a discipline is the study of the wealth of nations. Sometimes it will endorse the market and sometimes it will not. Always, however, it will protect its intellec-tual autonomy from the endorsement of any single instrumentality in particular.

(b)   Economics and Sociology

The economic is a city. The social is a lens. Economics is concerned with production, consumption, distribution and exchange. Sociology is concerned with interdependent perceptions and interpersonal relation-ships. There are few if any economic activities which do not presuppose the interdependent and the interpersonal. The *enfant sauvage* being an exception, Wild Peter being an anomaly, the observer would therefore do well to contemplate his city with the lens that makes it visible rather than assuming that the isolated study of the isolated individual will somehow produce a realistic image of an articulated whole.

Max Weber defines sociology as 'a science which attempts the inter-pretative understanding of social action in order thereby to arrive at a causal explanation of its course and effects' (Weber, 1947:88). His definition is in two parts. Subjectively speaking, precisely because human action has personal 'meaning' that sets it apart from the mechanistic reactions observed in the physical sciences, the sociologist must employ imagination, sympathy, empathy in such a way as to understand both the rational and the non-logical processes that make the act intelligible in terms of the ideas and the affects (intended or sub-conscious) that motivate the performance. Then, objectively speaking, the sociologist must complement interpretation with empiricism in such a way as to identify the group patterns which emanate from the individuals' minds – the lateral standardisation which ensures that a common situation provokes a common response, the temporal standardisation which builds consistency over time into the matrix of mutual orientation, the rewards and punishments which are seen to produce predictability and to repress conflict. Weber's conceptualisation is evidently an amalgam of psychology (the practitioner putting himself into the mind of the actor in order to establish in what way the subject takes others into account) and of statistics (the practitioner collecting information on recorded uniformities and correlations in order to make conditional forecasts of probable causes and effects). Its theoretical *ex ante* is always the individual – 'For sociological purposes there is no such thing as a collective personality which "acts"' (Weber, 1947:102) – but its empirical *ex post* can be as aggregative as the nation. It is of direct relevance to an understanding of the economic process. The banks, the corporations and the unions are dwellers in the city of value-added. *Verstehen* plus extrapolation make up the lens without which their behaviour-patterns would be seen as random if indeed they were seen at all.

Emile Durkheim, like Max Weber, was the source of important insights which help to circumscribe the social perspective. Beginning with the whole and not with the cell, it was Durkheim's strongly-held conviction that the collective reality dominates the atomistic – that 'there can be no sociology unless societies exist', that 'societies cannot exist if there are only individuals' (Durkheim, 1897:38). Durkheim rejected all forms of utilitarian libertarianism which sought to make the shared no more than the sum of the parts. His refusal to make the *sui generis* of the life in common no more than an emanation from the irreducible body and the essential mind was re-stated by the economist Commons when he insisted that a cake is not the simple aggregation of the original ingredients: '"Society" is not a *sum* of isolated individuals, like a census of population; it is a *multiple* of cooperating individuals.' (Commons, 1950:132). In place of a contextless factoring-down that treated the integrated team-member as if he were an isolated Wild Peter, Durkheim proposed a synthetic and not a reductionist approach which was built around the concept of a 'social fact'. A social fact is external to the actor, internalised through the learning process that schools the individual in language, religion and credit but nonetheless a mode of 'acting, thinking and feeling' which exists in the agent's consciousness because it has been implanted there by the general group mind outside: 'It is a group condition repeated in the individual because imposed on him. It is to be found in each part because it exists in the whole, rather than in the whole because it exists in the parts.' (Durkheim, 1895:9). A social fact is a constraint and not an object of choice. Conformity to the norms can be enforced by laws and punishments. Equally, it can be ensured – 'Air is no less heavy because we do not detect its weight' (Durkheim, 1895:5) – through habit and conscience, through exclusion and ridicule, through the institutional logic of the competitive process that deters the innovating genius from marketing what will not sell. Even in the wealth-orientated sector, Durkheim held, externality and constraint make the *I* a cog in the *We*.

The truth is the whole. This perception, common to Durkheimian sociology and to *Gestalt* psychology, led Solomon Asch to emphasise the explanatory power of interconnectedness and holism, situation and surrounding: 'If actions and experiences are in relations of interdependence, it follows that we must study them in terms of the units of which they are a part. . . . No error in thinking about social facts is more serious than the failure to see their place and function.' (Asch, 1952:60, 61). Objects look different depending on the colour of the background and the angle of the support: 'When the phenomena being observed have order and structure, it is dangerous to concentrate on the parts and to lose sight of their relations.' (Asch, 1952:60). Objects differ in associations depending on whether the remembered setting was a positive one (like the family circle or the peace-pipe) or a focus for revulsion (like aversion therapy employed to condition a reflex): 'There is scarcely an object in our surroundings that we do not perceive differently because of earlier contact with it, and there are few actions that have not been modified by past events.' (Asch, 1952:90). Awareness and interpretation, Asch argues, are best understood not as isolated and one-off but rather as relational and habituated. Applied to economics, what this means is that each action or motive should be seen not as 'natural, permanent, and inevitable' but rather as contingent and relative, the product of particular conditions and of the inter-personal relationships that those uniquenesses engender: 'The first lesson we must learn is that we may not take for granted any concept of man as self-evident, as, for example, the assumption of classical economics that the profit motive is the central fact of economics.' (Asch, 1952:7). Historical, anthropological, inductive, inter-related – what follows from Asch's situational relativism is the strong possibility that different societies ought to study different texts rather than being unified in their economics by the world-view of a middle-class, middle-aged American who has made his money in business.

Asch seeks to show that economic activity is fully integrated into the encompassing matrix of social interaction. His view of wealth-creation as a social fact is shared by Morton Sahlins, who looks to the economy for cultural reproduction and not only for material effectiveness: 'Men do not merely "survive". They survive in a definite way. They reproduce themselves as certain kinds of men and women, social classes and groups.' (Sahlins, 1976:168). Writing explicitly about the hunters and gatherers whose economic production is based upon the commensality, cooperation and cohabitation of domestic communism, Sahlins stresses that the economy in such conditions is a function of the society, not a separate structure or system: 'Even to speak of "*the* economy" of a primitive society is an exercise in unreality. Structurally, "the economy" does not exist. Rather than a distinct and specialized organization, "economy" is something that generalized social groups and relations, notably kinship groups and relations, *do*.' (Sahlins, 1972:76). Sahlins is here referring specifically to the household solidarity of the pre-market community. The more general proposition, that wealth-creation is a part of the matrix of sign and symbol, is, however, for him a fact of life.

Thus, addressing himself to 'bourgeois society as much as the so-called primitive', Sahlins states that 'material aspects are not usefully separated from the social, as if the first were referable to the satisfaction of needs by the exploitation of nature, the second to problems of the relations between men' (Sahlins, 1976:205). Mediated through the extended family or mediated through buying and selling, it is 'meaning' that imposes the order – that specifies the division of labour between men and women, that treats cattle as food and dogs as carrion, that legitimates the relationships between the owners and the workers. It is 'meaning', for that matter, that is responsible for the economist's perception of material scarcity itself – the reason why acquisitive man is driven by infinite wants to perpetuate an insatiable demand ('Economic man is a bourgeois construction') while primitive man is able to content himself with the psychological freedom of 'want not, lack not': 'His wants are scarce and his means (in relation) plentiful.' (Sahlins, 1972:11, 13). It is, Sahlins says, concept and ideology that bind together material goods and social relations in a joint product that cannot usefully be redivided into its elements. Mind and matter, economy and society, Sahlins is in favour of a theory of human behaviour that refuses to treat wealth-creation as a thing apart.

(c) Towards Sociological Economics

Wealth-creation must not be treated as a thing apart: 'As Adam Smith well understood, economic life is deeply embedded in social life.... It cannot be understood apart from the customs, morals, and habits of the society in which it occurs.' (Fukuyama, 1996:13). Economic life, Francis Fukuyama argues, cannot be understood unless it is given its context in comparative culture: 'Economics ... is grounded in social life, and cannot be understood separately from the larger question of how modern societies organize themselves.' (Fukuyama, 1996:xiii). Fukuyama uses the phrase 'cannot be understood'. There is no mistaking his message. Economic models which are too abstract and too formal, Fukuyama is saying, will not be able to provide an adequate account of how the economic system actually operates.

Fukuyama's call for breadth echoes the perspective of George Akerlof, who wrote as follows in support of an economics that models more than why the quantity demanded increases when the price of a complement falls or 'why you can always get spinach in New York' (Akerlof, in Swedberg, 1990:68): 'Just as traditional French cooking does not use seaweed or raw fish, so neoclassical models do not make assumptions derived from psychology, anthropology, or sociology. I disagree with any rules that limit the nature of the ingredients in economic models.' (Akerlof, 1984:3–4). Akerlof's endorsement of openness in turn recalls the eclecticism of J.K. Galbraith, always in search of the tool best suited to the job in hand, always prepared to bypass the established division of academic labour on the grounds that 'the world to its discredit does not divide neatly along the lines that separate the specialists' (Galbraith, 1967:393). Believing as he does that 'the boundaries of a subject matter are conventional and artificial' (Galbraith, 1967:26), Galbraith is unconvinced about inter-disciplinarity lest the institutionalisation of trespass be taken as a *de facto* recognition of irrational frontiers. What is required, Galbraith maintains, is not respectful collaboration between hermetically sealed disciplines but rather the unbiased investigation that studies whole phenomena without the schooled complacency of invariant professionalisation: 'Modern economic life is seen much more clearly when . . . there is effort to see it whole.' (Galbraith, 1967:25).

Thinkers such as Fukuyama, Akerlof and Galbraith, building on earlier authors like Smith, Marx and Schumpeter, favour a broad and eclectic approach to the study of the wealth of nations. Their emphasis on a socially informed economics which does not assume any single institutional structure, normative orientation or objective function clearly differentiates their interpretation of the livelihood of man from the less cultural, more mechanistic economics of the neoclassical orthodoxy. The neoclassical economics speaks when it ought to listen. The first defining characteristic of a socially informed economics is therefore a negative one, that it is sharply critical of an over-confident mainstream that takes too much for granted. The second defining characteristic is more positive. A socially informed economics is the economics of perception, interaction and process. Anthropocentric rather than reiocentric, it is the economics of people and of goods and services only in so far as they relate to people.

The neoclassical economics is concerned with maximisation subject to a resources constraint. It makes extensive use of mathematical logic including differential calculus. It tends to focus on the atomistic choice of a single individual (maximising utility) or a single firm (maximising profit). It explains how action disrupts equilibrium and how reaction re-establishes it. It adopts a deductive methodology which reasons from the twin axioms of instrumental rationality and personal self-interest. It generally assumes that human nature, property-rights, consumer preferences are all exogenous and stable over time. It usually takes markets to be competitive and information to be adequate. It is sympathetic to the obsessive economising of the means–ends posture: no science which takes its teleology from the poverty of nations can tolerate inefficiency or criticise the careful calculativeness which optimises the welfare squeezed from a given endowment. It is favourable to consumer sovereignty, revealed preference and the freedom of choice: its theories of highest-attainable need-satisfaction presuppose voluntary exchange, market-clearing prices and an invisible hand as often as possible unfettered by State intervention. Above all, it is value-free. Philosophers treat constructs like autonomy, non-satiety, interest, efficiency, choice as value-laden and open to debate. Not so the neoclassical economics. In neoclassical theory the constructs are not value-judgements at all but simple facts of life.

The neoclassical economics is persuaded that its background assumptions are relatively plausible. It has no serious doubts about the real-world relevance of economic men and women who make it their business to claw together their value for money. Even if the preconceptions were themselves dubious, moreover, that in itself would not necessarily affect the practical usefulness of the neoclassical axiomatics as seen by Dewey-like pragmatists interested most of all in results. Thus Milton Friedman, making clear that knowledge and understanding are not the scarce utilities that the economist most wishes effectively to maximise, has said that assumptions are 'good' not if they are 'true' but if 'the theory works' – 'which means whether it yields sufficiently accurate predictions' (Friedman, 1953:15). Social economists object in vain, Friedman would say, when they complain that the *let-us-assume*s are psychologically impoverished and culturally deprived. Prediction is the aim, explanation is not, and description is of little or no value to the economist who has a function to fulfil: 'The more significant the theory, the more unrealistic the assumptions.' (Friedman, 1953:14). *After God coughs he spits* – an economist who uses that nonsensical correlation to forecast rain on the basis of thunder can make a lot of money selling umbrellas in the Strand.

The neoclassical economics judges its success by the dual standard of rigour in presentation and accuracy of prediction. It is in the circumstances insensitive to the criticism that it is too quick to pyramid deductions without first 'performing the hard work of observing people' (Simon, 1959:254). The economic mainstream, Herbert Simon writes, is too quick to economise on the *minutiae* of man as he really is – on the raw data, qualitative as well as quantitative, that must so often be hewn out at first hand by means of interviews, questionnaires, case-studies, attitudinal surveys and participant observation. The mainstream economist, Herbert Simon continues, is too quick to shelter behind a naive caricature of rationality and interest, invariant in time and space. It brushes aside the multiplicities of contingency on the grounds that a person who makes a special study of scarcity simply 'doesn't need a theory of human behavior': 'He wants to know how people *ought* to behave, not how they *do* behave.' (Simon, 1959:254). Simon has little enthusiasm for so inward-looking a professional agenda, more concerned with abstract reasoning than with anthropological evidence, all-too-prone to ignore topics which are unsuited to symbolic simplification. What is needed, Simon believes, is a broader programme, committed to no specific *a priori* but open instead to the never-ending input of new findings. The neoclassicist's response to the empiricist's call for data is not difficult to anticipate. Induction is good in its place but statistics are only a means to an end. Historians collect information for its own sake. Economists buy only what they need to supply galoshes and not ice-creams in the Strand.

Social economics shows a greater awareness of relativity and situation, neoclassical economics a greater confidence in absolutes and universals. Social economics has therefore a greater attachment to fact-gathering using only tentative hypotheses, to explanations that accommodate the evidence collected rather than imposing upon it the standard meaning supplied from stock. Social economics, more specifically, directs its fact-gathering and its explaining to three closely connected areas of social science inquiry.

First, perception. The economy is refracted through the mind. Chemical reactions do not think and physical quantities do not feel. People are different. Social economics seeks to understand the ideas and the motives that lie behind the wealth-related choices. It is especially concerned with the patterned responses of individuals in groups. In its campaign to study the wealth-related through mental states at once interdependent and inter-personal, its quest recalls the 'interpretative understanding' of Weber, the 'collective representations' of Durkheim, the codes of Asch, the symbols of Sahlins – and the deep-seated socialisation which leads Parsons and Smelser to say this about the significance of the innate psychological essence: 'The individual is not the defining unit for the maximization of utility.' (Parsons and Smelser, 1956:22). Society dwelling within whispers to each of us the choices that it has programmed us to make. Social economics makes a study of the perceptions, the innate and the common alike.

Veblen took exception to the image of man as a 'lightning calculator of pleasures and pains', a 'homogeneous globule of desire of happiness' (Veblen, 1919:73), that he found in the economics of the utilitarian hedonists. The flattening of rounded human nature into the textbook simplification of the ideal-typical capitalist was, he contended, both unsupported and misleading. His doubts and criticisms were later shared by Coase, who found little connection between the economist's stereotype and the real-world mindset: 'The rational utility maximizer of economic theory bears no resemblance to the man on the Clapham bus.... There is no reason to suppose that most human beings are engaged in maximizing anything unless it be unhappiness, and even this with incomplete success.' (Coase, 1988:3, 4). A more useful focus would therefore be real perceptions in place of the imputed perceptions that the man on the Clapham bus might not recognise to be his own.

The contents of the human mind are notoriously difficult to observe. Social economics does the best that it can, using the empathetic understanding of Weberian *Verstehen* to discover what actual human beings are actually thinking and feeling. Its search for subjectivity and meaning, however fuzzy, impressionistic and inexact, is well captured by Commons in the following invitation to enter into the state of mind: 'What the economist wants is *understanding*, and he wants *measurement* only as an aid to understanding. The subject-matter with which an economist deals is not a mechanism or organism whose motions the investigator cannot *understand* – it is human beings whose activities he can fairly well understand by putting himself "in their place".' (Commons, 1934:723). Concerned with *why* as well as with *what, how, how much*, the economist like the psychoanalyst is obliged willy-nilly to invite his charges on to the couch.

Social economics picks up the degree and nature of rationality, together with the extent to which instrumentalism is legitimated by collective values. Social economics assesses the particular mix of malevolence, benevolence and commercial self-interest that it identifies in representative individuals acculturated into unique social groups. Social economics studies the relative impact of intrinsic satisfactions, peer-group emulation and want creation through advertising and salesmanship on the consumer's estimation of material scarcity. Social economics studies the balance of business profit-seeking and of other human objectives in the utility-function of the individuals who make up the firm. Social economics, in short, builds up a picture of perceptions in context which, useful or not for the sale of umbrellas in the Strand, makes a humanitarian contribution to the elucidation of why people do as they do when they supply and demand.

Second, interaction. The economy can be conceptualised as isolated individuals making discrete decisions, as rootless anonymities bound together in a coordinated whole through the self-regulating automaticity of the sensitive price-mechanism. The economy can also be viewed as role-playing and social expectation, integration and consensus, history and situation. Social economics, rejecting the libertarian universalisation which identifies economic activity with free-standing exchange, is favourable to the latter perspective. In place of price theory, gravity and natural law, it proposes that structure and overlap be made the primary focus of the inquiry into the wealth of nations.

Thus Etzioni, criticising market liberalism for assigning excessive importance to the detached choice-maker, argues that 'individuals act within a social context' that is 'not reducible to individual acts': 'Social collectivities . . . are the prime decision-making units.' (Etzioni, 1988:4, 5). The patterns and sequences are external and constraining in the purest Durkheimian sense: 'Decisions of the kind economists routinely study – what people buy, how much they invest, how hard they work, and so on – largely reflect their society, polity, culture and sub-culture, class, as well as collectivities to which they used to belong.' (Etzioni, 1988:181). Extreme reductionists would therefore do well to remember that the I might not after all be the fundamental unit of social choice: 'There is no historical or logical reason to assume that fully formed individuals preceded the community or shared rules. Indeed, . . . the individuals would not exist, if there were no community and no rules.' (Etzioni, 1988:199). Internalisation of the patterns and sequences at least ensures that the shared identity will not necessarily be perceived as a bond that is imposed: 'Instead, the social context is, to a significant extent, perceived as a legitimate and integral part of one's existence, a We, a whole of which the individuals are constituent elements.' (Etzioni, 1988:5). Besides that, the social I, not merely the passive repository of the macrocosm's values, retains the capacity to exercise his active creativity in response to a changing world. The social I is evidently neither under-socialised (in the sense of a calculative contractarianism that regards the community simply as an 'aggregation of individuals temporarily joined for their own convenience') nor over-socialised (in the sense of prescriptive totalitarianism such as makes the 'shared union' and not the free agent the single 'source of authority and legitimacy') (Etzioni, 1988:8). The social I is instead a creature of the middle ground, a creature of balance who flourishes best when making the most of the 'creative tension' that is the dialogue between the free innovator and the encompassing We: '*The individual and the community make each other and require each other*. The society is not a "constraint", nor even an "opportunity", *it is us*.' (Etzioni, 1988:9). Etzioni's approach to the capitalist economy is clearly not the approach of the economic maximisers. A study of I and We, the central theme in his social economics is the interaction of free individuals within the matrix of the group.

Karl Marx too saw the wealth of nations as the interactions of people: 'It is plain that commodities cannot go to market and make exchanges of their own account. We must, therefore, have recourse to their guardians, who are also their owners.' (Marx, 1867:84). Emphasising the systemic patterning of ownership and class, Marx grouped agents in terms of economic resources and productive function: 'The characters who appear on the economic stage are but the personifications of the economic relations that exist between them.' (Marx, 1867:85). He also advised that economists should delve beneath the superficiality of market price, lest the 'social relation between men' be falsely perceived in the 'fantastic form of a relation between things' (Marx, 1867:72). Marx, convinced that all value is created by labour and that commodity fetishism mystifies the alienation of the surplus by the *bourgeois* class, drew attention to the economic importance of variables such as power relationships, ideological convictions, property rights and political linkages that were later to be defined out of economics altogether and buried in the *ceteris paribus* pound. Marx saw little reason to assume other things to be constant when in truth they were at the cutting edge.

Third, process. Social economics studies perception and interaction. It also studies the changes in perception and interaction that occur over time. Perception and interaction, like the wealth of nations itself, are not outcome and endstate, equilibrium and destination. Rather, they are history and evolution, development and process. It is therefore important to trace out the changes both in ideas (such as achievement and contract) and in phenomena (such as multinationalism and computerisation) in order to situate observed occurrences in a restless context that always flows on.

The context flows – but much within that flowing context flows on with a lag. Temperamental conservatives like Daniel Bell draw great inspiration from the image of past generations come back to defend the traditional beachheads alongside their present-day successors who have inherited the title: 'When one is cut off from the past, one cannot escape the final sense of nothingness that the future then holds.' (Bell, 1976:50). Temperamental modernisers like Karl Marx, on the other hand, are unsentimental and unsympathetic in respect of vestigial institutions which have become an impediment to the progress of the new:

'Men make their own history, but they do not make it just as they please; they do not make it under circumstances chosen by themselves, but under circumstances directly found, given and transmitted from the past. The tradition of all the dead generations weighs like a nightmare on the brain of the living.' (Marx, 1852:315). Either way, the inertia of custom is an important topic in the conservative capitalism of socialised men and women who address the future through the responses they have learned.

Process means the habituated, the time-dominated and the familiar. Social economics clearly has no *a priori* expectation that choice, however rational and economising, will take place without memory. Process also means the mutability of the continuous, the sequencing of the unplanned. Social economics in that sense is concerned with the development of new conventions even as it is sensitive to the resistance of the *status quo*. Self-perpetuation on the one hand, the challenge to routine on the other – Veblen was able to resolve the apparent contradiction between stability and flexibility, rigidity and novelty, by situating the 'altering' and the 'fortifying' alike within the matrix of the evolutionary scheme: 'The situation of today shapes the institutions of tomorrow through a selective, coercive process, by acting upon men's habitual view of things, and so altering or fortifying a point of view or a mental attitude handed down from the past.' (Veblen, 1899:132–3). Today's experiences sometimes threaten yesterday's habits and sometimes reinforce them. The evolutionary perspective elucidates the balance of the currents within the flow of a social process that never reaches an end.

4.2 HABIT AND HISTORY

Perception and interaction, inseparable from process, are often the norms and canons of a group life-style that was carried over from the past: 'Institutions are an outgrowth of habit. The growth of culture is a cumulative sequence of habituation.' (Veblen, 1919:241). The neo-classical economics, Veblen wrote, was wrong to ignore the cumulative causality and the predetermined choices which were the consequence: 'The postulates of marginal utility, and the hedonistic preconceptions generally, fail at this point in that they confine the attention to such bearings of economic conduct as are conceived not to be conditioned by habitual standards and ideals and to have no effect in the way of habituation.' (Veblen, 1919:243). A more realistic approach, Veblen argued, would be to make the habituation of ideas and actions a central topic in the study of the wealth of nations: 'Any science, such as economics, which has to do with human conduct, becomes a genetic inquiry into the human scheme of life; and where, as in economics, the subject of inquiry is the conduct of man in his dealings with the material means of life, the science is necessarily an inquiry into the life-history of material civilization.' (Veblen, 1919:241). A behavioural science such as economics is necessarily an inquiry into the legacy of history, into the 'habits of thought accumulated through the experience of past generations' (Veblen, 1914:7). A wealth-orientated subject such as economics is necessarily an inquiry into the on-going dialogue between hereditary traits and traditional expectations: 'The economic life history of the individual is a cumulative process of adaptation of means to ends that cumulatively change as the process goes on, both the agent and his environment being at any point the outcome of the last process.' (Veblen, 1919:74–5). A behavioural science, a wealth-orientated subject, economics, Veblen stressed, was not static and spot but rather the economic history which was the moving picture of the society at work.

Veblen, in his interpretation of economics as economic history, assigned considerable importance to cultural lag and self-reinforcing regularity: 'Men's present habits of thought tend to persist indefinitely, except as circumstances enforce a change. These institutions which have thus been handed down, these habits of thought, points of view, mental attitudes and aptitudes, or what not, are themselves therefore a conservative factor.' (Veblen, 1899:133). Present-day choices, even where the calculus is conscious, purposive, rational, are still most unlikely to be made *ab initio*, to proceed without the memory of precedent or the pressure of personal contact. Embedded in the customs and the patterns of the group, standardised routines and legitimated practices are a source of repetition and replication. They are a reminder that it is not only income that can constrain, not only the State that can constrict. They are also a reminder that present-day obedience can be a shared response not to a current but rather to an embodied stimulus. In the words of Douglass North: 'History matters. It matters not just because we can learn from the past, but because the present and the future are connected to the past by the continuity of a society's institutions. Today's and tomorrow's choices are shaped by the past.' (North, 1990:viii). History matters. Tradition matters. The challenge of 1530 beckons. The door to 1241 is open wide.

As formal as laws, as diffuse as codes, transmitted usages are a cultural dimension which the unbiased inquiry into the wealth of nations cannot afford to neglect. The probable impact of the cultural conservatism upon the performance of the capitalist economy is a topic about which it is more difficult to be categorical. There is an undeniable temptation to predict stagnation and statics on the basis that the incentive structure which is the most conducive to fitting in will not be the incentive structure which is the most congenial to dynamic advance: 'The organizations that develop in this institutional framework will become more efficient – but more efficient at making the society even more unproductive and the basic institutional structure even less conducive to productive activity.' (North, 1990:9). An excess of cultural baggage probably does have this deadweight effect on the rate of productive advance. Importantly, however, a deficiency of cultural baggage may be said to have the same inhibiting impact. Some social habits, the vestiges of history, are in truth not social limits to growth but instead valuable inputs in the nation's production-function.

(a) The Frame of Reference

Raw data must be selected and processed. Overload, not scarcity, is the problem – but the filter of culture provides a guide and a weighting-scheme: 'Culture provides a language-based conceptual framework for encoding and interpreting the information that the senses are presenting to the brain.' (North, 1990:37). Even a map which was drawn up in the past can be less confusing than to be surrounded by knowledge with no map at all. Especially will this be so where change is slow, incremental and continuous. Marginalism in the sense of gradualism makes possible reasonable assessments using tried-and-tested schemata. Revolutions and impulsiveness make the choice and classification of data that much more difficult.

Where *natura non facit saltum*, information can be deployed with the efficiency born of experience and unnecessary costs can in that way be avoided. Different people experience different realities: people at the margin will have to make use of modified filters. External realities themselves move on: theories at the margin must be updated in order to retain their explanatory power. Difference and development are at the margin moderate exceptions to a rule that is constant. Where *natura non facit saltum*, however, the exceptions are less likely to call into question the value of the schema than would be the case where a radical breach occurred with the beliefs and practices of the past. Japanese culture remained recognisably itself despite the devastation and the trauma of the Second World War. Informal Russian codes showed a remarkable resilience when exposed to the laws and edicts of the Soviet social engineers. A cultural breach must evidently be a radical one indeed.

Situating new stimuli in the context of habituated images, blotting out unexpected occurrences because they lack a home in the familiar framework, people fall back on existing structures when they seek to make sense of external reality. The procedures can be as individual as the private and personal rule of thumb, as social as the common and shared selective standard. It is the contention of the socially informed economist that the common counts for much, that preexisting categories can be a collective property rather than simply an idiosyncratic heuristic – and that people, free to think, very often exercise their option to reason and to construe within the limits set by 'information generating devices', by 'practices which encode expectations' (Hargreaves Heap, 1989:72), that are no less than the shared institutions of a group with an identity of its own: 'They refer to the commonly held patterns of behaviour and habits of thought, of a routinized and durable nature, that are associated with people interacting in groups or larger collectives. Institutions enable ordered thought and action by imposing form and consistency on the activities of human beings.' (Hodgson, 1993: 253). Stable and inert, the shared prisms act as a restraint on individual vision but also promote the inter-temporal cohesion of a social aggregate that views as one.

(b)   The Normative Guide

Institutions chart raw data and channel perceptions into permitted patterns. They also influence behaviour and 'impart some regularity to the practices of human action' (Hargreaves Heap, 1989:72). Thought or action, mind or matter, the customary and the conventional standardise normative guidance and encourage predictable performance. Institutions, 'through the operation of tradition, custom or legal constraint', tend, Hodgson writes, 'to create durable and routinized patterns of behaviour' which are the *sine qua non* for the anticipation of response: 'It is this very durability and routinization, in a highly complex and sometimes volatile world, which makes social science with any practical application possible at all.' (Hodgson, 1988:10). Capitalism involves spontaneity, novelty, strategy and imagination. Conservatism makes capitalism possible by ensuring that entrepreneurial initiatives will be complemented by a bedrock of interactions neither uncertain nor unforeseeable.

Institutions systematise individuality and make conduct determinate. They do this, as Axelrod explains, by a mix of prescription and punishment: 'A norm exists in a given social setting to the extent that individuals usually act in a certain way and are often punished when seen not to be acting in this way.' (Axelrod, 1986:1097). Thus, in the case of a formal code, the courts and the police services are charged with the enforcement of the common law and the statute law. It is the duty of the protective infrastructure (a duty executed at a non-negligible enforcement cost) to detect violation and to compel compliance; while it is the option of the would-be defector to select a risk that carries a non-negligible expected value of sanction. Again, in the case of an informal rule, the fact that the standard is unwritten and diffuse need not mean that it will fail to acquire the status of a social imperative. Parsons and Smelser have described informal institutions as the 'ways in which the value patterns of the common culture of a social system are integrated in the concrete action of its units in their interaction with each other through the definition of role expectations and the organization of motivation' (Parsons and Smelser, 1956:102). Parsons and Smelser in their invocation of roles and motivation leave the reader in no doubt that even without the overhead of specialist enforcement the social discipline of all upon each will have a profound effect in defending the group's endorsements and taboos against the threat from individual choice. Businessmen who fail to pay bribes can find themselves excluded from contacts, contracts and concessions. Surgeons who undercut competitors can be cut off from professional referrals and hospital privileges. The traditional standards that endorse the corruption and make the rivalry taboo are not formal codes with a standing in law. Their impact on the gains from trade can for all that be just as predictable and just as strong.

Thus Akerlof has made social custom a possible cause of involuntary unemployment in a country where socialised employers, fair-minded and reputation-conscious, resist the auctioneer's invitation to impose the market-clearing wage. In paying above the odds to defend the 'just price', these past-perpetuating capitalists are *de facto* trading pecuniary advantage for a non-material gain which, assuming rational choice, is expected to leave them better-off in their own estimation. Profit is sold but utility is purchased: clearly, 'nonindividualistic-maximizing behavior may result in equilibria that are qualitatively different from those obtained from individualistic-maximizing behavior' (Akerlof, 1980: 72). Social approbation, sufficiently valued, can evidently be used to explain the failure of labour markets to adjust – and the persistence of (non-search) unemployment that can directly be attributed to the strict moral principles of employers who conform when the job-creating alternative would be to compete.

If the price of honour becomes too great, presumably even the morally-minded will budget anew in the light of the unacceptable disparity between the marginal cost and the marginal benefit. Where the majority respects the rigid money wage, the deviant can conclude mutually beneficial exchanges that not even a minimum wage law can entirely prevent. Where the consensus condemns interest-taking for money that is sterile, the usurer and the arbitrageur can reap the rent to odium that Adam Smith identified in the generous remuneration of the public executioner. Writing of differentials, Adam Smith observed that 'honour makes a great part of the reward of all honourable professions' and that 'disgrace has the contrary effect' (Smith, 1776:I, 112). His doctrine of compensating advantages may easily be extended to the wage-cutter and the interest-taker who renege on custom but catch up through cash. The economics of adherence is in such a perspective the economics of the next-best forgone: 'A custom that is fairly costless to follow will, once established, continue to be followed. . . . A custom that is too costly to follow, in terms of lost utility, will not be followed and therefore will disappear.' (Akerlof, 1980: 95). Obedience has a cost and adherence has a price. Hazarding a guess, Akerlof, like Marshall, would put his money on continuity and the median rule: 'I would tend to believe that usually the greatest returns go to those who do not break social customs.' (Akerlof, 1976:44). In the long-run the pressures may be irresistible: 'The usurer of the Middle Ages has turned into the banker of today.' (Akerlof, 1976:35). In the short run, however, the interest in acceptance probably exceeds the interest in interest, making social custom relatively secure.

(c) Stability as a Productive Input

Institutions situate raw data. Institutions systematise social action. Habits, in short, are a source of location and legitimation: 'Although the mix of rules and norms varies, . . . the combination nevertheless provides us with the comfortable feeling of knowing what we are doing and where we are going.' (North, 1990:83). The way of life is familiar, the biases and prejudices a part of the self. Looking backward while looking forward undoubtedly makes the community feel good about itself. Social survival is safe in the hands of the cultural conservatives. More open to debate is, however, the status of economic efficiency, allocative and dynamic.

Freud drew attention to the functionality of repression. His starting-point was the innate indolence, the in-bred lack of responsibility, which for him discredited the optimistic perfectionism of the utopian individualists: 'Human beings exhibit an inborn tendency to careless-ness, irregularity and unreliability in their work.' (Freud, 1930:93). Human nature is evidently not on the side of *homo faber*. The habit of discipline, however, puts backbone into the weakness of will: 'Order is a kind of compulsion to repeat which, when a regulation has been laid down once and for all, decides when, where and how a thing shall be done, so that in every similar circumstance one is spared hesitation and indecision. . . . It enables men to use space and time to the best advantage, while conserving their psychical forces.' (Freud, 1930: 93). Institutions focus action and permit economies in the labour of choice. The repeat purchase of a brand name spares the hesitation and indecision that would accompany the risk-assessment of unknown probabilities. The social logic that legitimises the established sequence conserves the psychic forces that would be wasted in the rationalisation into consistency of the cognitively dissonant. The habitual patterns and the regular reassures. As Durkheim writes, putting (social) bounds above (individual) inclinations: 'Man's nature cannot be itself except as it is disciplined.' (Durkheim, 1925:51). Acceptance liberates and choice enslaves. Durkheim, like Freud, is saying clearly that non-rationality will often be the most rational of all the options on offer.

Institutions 'define and limit the set of choices of individuals' (North, 1990:4). They also keep down the transaction-costs of interaction at the level of the group. As with constraint, so with coordination, the expectation must be of an economic gain. Learned rules of the road obviate the need for on-the-spot negotiation. Taken-for-granted rights eliminate the disruption from labour disputes. Knee-jerk shopping means that the processes and even the outcomes do not have to be thought through. Culture expects nurses and secretaries to be female (even if a man could process the work at twice the speed). Culture looks askance at training opportunities offered to low-return blacks (in that way making the vicious circle of stereotype into a self-fulfilling pro-phesy of under-achievement). It is not the thrust of the present point that cultural expectations such as these will necessarily make a useful contribution to economic advance – nor even that perpetuation *per se* will necessarily be more economical of scarce resources than would be scrapping and starting again. The present point is simply that, in a situation of relative *stasis*, the balance between the bargaining interests can be such that none of the contracting parties will regard it as cost-effective to press strongly for a restructuring of the agreement: 'Note that such a situation does not imply that everyone is happy with the existing rules and contracts, but only that the relative costs and benefits of altering the game among the contracting parties do not make it worth while to do so.' (North, 1990:86). It is, in such an equilibrium, more economical to retain the existing institutions than to incur the transaction costs of settling upon a different compromise.

Stability is economical in the negative sense that euro-denominated price-lists need not then be introduced nor Europe-standard plugs be fitted at a cost. Yet stability contributes to the economical use of scarce resources in another way as well. Rules and habits are an anchor in a sea of uncertainty. The same may be said of price and wage norms that constrict the amplitude of market adaptability. In the one sense as in the other the conditioned expectation inhibits the freshness of response. In the one case as in the other, however, the normative guidance may be said to be the precondition for the market to be able to function at all. Consider Schumpeter, arguing that tradition is 'an essential element of the capitalist schema' and that contract itself only acquires its legitimacy from the cultural values that were born before: 'No social system can work which is based exclusively upon a network of free contracts between (legally) equal contracting parties and in which everyone is supposed to be guided by nothing except his own (short-run) utilitarian ends.' (Schumpeter, 1942:139, 423–4). Consider Keynes, observing that conventional expectations make it less difficult to guess the outcome of a beauty-contest, maintaining that time and money are saved and mutual security is provided where the market participants face an unknown future with the knowledge of a known and a normal state: 'Although output and employment are determined by the producer's short-term expectations and not by past results, the most recent results usually play a predominant part in determining what these expectations are.' (Keynes, 1936:50–1).

Keynes's preferred illustration of lagged 'average opinion' and kinked mass psychology is the demand for money – transactionary, precautionary and speculative. Keynes, drawing attention to remembered bond prices and historical interest rates, showed that accustomed reactions can limit the instabilities that the battle of wits imposes on an uncertainty that recalls no standard: 'It might be more accurate, perhaps, to say that the rate of interest is a highly conventional, rather than a highly psychological, phenomenon. . . . *Any* level of interest which is accepted with sufficient conviction as *likely* to be durable *will* be durable.' (Keynes, 1936:203). Keynes's appreciation of the manner in which extrapolated probabilities provide boundaries and targets that make possible long-term business planning without the directive of the State is shared by Hodgson, who writes as follows not just of financial functionalities but of all nominal values in the capitalist market economy: 'The (partial) rigidity of prices and wages should not be treated as a restrictive assumption to be imposed upon a "more general" model. Rigidities are not a "special case". These so-called "imperfections" help to impose coherence and order on the market system. Markets function coherently *because* of these "imperfections", and not despite them as mainstream theorists presume.' (Hodgson, 1988:191). Rigid values reduce the risks of randomness and make economic relationships easier to anticipate.

Rigid values result from and perpetuate the economy's non-calculating correlations. They are also traditional images and familiar information, a feature of 'our common way of life' and somehow right and proper for that reason alone. The past is evidently a moral past, a cultural past and not just an economic past. In that sense the economic stability discussed with approbation by Keynes and Hodgson blends into the social stability that was at the heart of Schumpeter's conservative capitalism. We start from here because we start from there. As Hayek points out, we have no choice: 'Man's mind is itself a product of the civilization in which he has grown up and...is unaware of much of the experience which has shaped it – experience that assists it by being embodied in the habits, conventions, language, and moral beliefs which are part of its makeup.' (Hayek, 1960:24). Man's intellectual biography is not a prudent buy so much as an external accretion. The neoclassical economics is therefore too shallow where it fails to acknowledge the normative inheritance that makes the next round so dependent upon the authority of the previous encounters.

Hayek is positive about rule-following that transcends the case-by-case: 'In order to make ourselves act rationally we often find it necessary to be guided by habit rather than reflection.' (Hayek, 1960:66). So, and for not dissimilar reasons, is Viktor Vanberg: 'At least beyond the narrow confines of very small face-to-face groups, a viable social order seems not even conceivable if the rules on which it rests would only be obeyed in those instances where the particular situational constraints render rule-compliance in fact the utility-maximizing choice.' (Vanberg, 1988:13). Agreeing with Hayek that man by his nature is 'as much a rule-following animal as a purpose-seeking one' (Hayek, 1973:11), Vanberg strongly defends the contribution of acceptance that is not the short-run purchase of an in-period reward but rather the multi-period convergence on prescription by consent. Socially and economically alike, Vanberg stresses, precommitment in advance of play is the pre-condition for the generation of satisfactory outcomes. It is the *sine qua non* because the promise to obey is a constitutional commitment not susceptible to the continuous re-justification of the act-by-act calculus. As David Gauthier has put it so well: 'Duty overrides advantage, but the acceptance of duty is truly advantageous.' (Gauthier, 1986:2).

Institutions situate. Institutions guide. Institutions stabilise. The habits that are handed down through history may be said in these three ways to have a positive effect on economic performance. Yet not every observer will accept that the past belongs in the production function or that individualism and contract ought to be forced down roads which rationality and interest would never have selected. Just as some will say that institutions improve performance, so others will reply that produc-tivity is more likely to be stifled by a traditionalism that treats new angles as a threat.

The economiser's *critique* is in a real sense a difference of degree and not of direction. Most economisers are favourable, after all, to the dis-cipline of office routine, coordination through traffic-lights and the stability of annual instead of hourly pay-settlements. Few economisers would regard it as a prudent commitment of transaction costs to substi-tute continuous haggling for a bedrock of institutions such as these. What the advocates of the flexible response would, however, contend is that the economist should make it his study, treating the inherited as the exception, to live in the expected future and to start from here.

4.3 POLANYI

Karl Polanyi (1886–1964) was an Austro-Hungarian intellectual who, uprooting himself to England in 1933, turned in his fifties, sixties and seventies from the social-democratic journalist he had been in Vienna into an extra-mural lecturer at London and Oxford, a Visiting Pro-fessor at Benington College, Vermont, and a Professor at Columbia University. The formative years that culminated in *The Great Trans-formation* (1944) and *The Livelihood of Man* (1977), 'Our Obsolete Market Mentality' (published in *Commentary* in 1947) and 'Marketless Trading in Hammurabi's Time', 'Aristotle Discovers the Economy', 'The Economy as Instituted Process' (all published in *Trade and Market in the Early Empires* in 1957) had seen the breakdown of the international gold standard, the collapse of full employment, the rise of Fascist dictatorship, the two World Wars, the success of Roosevelt's New Deal, of Stalin's Five Year Plans, of Keynes's budgetary interventionism in restoring macroeconomic performance despite the perceived harm that had been done by the Enlightenment's *laissez-faire*. Herbert Spencer had championed the automaticity of gain-seeking capitalism against the background of the *pax Victoriana*. Karl Polanyi was the witness to more troubled times.

Polanyi was a man of passion and mission who turned to historical and comparative evidence in order to establish the economic causes of social dislocation. Closer to Tolstoy than to Marx, he did not see the crisis of his times in terms of subsistence wages, exploitation of labour, class conflict, the pro-bourgeois State, but rather as the direct consequence of an over-optimistic Victorianism which had unwisely decoupled the car from the track: 'The origins of the cataclysm lay in the utopian endeavour of economic liberalism to set up a self-regulating market system.' (Polanyi, 1944:29). The material disruption, the cultural degradation, were, Polanyi suggested, all but inevitable, given the over-confident reductionism that had disregarded Aristotle's practice of treating the economy as inextricably embedded in its inter-personal context. Economy is society and never a thing apart – this, as Stanfield indicates, was the essence of Polanyi's campaign to bend back the bent rod to make it straight again: 'His motive for studying the place of economy in society was to induce people to put the economy in its place and keep it there. He thought and felt . . . that this is the central problem of existence and the most imperative struggle of our times.' (Stanfield, 1986:25).

At the level of *analysis*, the crux of the economy is pattern-maintenance and the codes of community: 'The outstanding discovery of recent historical and anthropological research is that man's economy, as a rule, is submerged in his social relationships. He does not so act as to safeguard his individual interest in the possession of material goods; he acts so as to safeguard his social standing, his social claims, his social assets. He values material goods only in so far as they serve this end.' (Polanyi, 1944:46). What Polanyi is saying is that economic activity is intimately bound up with role-playing and group cohesion, with conformity and ties, with personal identity in the sense that it is understood by a cultural conservative such as Gray when he writes as follows about the 'unchosen histories' that ensure, for social individuals, 'that what is most essential about them is, in the end, what is most accidental': 'Human individuals are not natural data, such as pebbles or apples, but are artefacts of social life, cultural and historical achievements: they are, in short, exfoliations of the common life itself. Without common forms of life, there are no individuals.' (Gray, 1993:65, 136–7). Economists in such a perspective are economic sociologists who make it their business to comprehend the web of meanings and contacts that is spun when 'common life' takes its course in the office, the factory or the shop. Economists are evidently not economic technocrats, committed by their professional oath to the single, named maximand of efficiency, allocative and dynamic, which in turn leads them to put in a principled defence of competitive pricing and the freedom of trade. Man's economy is submerged in his social relationships. The economist should study that embeddedness – and should do so without imposing on his subjects some unique, prefabricated template that alone can shield them from the terrors of scarcity.

Polanyi was sharply critical of the narrow-minded fixation which sees in the *economic* nothing more than the *economising*: 'The economistic fallacy...consists in a tendency to equate the human economy with its market form.' (Polanyi, 1977:20). Polanyi saw no possible reason to shoe-horn his analysis into so monolithic, so universalistic, so intolerant a structure. Repeatedly, he sought to analyse phenomena in an unblinkered manner that did not prejudge the legitimacy of the institutions.

One illustration would be the non-judgemental openness that he brought to the tradition-furthering models of the 'just price' that had been developed by Aristotle and Aquinas: 'The rate of exchange must be such as to maintain the community.... Not the interests of the individuals, but those of the community were the governing principle. The skills of persons of different status had to be exchanged at a rate proportionate to the status of each: the builder's performance exchanged against [so] many times the cobbler's performance; unless this was so, reciprocity was infringed and the community would not hold.' (Polanyi, 1957a:88). Maine's 'status', not Maine's 'contract', is the core of equivalence in the sense of those conservatives from Hammurabi in Babylon to the present-day critics of market-pricing's fluctuating fickleness who expect from their exchange ratios the perpetuation of a satisfying social pattern and only secondarily the 'higgling-haggling' of supply and demand. The traditional differentials that monetise the accustomed social distance demonstrate the survival in contemporary collective bargaining of the perspective that allocation is not the only function of price. So does the Catholic doctrine (sometimes invoked to defend the minimum-wage law on the grounds of Christian charity) that payment must be sufficient to protect the self-respect of the worker and to discourage the disembeddedness of social exclusion. Polanyi (whose father, of Jewish origin, had converted to Protestantism) was brought up in Catholic Austria at a time when the theological mainstream was Leo XIII's sharply anti-individualistic *Rerum Novarum* of 1891.

Polanyi analysed economic relations without the prior specification that they must be market relations as well. The conventional price provides one illustration of his practice. The uniqueness of labour and land is a second. Manufactured commodities, Polanyi said, will often be sold for profit – but to subject people and nature to the same atomising contractualism 'is only a short formula for the liquidation of every one and any cultural institution in an organic society' (Polanyi, 1944:159). The separation of labour from non-marketed communal activity undermines the cohesion of the identity-forming whole and reduces the likelihood that good neighbourliness will respond quickly to personal deprivation in the way that it does in the less commodified community: 'It is the absence of the threat of individual starvation which makes primitive society, in a sense, more human than market economy, and at the same time less economic.' (Polanyi, 1944:164). The relegation of land to the standing of a business input challenges the rootedness in place of the stable allegiance and substitutes erosion, deforestation, dust-bowls, climatic change for the age-old nurturing of men by the surrounding environment: 'Nature would be reduced to its elements, neighborhoods and landscapes defiled, rivers polluted, . . . the power to produce food and raw materials destroyed.' (Polanyi, 1944:73). In respect of people, the recommendation (not least to the developing countries) would be to retain rural links and intermediate craftsmanship where the catastrophic alternative would be the 'smashing up of social structures in order to extract the element of labor from them' (Polanyi, 1944:164). In respect of nature, the premium must be on prudent abstention to the benefit of future generations, together with a recognition that land is too much the precondition for territorial solidarity for it ever to be liberated into unfettered exchange: 'To isolate it and form a market out of it was perhaps the weirdest of all undertakings of our ancestors.' (Polanyi, 1944:178). In respect of land as in respect of labour, the *economic* must not be shoe-horned into the *economising*. Nor ought all analysis to be refracted through the market lens that will so often be the inappropriate tool for the production and absorption of value-added.

Polanyi at the level of analysis interpreted the economy in terms of social interaction and not through the filter of purchase and sale. The focus being the common culture and not the homeostatic mechanism, it is only to be expected that, at the level of *public policy*, Polanyi saw no reason to follow the libertarians in espousing a dichotomy between social authority and the creation of wealth: 'The institutional separa-tion of politics and economics, which proved a deadly danger to the substance of society, almost automatically produced freedom at the cost of justice and security.' (Polanyi, 1944:254–5). The advocates of the self-regulating market had, Polanyi objected, been prepared to sacrifice the consensual valuation of family, ecology, health, harmony and integration in single-minded pursuit of the profit-seeker's freedom of enterprise. British experience in the Industrial Revolution shows what the consequences can so easily be – 'The effects on the lives of the people were awful beyond description' – but also that the society very rapidly had recourse to 'protective countermoves which blunted the action of this self-destructive mechanism' (Polanyi, 1944:76). More spe-cifically, it turned to the State to take a lead in insulating the going *social* concern from the perils associated with a detribalised commer-cialism that saw in the hunger of the masses no more than a functional incentive to work.

Thence came the 'right to live' of poverty-relief, factory-legislation to impose hours and conditions, laws to contain pollution, laws to give unions voice. The State intervenes to reduce unemployment. It taxes the windfalls of speculators. It gives support to the arts and the sciences. The State, it is clear, is no longer prepared to precommit itself to *laissez-faire* where it also grasps that 'the requirements of man's nature' (Polanyi, 1944:249) cannot properly be satisfied by means of anarchy and void. Looking backward, Polanyi writes, human society would have been 'annihilated', the human race extinguished (Polanyi, 1944:76, 249), had the State not stepped into the shoes left empty by the collapse of feudalism and of the traditionalism that followed it. Looking for-ward, Polanyi continues, the very survival of the industrial system pre-supposes the re-embedding of economic authority in the social matrix, and therewith in the democratic leadership that must rescue what so could so easily become 'veritable human refuse', a 'degraded rabble', from the 'loss of self-respect and standards' of the market society's 'cultural vacuum': 'The congenital weakness of nineteenth-century society was not that it was industrial but that it was a market society. Industrial civilization will continue to exist when the utopian experiment of a self-regulating market will be no more than a memory.' (Polanyi, 1944:157, 158, 250).

The future of the price-system in Polanyi's socially sensitive economy is not made entirely clear. On the one hand he says that the market must survive, 'to ensure the freedom of the consumer, to indicate the shifting of demand, to influence producers' income, and to serve as an instrument of accountancy'. (Polanyi, 1944:252). On the other hand he says that the free market must be transformed into an administered and a guided market, 'ceasing altogether to be an organ of economic self-regulation' (Polanyi, 1944:252). Polanyi evidently wanted the allocative efficiency of flexible values to be delivered in combination with the solidaristic unity of regulated institutions. He appears not to have expected that the two sets of benefits would in the end prove incompatible. Perhaps this was because he was opposed only to the market that was literally *self*-regulating, to the market that was the *sole* director of the fate of men and things, but not to the market that responsibly exercised its freedom within the reasonable limits of the self-conscious community. Perhaps it was because he did not equate the maintenance of a decent livelihood with the maximisation of money incomes and believed that felt well-being would often involve a collective choice to forgo some consumption at the margin, to purchase some pattern-maintenance, some non-material adaptation instead. What is clear at any rate is this, that the regulated market to Polanyi did not suggest either a return to pre-capitalism or an escape into Leninism. What Polanyi wanted was conservative capitalism and not the capitalist capitalism that, in his view, had disembedded society into loneliness, insatiability and lack of continuity.

Polanyi is not alone in advocating a socio-political response to the challenge of cowboy capitalism. Thus John Gray, a conservative on the middle ground, has made much of 'the cultural inheritance which is the matrix of a stable capitalist order' and has appealed for the involvement of the State: 'Any conservative government, in Britain or elsewhere, must express not only the individual freedoms embodied in market capitalism but also the cultural identities that are renewed across the generations.' (Gray, 1993:65, 273). By no means opposed to rising living standards or felt quality of life, Gray reminds the affluent of the needy and vulnerable. He supports his plea for social and welfare services with a reassertion of 'the patrimony of a common culture, which government may rightly act to reinforce', with an endorsement of the 'traditional Tory concern for compassion and community in one nation' which suggests something more than the minimal State: 'Vital as the market is as an expression of individual freedom, it is only one dimension of society in which individuals make choices and exercise responsibility.' (Gray, 1993:56, 63).

There are Eucken, Erhard and Röpke as well as Spencer, Hayek and Mrs Thatcher in Gray's call for 'a liberal market economy constrained (or supplemented) by an enabling welfare state' (Gray, 1993:66). What there is not is Michael Oakeshott – who as a conservative and a Conservative – wanted a government of law and little else: 'The disposition to be conservative in respect of government is rooted in the belief that... the only appropriate manner of ruling is by making and enforcing rules of conduct.' (Oakeshott, 1962:189). Oakeshott looked to the State to be conservative of the rules. Gray looks to the State to be conservative of the society that is the source of the rules. In seeking to defend the core culture against the value-incommensurability of enterprise gone wild, Gray strongly resembles Polanyi in his insistence that the economistic would do well to return to their roots in the social, the inherited and the shared.

5 Convention

I live up to your expectations and expect you to orientate yourself to mine. You adapt yourself to my expectations and expect me to plan on the basis of yours. My expected conformity is the cause and effect of your present-day choices. Your expected conformity is the effect and cause of my future-shaping initiatives. The future is unknown and unknowable. Institutionalised expectations, 'regularities in behavior which are agreed to by all members of a society and which specify behavior in specific recurrent situations' (Schotter, 1981:9), at least light up the midnight and make it into a dusk.

Chapter 3 on Inductive Conservatism considered extrapolation from past recurrences. Chapter 4 on Economy and Society drew attention to the shared and the common as an input and a constraint. Both the predicted and the interdependent come together in the present discussion of the convention that anchors the actions of the group: 'A convention is a regularity in behavior produced by a system of expectations.' (Lewis, 1969:118). A convention allows you to supply fixed points to me. A convention enables me to supply fixed points to you.

The subject of this chapter is fixed points codified into social rules. The subject is social rules – not mathematical rules, not the rules of hygiene, not the rules set out in a cookery book but rather the social rules that link up human minds. The chapter is divided into three parts. Section 5.1 examines the function of the rules and Section 5.2 their origin. Section 5.3, turning from sociological economics to ethical economics, explores the legitimation that converts a habitual sequence into a duty, an obligation and a welcomed state.

5.1 FUNCTION

The textbook treats the economy as equilibrium, utility, substitution, mobility, gain, competition, markets. The implicit assumption is that the price mechanism is the core, other social facts the periphery. The acknowledgement of the social rule calls into question the complacency of the *ceteris paribus*: 'Economies contain an information network far richer than that described by a price system. This network is made up of a whole complex of institutions, rules of thumb, customs, and beliefs that help to transfer a great deal of information about the anticipated actions of agents in the economy when those actions cannot be decentralized by prices or when price mechanisms are too costly to administer.' (Schotter, 1981:118). Some information is generated by means of allocative flexibility: 'Prices are mechanisms that provide information about the societal scarcity of resources.' (Schotter, 1981:157). Some information is passed on as a consequence of embedded mutuality: 'Institutions are mechanisms that supply information about the potential actions of other economic agents.' (Schotter, 1981: 157). Economies are guided not by one beacon but by two. Neither beacon can be presumed *a priori* to merit its relegation to the obscurity of the *ceteris paribus*.

It is the essence of the convention that it hands on messages. Each generation is able in that way to learn from past vintages and to educate future cohorts. In terms of conservatism, the convention is an embodiment of continuity and an affirmation that predecessors have descendants. In terms of capitalism, the convention complements price-signals and gives relative shortages a remembered baseline. Conventions allow actors to assign probabilities to each other's actions. They reduce the uncertainty that surrounds the coordinative process. Sometimes written, explicit, formal, sometimes diffuse, tacit, uncodified, what is crucial is the ability of the convention to enlist memory and recall in the cause of a stable solution. Its capacity to promote a mutual concordance of expectations is most easily understood when the discussion of its function is divided into two separable cases.

The first case relates to situations where all agree on the need for a rule and where none has an incentive to cheat.

The skull and crossbones is the recognised symbol for poison, SOS the accepted signal of distress, the white flag the customary offer of surrender. The American dollar serves as the medium of exchange in Boston (where 'coin' signifies coin). The Canadian dollar is the agreed-upon legal tender in Montreal (where 'coin' signifies corner). The Chinese eat food with chopsticks, the Russians with a knife and fork, the Indians with their fingers. Visual symbols, monetary assets, linguistic symbols, table manners are all illustrations of consensual counters where convention aligns expectations and coordinates without loss.

Thus it is a matter of indifference to vendors that Thursday by convention is the early closing day and Friday by convention is the market-day. What affects the vendors' pay-off is not the day in itself but rather the fact that potential buyers are aware of the convergence in practice. It is not a matter of controversy that the week is divided into seven days and not into ten; or that worshippers remove their hat in a cathedral but put on their hat in a synagogue; or that participants at a formal ball wear formal dress that would be unconventional enough to constitute a fashion statement if worn at a teenagers' discotheque. No more is it a matter of controversy that cars stop when the lights are red and go when the lights are green; or that motorists in Britain drive on the left while motorists in France drive on the right. Some vehicle-users will presumably favour a different convention, just as some franc-users will favour a European currency and some English-speakers will favour a world language. All vehicle-users will, however, be in absolute agreement that a single code is infinitely more valuable than any specific code in particular. Red or green, right or left, what matters most is that no one is killed or injured on the road.

A convention that has a monopoly has a function. The rule of 'ladies first', first-best or a Stone Age survival, facilitates understanding and focuses expectation. A common rhythm, in Hume's deconstruction of cooperative rowing, makes possible the forward motion of a multi-oared craft. The adoption of Wednesday as a national day of rest ensures that the nation as a whole gains access to one and the same non-working period. Choices are coordinated; explicit consent is not required; and no player has an incentive to cheat. The danger is mediocrity – as where all agree not to experiment with a rival to an existing rule because the *status quo* convention is believed to be communicating tolerably well. The danger is not evasion – since the traveller who holds up two fingers for victory in a crowded bar in Milan has only himself to blame for the semiological sub-optimalities which are bound to be the result.

The second case refers to situations where all acknowledge the functionality of a rule and where each, unilaterally, faces a temptation to defect.

Oligopolists will find it rational to agree to price-fixing within the cartel. Oligopolists will also find it rational to deviate and undersell so long as their partners hold to the convention. Neighbours will find it rational to consent to the communal draining of a nearby swamp. Neighbours will also find it rational to continue their private business if only their fellow stakeholders retain a commitment to the public good. Citizens will find it rational to encode truth-telling as superior to mendacity.

Citizens will also find it rational not to keep their word provided that a truth-telling community cannot identify defaulters who economise on the social compact. The oligopolists, the neighbours and the citizens are all in absolute agreement that a mutually beneficial state can be brought into being by a rule. Each oligopolist, each neighbour and each citizen is also aware that an even more attractive state is accessible to the free rider who consumes without making a contribution. What each can do, all cannot. The second case of coordination by convention refers to situations that have a tendency towards radical instability.

Red or green, right or left, the first-case convention save to the wantonly self-destructive has all the logic of a self-enforcing code. The fixed price, the drained swamp, the kept word, the second-case convention is forever at risk from the blinkered maximisation of ambitious isolates who prefer the exclusivity of the *optimum optimorum* to the lower-valued optimum that all can enjoy. In both cases there is unanimity of consensus as to the functionality of a rule. In the first case, however, it is in the interest of the individual to conform – and in the second case it is the study of the rational to leave it to the cooperative to bear the cost. Should all members of the community choose simultaneously to take without giving, not a pint of blood would be gifted (in the sense of Titmuss), not a vote would be cast (in the sense of Downs), not a cow would be withheld from an over-grazed commons (in the sense of Hardin). Conventions that influence actions make it possible to expect, to anticipate and to predict. Conventions that are subordinated to strategies, on the other hand, draw a veil of uncertainty over the supply of the attainable ideal that all are known to prefer to no supply at all.

Convention coordinates. It is able to fulfil this function precisely because it is conservative.

Consider first the first-case convention. Here no single equilibrium has an intrinsic superiority, but the going rule has the attraction that it already serves as a focus. The *lingua franca* is a *fait accompli*. The soup is eaten before the meat. The football is passed around without a bat. Even if the practice were initially a coincidence, time digs deep the rut. Mimicry and snowballing produce a convergence so complete that no participant would have an incentive to interrupt the regularity. Any rule will do so long as it is validated through adherence. Provided that the *status quo* retains its capacity to guide and to channel, there is no reason to think that the requisite adherence will not be forthcoming.

Consider now the second-case convention. Where the allies are also enemies, where collaboration is hedged about with conflict, there the historical experience once again will have an especially useful role to play.

The parties, for one thing, might have a past in common that has given them an in-depth education in each other's probable reactions. Tennis professionals know one another not from a one-shot game but from an iterated sequence of rounds or plays. Meeting the same opponent on more than one occasion, they are able to shape their current moves in the light of personal observations. A similar learning process may have been the criminal socialisation of two repeat prisoners, each given an incentive to implicate his confederate, each aware that his confederate has been given an identical incentive in his turn. Where the same confederates have previously been placed in the same cells, the much-discussed 'prisoner's dilemma' is much easier to resolve than where no dynamic supergame has made available a stock of expectations built up in the past.

Probability is not, of course, the same as incentive. Assuming, however, that both partners intend that their interdependence should be prolonged for an unlimited ('infinite') number of matches, it will be in the interest of both in the present to make an investment in mutual support for use in the future. A nation that frequently goes to war with another will see that it is signing its own death-warrant when it makes the 'no holds barred' of infanticide and gas its dominant strategy in a short run that could set a precedent. A duopolist, understanding that a ruinous price-war could result from beggar-my-neighbour advantage-seizing, will build upon pre-existing trust to ensure the perpetuation of the balance. And a prisoner with a history as well as a dilemma will act in the expectation that to betray today is to be betrayed-upon tomorrow. Past behaviour gives tentative guidance as to probable reactions. Prospective plays frighten returning contenders into loss-averting minimax: 'In the repeated game the repeated selection of (α_1, β_1) is in a sort of quasi-equilibrium: it is not to the advantage of either player to initiate the chaos that results from not conforming, even though the non-conforming strategy is profitable in the short run (one trial).' (Luce and Raiffa, 1957:98). The nation that first uses germ-warfare *could* poison away its opponent. The duopolist who under-cuts *could* end up a monopolist. The prisoner who implicates *could* himself go free. Chaos is not the only possibility in the game-theoretic speculation. For cooperation to be more powerful than defection, the fear of loss must evidently be greater than the hope of gain. Uncertainty makes cowards of the dyads all – and the result is the incentive to act with restraint.

Recurrence in the two-party game mobilises probability and provides incentive. More complex – and more common – is the generalised, multi-person environment where the individual atom is unnoticed and insignificant. Each worker in a trade can enjoy the benefits of collective bargaining without paying the subscription to join the union. No soldier in a battle can contribute so much to the outcome of the war as to give him a rational reason not to desert. What one can do, all cannot. Across-the-board breach would mean no union and no battle. Choices, however, are made by the discrete and not by the omniscient. Isolated individuals correctly perceive that each makes no real difference to the history of the whole. Isolated individuals have therefore a rational reason to abstain and not to supply.

Yet isolation is not without its limits; and individuals do interact with others in patterned situations already in possession of a charter. A club over time generates the rules that it needs to keep its members in line. A society with a past and a future does the same. It is in the circumstances unrealistic to deduce predictions about litter-droppers, Good Samaritans, taxpayers and promise-keepers on the assumption that the agents are calculating *ab initio* and on their own. Convention is conservative. Even the isolated are not alone.

Thus, as new participants enter the open-ended pool (gradually taking the place of existing players who phase themselves out), each becomes aware of the rules that circumscribe choices both in the (micro) club and in the (macro) society: 'As the games we analyze are repeatedly played, the players develop certain societally agreed to rules of thumb, norms, conventions, and institutions which are passed on to succeeding generations of players.' (Schotter, 1981:12). With the standards go the sanctions that make the ideals effective as informational and regulatory mechanisms. Negatively speaking, there is the fear of retaliation, ostracism, a loss of 'face', a guilty conscience (and 'you have to live with yourself') that deters the free spirit from distancing himself too greatly from the crowd. Positively speaking, there is the love of the approbation, the fellowship, the solidarity, the acceptance that are the private rewards accruing to the loyalty of the team-player who does his duty. Even where the group is large and amorphous, each anonymous deviant can suffer from spoiled identity as if stigmatised by an 'Impartial Spectator' when he abstains from his union-subscription or absents himself in time of war. Nor should it be forgotten that the large group will very often be made up of sub-sets of smaller ones, personal and face-to-face. As Dennis Robertson writes, explaining why Alfred Marshall believed that the fear of 'incurring odium from other producers for spoiling the common market' (Marshall, 1890:380) would prevent even the perfect competitor from responding to excess supply with a price cut to the average variable cost: 'It seems to be not so much of their trade policy that Marshall's typical producer moves in fear, as of their personal behaviour to him (and no doubt to his wife) when he meets them outside the chapel or in the club.' (Robertson, 1956:15). The convention is enforced by the horizontal pressures that also prescribe sober dress in the Exchange and prohibit drunken debauchery on the Sabbath. The pressures are the personal pressures of all upon each. The public good of the inflexible price is protected from supply and demand as a result.

Enforcement, needless to say, will often take the form of top-down authority and not simply of informal interaction. The vertical can easily be a world away from the horizontal: witness the practice of a clique of dictators which propounds its laws to suit itself. The horizontal can, however, also provide the *raison d'être* and the legitimation for the vertical: where all acknowledge the functionality of a rule but each, unilaterally, has an incentive to cheat, it will be the democratic defence of coordination by compulsion that it leads to the best-attainable fulfilment of consensually-held expectations. Consensus and coercion can in such circumstances work hand-in-hand to ensure that group members who demand their share will also supply their share. Consider the stakeholders in collective bargaining, aware that self-interest can be self-defeating where all make the choice to default: 'If the members of a large group rationally seek to maximize their personal welfare, they will *not* act to advance their common or group objectives unless there is coercion to force them to do so.... Some form of compulsory membership is, in most circumstances, indispensable to union survival.' (Olson, 1965:2, 3). Consider the front-line combatants, each prepared to do without the option of running away if all agree to the same binding discipline: 'It is not irrational for the mortarmen themselves to ask for the laying of the mines around their posts (provided they are given no map of the locations), thus assuring their solidarity in battle.' (Ullmann-Margalit, 1977:33). Coercion by consent in instances such as these is not the road to serfdom but rather the liberating guidance that brings into being the mutually-beneficial state.

5.2   ORIGIN

Conventions assist individuals to meet one another's expectations. First-case conventions do so in circumstances where all parties stand to gain from the coordination and no party loses welfare because of the norm. Second-case conventions do so in more rivalrous conditions where the individual's first-best is incompatible with the collectivity's first-best and each must therefore settle for a personal second-best instead.

Conventions have the clearly defined function of imposing a stable and predictable pattern upon actors who, stranded like *homo economicus* in a choice-calculus built around appropriable utilities, would not otherwise be in a position to synchronise vital interdependencies in the area of collective action. The topic to be discussed in this section is the origin of the rules. The account is divided into three sub-sections: 'Evolution – the First Case', 'Evolution – the Second Case', and 'Decree'.

(a) Evolution – the First Case

The process, as Ullmann-Margalit says, is a gradual one: 'Norms do not as a rule come into existence at a definite point in time, nor are they the result of a manageable number of identifiable acts. They are, rather, the result of complex patterns of behaviour of a large number of people over a protracted period of time.' (Ullmann-Margalit, 1977:8). The process is a spontaneous unfolding. It is not the record of human design or of *ex ante* covenanting but rather the history of an invisible hand which gravitates without direction to unintended outcomes. The norms are validated *ex post* because they are already the standard practice *de facto*. No further justification than the success of the *status quo* would appear to be required for the *what is* to turn into *what ought to be*, as the cause and effect of expectations conditioned gradually through the repetition of regularities.

In respect of the first-case convention, the precedent can become established simply because it yields a perceived high return to the rational decision-maker. Thus individuals agree to trade in the currency that is the most widely accepted and they forgo right-hand driving in a nation where left-hand driving has emerged as the high-frequency solution. Individuals in this way invest in the continuity of inherited channels and spare each other the cost of search: 'At any equilibrium point, not only does no player have any incentive to change his behavior, given the behavior of the other players, but no player wishes that any other player would change either.' (Schotter, 1981:22). The conspicuous and the focal are able to bring about a satisfactory coordination of performance. That in itself is a good reason for the individual economiser to abandon his quest for the best-conceivable rule in favour of the rule that iterated interaction has identified as the most prominent standard.

The rule that is adopted may or may not be the convention that would have been prescribed by an omniscient maximiser. It sheds little light on the evolutionary process to speculate on what a Great Planner would have to say about something that will frequently have never been planned: 'Institutions are often bastard children whose true parents are hard to trace.' (Schotter, 1981:14). What is more valuable, historically speaking, is to reconstruct the skein of accidents that produced the real-world convergence. The explanation is likely to involve the concept of critical mass. Wishing to communicate, rational individuals select the language that promises them the highest success-rate. Wishing to trade, rational individuals choose the money-asset that most other individuals are observed to employ. B copies A, C imitates B; and thus does concordance emerge without the need for the code to be the best conceivable.

What best explains the adoption of the code is the bandwagon *per se* and not the optimality of the rules. The result is that it is good English to pronounce 'through' as 'thru' but bad English to write 'rough' as 'ruff'. The convention may have luck rather than logic on its side, but at least it supplies the common knowledge that makes prediction possible and directs conformity to its target. The consensus that it enjoys is derived from its capacity to create a system of mutual expectations. Unlike fads and fashions, therefore, unlike the moving momentum that accompanies the launch of new products, it will only retain its support so long as it remains a self-perpetuating fixity. Provided that it fulfils its coordinative function, however, there is likely to be a majority of opinion in favour of the tried-and-tested that will prove a significant obstacle to the trial-and-error of the entrepreneur in pursuit of an even better rule. Dissatisfaction at the margin will always find its voice: witness the unofficial status of the US dollar as a *de facto* world currency. Even so, it is undeniable that evolution will proceed more slowly once the custom has made regularity its own justification than when the society is in active search for a viable median.

(b) Evolution – the Second Case

The first-case convention relates to fitting in without losing out. The second-case convention is more conflictual. The best-possible outcome for country A is for A to levy a tariff and for B to practise free trade. The best-possible outcome for country B is for B to levy a tariff and for

A to practise free trade. The worst-possible outcome for both A and B is for both countries to levy a tariff and for neither to practise free trade. The best-attainable outcome for both A and B is for both countries to practise free trade and for neither to levy a tariff. The second-best scenario is clearly the mutually advantageous plan of campaign. Yet each partner, aware of the existence of the best-possible option, is in no doubt as to the incentive to defect. A convention would promote cooperation and discourage exploitation. The question is whether such a convention will emerge automatically, without the need for a third party to put its authority behind the compromise and the self-denial.

Axelrod believes that it will, and not least because of the nature of rational self-interest itself. Out go the traditional supports of other-regarding activity: 'There is no need to assume trust between the players: the use of reciprocity can be enough to make defection unprofitable. Altruism is not needed: successful strategies can elicit cooperation even from an egoist. Finally, no central authority is needed: cooperation based on reciprocity can be self-policing.' (Axelrod, 1984: 174). In come the calculator's preconditions of memory, transparency and continuity. The shadow of the past – because observation of deeds is the basis for the appropriate response: 'Just as the future is important for the establishment of the conditions for cooperation, the past is important for the monitoring of actual behavior.... Without this ability to use the past, defections could not be punished, and the incentive to cooperate would disappear.' (Axelrod, 1984:182). The transparency of the interaction – because tacit cooperation will not evolve where the continuing associate cannot be identified: 'An individual must not be able to get away with defecting without the other individuals being able to retaliate effectively.... The response requires that the defecting individual not be lost in a sea of anonymous others.' (Axelrod, 1984:100). The durability of the relationship – because a player in the final move of a finite game has no further stake in non-provocative abstention: 'The very possibility of achieving stable mutual cooperation depends upon there being a good chance of a continuing interaction.' (Axelrod, 1981:309). Once the final round is known in which the players no longer have the need to hold back, the next-to-last round in its turn becomes a playing-field in which it is rational to cheat. As with the one-off play, so with the finite series, cooperation unravels once there is no unbounded future to shape and influence. Given the prospect of continuity, however, given the known partner and the history of the sequence, it is Axelrod's belief that natural selection may be expected to throw up the mutually beneficial scenario. Not least may it be expected to do this because of the nature of rational self-interest itself.

Axelrod gives the example of the live-and-let-live strategy that evolved in the front-line trenches of the First World War. Friendship was obviously not the reason why the soldiers on both sides avoided the practice of shooting to kill; and nor was verbal communication or explicit contract (a sure route to execution for treason) the basis for their mutual support. As Axelrod explains the position, the key to the confidence is to be found in the non-random iteration of a sequence without end in which today's victim may be expected tomorrow to repay the defection in kind: 'What made this mutual restraint possible was the static nature of trench warfare, where the same small units faced each other for extended periods of time.' (Axelrod, 1984:21). Neither side took the initiative to kill – its first-best of exploitation was an outcome that remained blocked off by interest. Neither side had the experience of betrayal without warning – at least its third-best did not emerge as the unexpected pay-off to trust misplaced. What happened instead was that the second-best evolved and that the guns missed their aim as if guided by the Golden Rule.

The orientation was selfish but the outcome was cooperative. The prospect of repeat business evidently brought about the same equilibrium as did the sermons of the early Christian communists. It was able to do so, in Axelrod's perspective, by virtue of gain-seeking rationality in a pattern characterised by sequence, recognition, perpetuity, compromise and relativity. It was able to do so, more specifically, by virtue of tit-for-tat: 'TIT FOR TAT . . . is nice, forgiving, and retaliatory. It is never the first to defect; it forgives an isolated defection after a single response; but it is always incited by a defection no matter how good the interaction has been so far.' (Axelrod, 1984:46).

Playing by the tit-for-tat rule, the rational gain-seeker will always retaliate if once provoked. He in that way communicates to a would-be aggressor testing him for weakness that his refusal to be the first to cheat does not mean that he is slow to anger or can be used as a doormat by a bully. Yet he will always adopt the practice of early forgiveness as well lest a once-for-all response spiral into an unending disequilibrium of echoing instabilities: 'When a single defection can set off a long string of recriminations and counterrecriminations, both sides suffer.' (Axelrod, 1984:38). The end product of short-lagged memories and stage-by-stage reciprocation is that both parties do equally well in the tit-for-tat tournament and that no party ever scores better than the other or actually wins. A dead Tommy meant a dead Fritz. A living Fritz meant a living Tommy. Tommy and Fritz in the front-line trenches saw clearly that the success of the self depended upon the success of the other. The evolution of their cooperation pays tribute to the perceived interdependence of their – second-best – rewards.

The prediction is an optimistic one. Country A does not make first-strike use of its nuclear arsenal. Country B resists the temptation to levy a tariff. Tommy and Fritz find a life-saving alternative to kill-or-be-killed. Rationality in isolation throws up the worst-possible outcome. Tit-for-tat leads to the best-attainable state of affairs – and to the survival of the players who are the best-adapted to the mutually rewarding game: 'An individual able to achieve a beneficial response from another is more likely to have offspring that survive and that continue the pattern of behavior which elicited beneficial responses from others.' (Axelrod, 1984:22).

The prediction is cooperation: 'If everyone in a population is cooperating with everyone else because each is using the TIT FOR TAT strategy, no one can do better using any other strategy.' (Axelrod, 1981:312). The equilibrium that evolves is apparently also the optimum that maximises the mutuality. The conditions, however, are restrictive and problematic.

The condition of stable sequence is called into question by the entry of newcomers and mutants without a track record that links the future to the past. Once put in place, the cooperative norm enjoys the not inconsiderable protection of self-perpetuating momentum. Business life, however, is change; and active competition is bound up with novelty and alertness. New entrepreneurs launching new projects threaten the modal value and make extrapolation difficult. At each stage a new tit-for-tat process must take place, and take place behind the veil of unknowledge that always envelops a trading-partner without a reputation. Stable sequence harmonises interests. Opportunism breaks moulds.

The condition of easy recognition is put under pressure in a large-group context. Two politicians know whom to blame when a vote-trading promise is not kept. The transparency of the dyad makes each a man of his word. Identification is more difficult when the pair swells up into a crowd. The litter-dropping citizen cannot generally be made the subject of a generalised tit-for-tat.

The condition of expected perpetuity loses its force where the standard practice is the discrete interaction: 'When the players will never meet again, the strategy of defection is the only stable strategy.' (Axelrod, 1984:92). The evolution of cooperation presupposes that the relationship will last long enough for default to be made the focus for retaliation. A relationship without a future provides no incentive for a rational actor to make an investment in self-denial.

The condition of second-best compromise is weakened by the acknowledgement that much of human behaviour is not loss-averting (the gambler gains little satisfaction from half a prize, the chess-player from a perpetual draw) and much of human motivation not *zweckrational* in nature (as where envy, malice, insecurity, anger engender the excessive retaliation of 'two tits for a tat' that leads not to damping-down but to the pleasures of the feud). Tit-for-tat, neoclassical in inspiration, underestimates invidious comparison and overestimates the extent to which the future is seen as a highly-ranked consumable. Tit-for-tat in that way tends to bias upward the likelihood of cooperation.

The condition of moral neutrality is challenged by the presence of competing schemata. Thus the Christian rule of 'Turn the other cheek' (in contrast to the tit-for-tat standard of 'an eye for an eye') can be a cause of never-ending harm to oneself and one's community where the defector is never deterred by toughness. Also, one interpretation of 'Do unto others' would be that one should always cooperate: this, after all, is the conduct that each would want and expect from one's fellows. It is too easy to dismiss such absolutes as unilateral constraints that are intrinsically self-destructive – that bad people will crowd out good people in a way that would not happen if good people acted on the basis of expediency alone. Yet the fact is that 'Turn the other cheek' and 'Do unto others' do exist. Such alternatives may stand in the way of the retaliation needed for tit-for-tat, proceeding not on the basis of a single signed treaty or social compact but through a sequence of small moves, steps and stages, gradually to build up the confidence that is needed.

The conditions of sequence, recognition, perpetuity, compromise and relativity are restrictive and problematic. Taken together, they limit the extent to which cooperation may confidently be predicted on the basis of tit-for-tat. It must also be observed that the underlying logic of tit-for-tat presupposes a degree of comprehension and awareness which the real world might not find it easy to match. Thus retaliation loses its peace-making function where the defector does not understand the warning signal or glimpse the cooperation to which he is being invited to return. Cooperation, again, can prove an economic waste where the donor does not recognise when the life-span of the relationship is nearing its end (when the firm to which he gives a loan is about to go bankrupt or the politician who precommits with him to 'logrolling' is about to lose his seat). It is all too easy in the tit-for-tat game for important information to be brushed aside as *ad hoc* or random. Especially will this be a risk where the players communicate exclusively through deeds and not at all by means of words. Unlike a game such as poker, success here depends on intentions being made clear and not kept concealed. Yet it is precisely that knowledge of what is happening and of what other players will do that is in the real world in such deficient supply.

One consequence will be the incorporation of a discount factor. Apparent niceness could be a strategic investment in a post-dated betrayal. Alter might die or cease trading before ego receives the counter-gift expected from present-day abstention. The early-returns option of 'the bird in the hand' offers immediacy and certainty that deferred gratification can never promise. The risk of loss through exploitation will by the minimax averter be seen as subjectively more urgent than will be an equivalent chance of gain through defection. Considerations such as these suggest that the evolution of cooperation will be subject to a discount factor. Perhaps they also imply that the weighting scheme, personal and uncommunicated, will introduce complexities so great into the sequence as to impede predictable convergence on the second-best standards that are functional for social order.

The second-case convention can possibly evolve via tit for tat in the small-group context. The large group is, however, more vulnerable to the interest-seeking of rational calculators without an incentive to contribute. There is no iterated interaction in the mass-society context, no transmission of reputation, no recognition of past partners, no opportunity for sustained observation. Extrapolation cannot be made from historic rounds that never took place into future meetings that are eminently unlikely. Interactants in the circumstances have no reason to invest in the modification of one another's payoffs – and considerable reason to ride free on one another's lack of knowledge. As Fred Hirsch writes: 'Only *I* can see everywhere I litter.' (Hirsch, 1977:139). *A priori* the commons should long since have disappeared beneath the refuse.

Yet it has not. Self-policing citizens deposit rubbish in bins, just as unknown strangers eschew falsehood, donate blood and turn out for rallies. There is little point in observing that such persons are uneconomical of scarce resources since they volunteer for a payment that they could have avoided. Sometimes called Samaritans, sometimes called 'suckers', the evidence suggests that such persons demonstrably respect the cooperative convention despite the fact that it is manifestly not enforceable through the pairwise recollection, the personal targeting of tit-for-tat.

Cooperation can *exist* in the large-group context. Whether it will also *evolve* in a social setting typified by the anonymous and the one-off must be a good deal more doubtful. Large groups are admittedly made up of smaller ones. It might in that sense be the fear of face-to-face sanctions that keeps down the litter, the probable rudeness of the taxi-driver that lies behind the tip. Perhaps it is true that it is only when the large group is factored down to its smaller components that the pressure to conform can properly be said to produce the second-case convention. If so, however, then the point is not weakened but strengthened that personal interaction – and ingrained sensitivity to an expression of disapproval that carries with it no threat of business withdrawn – is the probable locus of normative evolution.

Once the norms are in place, of course, the everyday usage acquires a momentum of its own. Salient and conspicuous, the modal practice is absorbed through simple repetition, reinforced by informal constraint, passed on to children through lessons and role-models. The members of a community share a background knowledge of what 'works' in a given context: their actions and expectations are in that way channelled into regularities without the need for each to conduct a separate search. The prescription irrespective of its content has a common continuity that over time gives it the status of a binding force: it becomes a part of the social identity and enjoys the support of all who want the group to preserve its defining uniqueness. What this means is that conservatism is protective of that which has evolved – and that a norm once in place acquires a self-reinforcing function which it would be inappropriate to confuse with origin.

Greeks communicate in Greek even if some privately find French the superior syntax. The self-perpetuating nature of the norm is clear enough in respect of the first-case convention. The same conservatism, importantly, may be said to protect the more conflictual fabric of the second case as well. Norms are integrated into the cohesion and solidarity of an on-going collectivity: to litter the commons is to let down the team. Norms are also a part of the self: to betray a trust is to stigmatise the image. Conservatives, put simply, arrive with baggage at the moment of choice. Unable to speak a mother-tongue that is not Greek, unable to separate the essence of identity from the socialisation that has shaped it, conservatives often find that the core of their choice is no choice at all. Thus it is that the socialised mortarman, recognising his self in his duty and afraid of shame or guilt, is accepting of death even if his fellow mortarman elects to desert and run: 'In other words, one is here better off remaining and fighting, *whatever the other does*.' (Ullmann-Margalit, 1977:37). The past stands behind him and restructures his compensation-package. Giving up his life, casting his vote, bagging his litter, he voluntarily gravitates to the cooperative norm. He does so because, internalised through the past, it is all he has to use as a map.

(c) Decree

Sometimes a governor, short-cutting the evolution of habits and precedents, will promulgate a standard of practice from above: 'In certain novel co-ordination problems a solution is likely to be dictated by a norm issued specifically for that purpose by some authority.' (Ullmann-Margalit, 1977:83). First-case illustrations of such imposition would be the decimalisation of the coinage, the unification of competing currencies, the allocation of radio-frequencies. Clearly, even if all agreed that the new rule were the superior one, it would be difficult for isolated individuals unorchestrated by an external third party to initiate a change away from the convention of driving on the left. Second-case illustrations of freedom through coercion would be legal sanctions to enforce binding contracts, make tax compulsory, uphold the closed shop. Common goals, Mancur Olson observes, are often only attainable by means of coordinative control: 'The union member, like the individual taxpayer, has no incentive to sacrifice any more than he is forced to sacrifice.' (Olson, 1965:91). Consensus is evidently not enough for the public good to be in adequate supply. Thence the argument, in Mancur Olson's perspective, for expectations to be made consistent by decree.

Decree will often follow the contours of preexistent traditions and customs. In such circumstances it will not be creating a new code but rather formalising an implicit contract. Decree, alternatively, will sometimes demand concerted action that has not yet been put to the test of individual opinion. Verbal communication being difficult and the bargaining of consent being costly, it is conceivable that the subjects will want *ex post* to legitimate the lead that produced the generally more satisfying reconciliation of interest. Just as conceivable, however, is the possibility that they will resent the new rule and complain that it flies in the face of democratic preference. Condemned not to spit in public places and saddled with a two-girl family which the philosopher-ruler prevents them from augmenting, the subjects might object that the collectivity's interests were perhaps being served but that their personal rankings were not being respected. Coercion being what it is, there is no guarantee that their protests will have any real consequences.

An equilibrium need not be an optimum. A minority's choice need not be a social norm. The possibility that a decree from above might be other than a codification of consensus is the essence of the Marxian contention that political sway both reflects and perpetuates the class-based exploitativeness of the capitalist economic system: 'Our epoch, the epoch of the bourgeoisie ... has simplified the class antagonisms. Society as a whole is more and more splitting up into two great hostile camps, into two great classes directly facing each other – bourgeoisie and proletariat. ... The executive of the modern state is but a committee for managing the common affairs of the whole bourgeoisie.' (Marx and Engels, 1848:205–6, 207). The first-case convention makes non-conflictual choices consistent with one another. The second-case convention promotes a second-best agreement despite the destabilising frictions of uncertainty and strategic interaction. The Marxian world-view challenges the complacency which surrounds the derivation of both conventions. Where society is a twin-peaked distribution of production-based circumscriptions (and not simply an unstructured summation of factored-down individualities), it will be the contention of the Marxians that a norm which furthers the interests of one class will frequently only do so where it diminishes the welfare of another. An equilibrium need not be an optimum. Decree buttressed by coercion is especially open to the accusation that it has a discriminatory bias.

Thus the protection by the State of private property-rights is often taken to be a positive-sum game: A is prevented from mugging B but B in turn is prevented from expropriating A. The Marxians, not persuaded as to the legitimacy of the *status quo* endowments, do not accept that the convention being enforced is in truth an even-handed one. Existing claims are unequally distributed, some groups inherit a privileged head start – and capital accumulation is itself the direct consequence of labour-power alienated to produce surplus value for the haves. To protect such property against its progenitors, the Marxians will say, is to legislate not for a (second-best) compromise but for a (first-best, third-best) imbalance that favours the materially better-situated ranks.

Convention by coercion in such circumstances will evidently not resolve class-conflicts so much as paper over the cracks. In the long run, of course, the familiarity of the imbalance might take the edge off the resentment. So might a public perception that the business interest is the national interest. Long habituation might convert a felt injustice into a core element in the nation's approach to the problem of coord-ination. Should it be able to do so, false consciousness in the world-view of the Marxian economic determinist would then be a cover for a controversial and disturbing partiality in the theory of conservative capitalism.

Decrees can perpetuate inequalities in the Marxian interpretation of the capitalist State. Decrees by the same token can correct inequities where the conventions that evolve are functional for the club but a dis-welfare for the encompassing whole.

Thus loyalty within the cartel means higher prices and restricted quantities. Honour among thieves means fewer arrests and fewer betrayals. Cooperation within the lobby means rents for the produ-cers and inflation in the shops. In cases such as these, it is clear, the majority of the clients and the citizens would be on balance better-off if each team-member were to redirect his gain-seeking from the club to the self. As Mancur Olson states, explaining the slow growth and crowded agendas that he identifies in stable societies, uninvaded, undefeated, unrevolutionised: 'Stable societies with unchanged boundaries tend to accumulate more collusions and organizations for collective action over time. . . . On balance, special-interest organiza-tions and collusions reduce efficiency and aggregate income in the societies in which they operate and make political life more divisive.' (Olson, 1982:74).

Distributional coalitions can reduce the welfare of non-members. The free rider in such circumstances can evidently be a public bene-factor; while conservatism can apparently work to the detriment of cap-italism. In such circumstances at least, the well-being of the community will actually be enhanced by selfish individualists who deny themselves nothing for which the group does not pay.

The invisible hand would enlist the greedy and the treacherous in the service of the flexible, the adaptive response. Yet expected retaliation remains an ever-present obstacle to the desirable externalities that would be the consequence of self-interested withdrawal. Particularly where they are not in a position to communicate directly, to precommit inter-temporally, to make enforceable contracts, the greedy and the treacherous will simply not know how much defection is safe without exposing themselves to sanctions. It is the function of decree to put backbone into their private-spirited avarice.

Restrictive practices legislation enables low-cost interlopers to under-cut. The separation of imprisoned confederates works against long-term banding. The rotation of civil servants (analogous to the repositioning of front-line troops) discourages symbiotic capture on the part of suppliers and persuaders. Success-indicators incompatible with tit-for-tat (pay proportioned, say, to front-line kills) break up cosy accommodations. Public-sector tendering solicited from abroad reduces the scope for tacit collusion that is favourable to price-fixing where the short-list is consistently the same. Political service restricted to two successive Parliaments increases the turnover of office-seekers and diminishes the extent to which favours can be enjoyed on credit. Just as the State can produce a united front to keep down pollution, so, it is clear, can it attack a united front that stands between private vices and the public virtues that the community expects from interest. Cooperation will not always be compatible with consensually-defined objectives. Where it is not, the visible hand will do well to weaken the convention and not to reinforce it. Weakening the convention, the visible hand also contributes constructively to the universalisation of morality in the society as a whole.

5.3   LEGITIMATION

A regularity is a statistic and not an obligation. A habit is a fact and not a duty. Simple replication is not enough to make a predictable recurrence into a normative *ought to be*. For an empirical sequence to acquire the status of a social norm, something more is required than behaviour which repeats itself and patterns which conform. What is required is that there be perceived legitimacy surrounding the convention, that the individual feel bound by the convention because there is something in it that he believes rightly to command his allegiance. For a social convention to be magnified into a social norm, it must be able to appeal to inner conviction. It must offer the intrinsic rewards that a commitment which is more constraining than a preference will always pay to the social actor who acknowledges the discipline.

Legitimacy relates to *ought-ness* and not to *is-ness*. It is not concerned with regularities which are restricted to the individual's *de gustibus* ('Jack always drinks coffee before breakfast') or which are subject to the falsification of a scientific test ('Jill always uses a size-3 lathe to minimise waste'). Respect for Jack's preferences and Jill's valuation of efficiency have all the authority of collective representations. The coffee and the lathe *per se* do not. Nor, indeed, does the legal contract which lies at the heart of the exchange nexus. As Durkheim observes, the market's *quid pro quo* is not self-legitimating in a vacuum but validated instead by the customs and attitudes which predate and surround it: 'In sum, a contract is not sufficient unto itself, but is possible only thanks to a regulation of the contract which is originally social.... Society lends it an obligatory force.' (Durkheim, 1893:215). The rightness, Durkheim is saying, is derived from community and confirmed by agreement. It owes nothing to the shopper's in-store comparison of the utilities and the costs at the margin.

Legitimacy relates to *ought-ness* and imposes a limit. Yet the incorporation of the non-tradeable and of the binding does raise a conceptual problem in the context of the present chapter. The first two sections, unsentimental and calculative, explored the function and evolution of convention using the commercial logic of instrumental rationality and self-interested individualism. This third section is faced with the more difficult task of explaining why choosers might find it a duty not to choose, why capitalists might make it an obligation to be conservative of the past. This third section must evidently explain the multi-period constitutionalism of the non-ego constraint, and must do so without falling back on the in-period expediency that causes the coffee to be replaced by tea and the size-3 to be swapped for the superior tool. The first two sections suggest that society buys the norms that best do the job – and scraps them ruthlessly when they outlive their productivity. This third section considers the circumstances in which yesterday will be able to perpetuate its standards – and to inspire an agreed-upon *ought-ness* even in the absence of the teachers, the revelations and the books.

James Buchanan is one of many sceptics and agnostics who have defended an open-ended ethical relativism. The reason, as Buchanan sees it, is that there is no honest alternative in an age of pluralism and doubt: 'Values are widely acknowledged to be derived from individuals, and there are not absolutes. God has been dead for a century, and attempts to revive him are likely to founder.' (Buchanan, 1986:12). God being dead, it is individuals and individuals alone who hold the sacred keys to the 'good society', the 'public interest', the 'Social Welfare Function' and the 'General Will'. Only the individual can articulate a value. Only the agreement of individuals can legitimate an *ought-to-be* that is more than an *is*.

Individuals have preferences but they also need conventions: 'We require rules for living together for the simple reason that without them we would surely fight.' (Brennan and Buchanan, 1985:3). Individuals value freedom but they also value order: 'It is rational to *have a constitution.*' (Buchanan and Tullock, 1962:81). Individuals want pre-commitment but they also demand consultation: 'The essence of any contractual arrangement is *voluntary* participation.' (Buchanan and Tullock, 1962: 250–1). What all of this adds up to is *ought-to-be*s by consent and a set of rules that all participants in the veil of uncertainty that precedes the opening of play take to be the most suitable standards to govern their game: 'A "fair rule" is one that is agreed to by the players in advance of play itself, before the particularized positions of the players come to be identified. Note carefully what this definition says: a rule is fair if players agree to it. It does not say that players agree because a rule is fair.' (Buchanan, 1986:126). No one would say that the shared *ought-to-be*s agreed upon democratically through the rule-making process are the same as the normative codes that would have been promulgated by a *deus ex machina*, omniscient, beneficient and supported by a hierarchy of unimpeachable Great Books. No one would say it because no one can know it. Stranded in unknowledge and starting from here, the only certainty is individual opinion harmonised into the consensus of opinion: '"Truth", in the final analysis, is tested by agreement. And if men disagree, there is no "truth".' (Buchanan, 1977:113). It isn't much. It is, however, the only game in town.

Buchanan derives legitimacy from agreement. It will be interesting, building on his market-like model of the citizen buying morals just as the butcher buys beer and bread, to ask whether the logic presented in the first two sections of this chapter will be sufficient to inspire the legitimacy that is the subject of this concluding part. The question, in other words, is whether the individual will gravitate to the ethical standards derived in the first two sections from rationality and self-interest or whether he will hold out for a conservatism that is less explicitly the product of the capitalist ethos.

The first section of this chapter defined the function of convention to be the coordination of expectation without the conflict of interest: 'A social norm is a prescribed guide for conduct or action which is generally complied with by the members of a society.' (Ullmann-Margalit, 1977:12). A first-case convention makes choices concordant and brings about a jointly-desired state of affairs: thus 'under the clock' or 'Grand Central Station' will be treated as likely meeting-places by individuals who lose their travelling companions. A second-case convention defuses tensions and leads to a second-best situation which is ranked by the insurance-prone above the gamble of the first: the Biblical Commandment 'Thou shalt not steal' is a clear instance of an injunction which will make sense even to a thief, himself the possible target of another thief's aggression. Both the first-case and the second-case convention would appear easily compatible with a social consensus that, as in Buchanan's legitimation of ethics through agreement, magnifies the *is* into the *ought to be* that then becomes a mode of social control.

The second section of this chapter turned to the evolution of the rules and to their codification in decree. Tit-for-tat suggests that cooperation emerges as an unintended consequence of narrow maximisation; while threats and punishments ensure that conditioned expectations will not permanently be thrown off course by non-beneficial deviation. The endstate is an equilibrium more satisfying to each than any alternative outcome that he could have produced on his own: 'In an equilibrium combination, no one agent could have produced an outcome more to his liking by acting differently, unless some of the others' actions also had been different. No one regrets his choice after he learns how the others chose. No one has lost through lack of foreknowledge.' (Lewis, 1969:8). An equilibrium need not be an optimum. That said, there is reason to hope that the rule that produces such a situation will win sufficient acceptance to be adopted as the norm.

*Ought-to-be*s by agreement are not incompatible with the *ought-to-be*s of Jesus and Kant. All that is required is that the persons to be subject to the norms should be consulted about the rules and should give their assent.

That done, of course, the electors pass from the realm of consequentialism into that of deontology. Motives count, immediate advantage does not, and even in the prisoner's dilemma there is conscience and there is sacrifice: 'A moral man is one who, in a PD-structured situation, chooses the co-operative action on the assumption that the other is also going to make the same choice, and who, moreover, does not deviate from this choice even if he be certain that the other cannot, for some reason, punish him later by deviating too.' (Ullmann-Margalit, 1977:41). A moral man refuses to seize the short-run gain because he has already made an investment in the long-run convention. A moral man behaves *as if* he is constrained by law when in fact he is only constrained by self. A moral man, in short, is a natural conservative. What this chapter has shown is that, rational and interested, he may be a natural capitalist as well.

6 Evolution and Economy

The starting-point is not price theory, comparative statics or equilibration at the margin. Instead, it is social selection, perpetual motion and adaptation to circumstance: 'The life of man in society, just like the life of other species, is a struggle for existence, and therefore it is a process of selective adaptation. The evolution of social structure has been a process of natural selection of institutions.' (Veblen, 1899:131). Social life, Veblen said, closely resembles organic life in that it is locked into cumulative causation, disequilibrium states and mutation to avoid extinction: 'The economic life history of the individual is a cumulative process of adaptation of means to ends that cumulatively change as the process goes on, both the agent and his environment being at any point the outcome of the last process.' (Veblen, 1919:74–5). Economic activity, Veblen argued, is better understood in the Darwinian context of biological development than it is when flattened into the mathematical mechanics of Newtonian physics. Alfred Marshall wrote that 'the central idea of economics' could be nothing other than 'that of living force and movement': 'The Mecca of the economist lies in economic biology.' (Marshall, 1890:xii–xiii). It is a viewpoint which would be shared by Veblen and by other anthropocentric economists whose focus is the evolution in the structures, the parameters and the rules of the game.

Marshall was a meliorist who believed that change was on the side of betterment, both material and moral: 'In every age of the world people have delighted in piquant stories, which tell of some local or partial retrogression; but, if we look at the broad facts of history, we find progress.' (Marshall, 1873:115–16). So, taking a different view of what betterment would actually mean, was Karl Marx: 'Centralisation of the means of production and socialisation of labour at last reach a point where they become incompatible with their capitalist integument. Thus integument is burst asunder. The knell of capitalist private property sounds. The expropriators are expropriated.' (Marx, 1867:763). Both Marshall and Marx expected the pursuit of the wealth of nations to be at once the cause and the effect of institutional upgrading. A more neutral, more scientific stance would, however, be to separate the evolution from the optimism, the economics from the philosophy. Evolutionary economics would then track the phenomena and explain the norms but would not venture to say if the changes had an *ought-to-be* value in and of themselves.

133

The task would be a difficult one, given that adaptation and survival both carry their own legitimation in a way that dysfunction and death most palpably do not. Difficult or not, the alternative to a detached analytic will often be an unappealing complacency that substitutes *whatever is, is good* for an open-minded inspection of such facts as can be found. Evolutionary economics is an orientation which looks for explanations not in the 'self-balanced mechanism' but in the 'cumulatively unfolding process' (Veblen, 1919:173): 'The question now before the body of economists is not how things stabilise themselves in a "static state", but how they endlessly grow and change.' (Veblen, 1943:8). Evolutionary economics studies growth and change. It does well to do so impartially, postponing the evaluation of welfare and teleology until its more positive inquiries have been completed. Yet meliorism is in the air. The evolutionary economics of Alchian and of Friedman (discussed in Section 6.1) and of Hayek (discussed in Section 6.2) illustrates just how difficult it is in practice to separate the logic from the purposiveness which (the subject of Section 6.3) confers upon the phenomena and the norms their moral worth.

6.1   ALCHIAN AND FRIEDMAN

Neoclassical economics begins at the beginning, with rational decision-makers who maximise profits and optimise pay-offs. Alchian's evolutionary economics begins at the end, with 'impersonal market forces' which test for relative efficiency and reward performance by means of realised returns: 'It does not matter through what process of reasoning or motivation such success was achieved. The fact of its accomplishment is sufficient. This is the criterion by which the economic system selects survivors: those who realize *positive profits* are the survivors; those who suffer losses disappear.' (Alchian, 1950:213). The economic system selects the winning businesses just as the natural environment selects the best-adapted plants: 'Plants "grow" to the sunny side of buildings not because they "want to" in awareness of the fact that optimum or better conditions prevail there but rather because the leaves that happen to have more sunlight grow faster and their feeding systems become stronger.' (Alchian, 1950:214). Decision-makers like to attribute business success to intelligent foresight and the *ex ante* calculus of advantage. It is Alchian's message that, given radical uncertainty and acknowledging the randomness of luck, the outcomes *ex post* alone reveal the truth about 'the economy's realized requisites for survival'

(Alchian, 1950:216). For executives as for vegetables, success lies in adaptation and the structure is the entity that selects.

Alchian's emphasis is on the logic of the whole and not the careful consciousness of the part: 'The suggested approach embodies the principles of biological evolution and natural selection by interpreting the economic system as an adoptive mechanism which chooses among exploratory actions generated by the adaptive pursuit of "success" or "profits".' (Alchian, 1950:211). The economic system makes the choice; but still the outside observer can use the rational orientation to predict the outcome. Even if runners selected their routes by chance, still the observer could predict the winner on the basis of the shortest road. Even if seeds were planted at random by the wind, still the observer could predict the most fecund on the basis of the soil. In neither case is the rational choice of the unit the real-world explanation of its success. In the one case as in the other, however, the observer who grasps the environmental constraints will be in a position to identify the best road and the best soil without relying in any way upon the maximising estimations of the units themselves. Thus may the assumption of rationality be retained as a central tenet of microeconomic theory despite the fact that the units themselves are so often handicapped by ignorance and uncertainty.

Successful outcomes in Alchian's perspective do not depend upon antecedent estimation. The reassurance is a welcome one since so many of human choices (consider Simon's conservative satisficing as a routine-repeating alternative to trying something new) would appear to dispense with the textbook conditions of reflection and comparison. In the words of Gary Becker, acknowledging the non-rationality but defending the assumption: 'The economic approach does not assume that decision units are necessarily conscious of their efforts to maximize or can verbalize or otherwise describe in an informative way reasons for the systematic patterns in their behavior.' (Becker, 1976:7). Rational choice yields good predictions – that test alone would satisfy Alchian and Becker, as it satisfies Milton Friedman, that 'rational and informed maximization' (Friedman, 1953:22) remains a valuable assumption despite its conspicuous lack of descriptive completeness.

Milton Friedman argues that accurate predictions are the economist's proper study, that full explanations, however illuminating in themselves, are simply not needed for the task in hand. He supports his contention that application should be ranked above understanding with the example of an expert billiard player: 'It seems not at all unreasonable that excellent predictions would be yielded by the hypothesis that the billiard player made his shots *as if* he knew the complicated mathematical formulas that would give the optimum directions of travel.' (Friedman, 1953:21). The winner does not actually make the calculations or follow the plan. There is no need for him to do so for the assumption of *as if* rationality to retain its predictive power. The balls have weight, the table has breadth, the cue has length. The player who wins the game will *de facto* be the fittest player, the player best adapted to the parameters of the situation. The possibility that he wins by luck and not by judgement in no way negates the value of the prediction *as if*: 'At a horse race with enough bettors wagering strictly at random, someone will win on all eight races.' (Alchian, 1950:215–16). The assumption of rationality identifies the best-suited moves. The prediction *as if* expresses the conviction that some seeds are bound to fall on fertile ground.

As with the billiards and the seeds, so with the capitalist entrepreneurs, the rule is that the situation speaks, the unit adapts, and the fittest survives. The condition for success is the satisfaction of the trading-partners who pay: 'Unless the behavior of businessmen in some way or other approximated behavior consistent with the maximization of returns, it seems unlikely that they would remain in business for long.' (Friedman, 1953:22). The customers must be satisfied or the firm will cease to trade – that much is a fact of business life. Less clear is the contribution that careful calculation will have made to the outcomes that succeed. So long as the *as if* construction accurately foreshadows the empirical result, Friedman and Alchian would say, there is no real need to probe more deeply into the secrets of the businessman's mind.

Were, however, the economic psyche nonetheless to be examined under the microscope, the likelihood is great that rational self-interest would reveal itself in the capitalist market to be something more concrete than just a simplifying *as if*. The reason, Max Weber makes clear, is the very nature of capitalism itself: 'Capitalism is identical with the pursuit of profit, and forever *renewed* profit, by means of continuous, rational, capitalistic enterprise. For it must be so: in a wholly capitalistic order of society, an individual capitalistic enterprise which did not take advantage of its opportunities for profit-making would be doomed to extinction.' (Weber, 1904–5:17). Trapped in the cage of events, the individual capitalist is likely to reflect, with Durkheim, that mind is weak before the laws of matter and that even free enterprise can be a system of constraint: 'As an industrialist, I am free to apply the technical methods of former centuries; but by doing so, I should invite certain ruin.' (Durkheim, 1895:3). *Ex post* the conservative industrialist will learn the cost of his conformity, just as *ex post* the snowflake will discover the difference between sun and shade. Importantly, however, there is an *ex ante* element in the rational self-interest of the competitive capitalist which is forever denied to the unthinking snowflake. In the same way that successful outcomes can be predicted on the basis of rationality *as if*, so, it is clear, can the competitive capitalist be modelled on the basis of conscious design to be alert and economical in order to survive.

Milton Friedman cites the instance of non-economic discrimination as a case where non-competitive conduct can cost the perpetrator his future. Friedman's point is that a non-competitive practice is a self-imposed handicap which is incompatible with the gain-seeking objective: 'A businessman or an entrepreneur who expresses preferences in his business activities that are not related to productive efficiency is at a disadvantage compared to other individuals who do not.' (Friedman, 1962:109). *Ex post* the ascriptive will be undersold by the economical: 'In a free market they will tend to drive him out.' (Friedman, 1962:110). *Ex ante* the rational will therefore economise on bigotry in order to remain in the game: 'The competitive publisher, for example, cannot afford to publish only writing with which he personally agrees.' (Friedman, 1962:17). The observed and the intended, the actual and the *as if* – the assumption is the 'single-minded pursuit of pecuniary self-interest by employers in competitive markets' and the expectation is profoundly pro-economical: 'This "assumption" works well in a wide variety of hypotheses in economics.' (Friedman, 1953:28).

Competitive capitalism is driven by circumstance to select only those institutions which will be functional to its sustained efficiency. Pulled by existing rivals and pushed by potential contestants, the business that does the best will be the one that is the quickest to dispense with the 'job for life', appointment by nepotism, promotion by seniority, the career-structure, the outdated product, the reflex-action supplier; while the one that does the worst will be the business that succumbs to what Arrow describes as the cause of the 'greatest tragedies of history' – the 'sense of commitment to a past purpose which reinforces the original agreement precisely at a time when experience has shown that it must be reversed' (Arrow, 1974:29). Competitive capitalism sells no tickets to past purposes and subsidises no passages for rituals and sentiments that can no longer pay their way. The survival of the fittest buys only the practices for which it has a use; while the invisible hand lays in no prizes to compensate the also-rans. The discipline is tough and much baggage must go. The social gain, in the eyes of the evolutionary marketeer who shares the neoclassical's high valuation of performance, will more than make up for the private disruption that the weeding out will cost: 'Competition in the face of ubiquitous scarcity dictates that the more efficient institution, policy, or individual action will survive and the inefficient ones perish.' (North, 1981:7). If tradition is good and disruption bad, then so, in another perspective, is scarcity bad and prosperity good. Adherents of that latter perspective would say of competitive capitalism that it does right to buy only the conservatism that serves its popular economic purpose.

The intellectual standard is conjectures and refutations. Its material counterpart is successive approximation. Popper saw clearly that the scientist and the capitalist had much in common in the feedback-adjusted hypothesis-testing which each made the centrepiece of his approach to 'problem-solving...by the method of trial and error': 'New reactions, new forms, new organs, new modes of behaviour, new hypotheses, are tentatively put forward and controlled by error-elimination.' (Popper, 1972:242). Success identified through experiment, imitation understandably occurs and accounts for the observed uniformity that characterises the survivors of an evolutionary process. The imitation of novelty that works clearly diffuses the track-record into a public good in an economic market that welcomes any hedge against uncertainty. With the hedge goes, however, a threat. Convention established, as Alchian observes, a question must be raised about 'the willingness to depart from rules when conditions have changed': 'What counts, then, is not only imitative behavior but the willingness to abandon it at the "right" time and circumstances.' (Alchian, 1950:218). Lacking that willingness, innovation followed by conventionalisation can easily mean the local maximum that settles for the horse and cart rather than the global maximum that reaches out for cars and jets.

Friedman would look to the 'creative destruction' of competitive capitalism for the dynamic that keeps alive the entrepreneurial spark. So would Joseph Schumpeter. Schumpeter was a reader of Marx and Darwin and a theorist of continuous change: 'In dealing with capitalism we are dealing with an evolutionary process.' (Schumpeter, 1942:82). Unlike Friedman, however, he was unable to predict a perennial reappraisal of consumer goods and methods of production in the complacent era of the large corporation and the bureaucratic elite. Looking to the future, Schumpeter expressed himself most memorably about the institutional stagnation to which he believed that organisational ossification must inevitably lead: 'Can capitalism survive? No. I do not think it can.' (Schumpeter, 1942:61). But perhaps he was wrong.

6.2 HAYEK

Hayek was a libertarian and an economist. An advocate of evolution through entrepreneurial spontaneity and market search, he was sharply critical of backward-looking philosophy with a 'fondness for authority', a 'lack of understanding of economic forces' and – probably the main reason why Hayek once entitled an essay 'Why I Am Not a Conservative' – a serfdom-fostering 'fear of trusting uncontrolled social forces': 'One of the fundamental traits of the conservative attitude is a fear of change, a timid distrust of the new as such, while the liberal position is based on courage and confidence, on a preparedness to let change run its course even if we cannot predict where it will lead.' (Hayek, 1960: 400). The conservative wants to know the endstate before entering into the process. The liberal accepts that the destination will be shaped by the circumstances of the journey but encourages the travellers despite the uncertainty to exercise their freedom of choice.

Knowledge is dispersed and the future behind a veil. The careful balancing of costs and benefits, the mathematical calculus of the maximum pleasure, must logically give way to bounded rationality or even to no rationality at all in a kaleidoscope world where internal consistency and the pure abstractness of choice are superseded by the risky, the fragmented, the uncoordinated and the unforeseen. As Hayek puts it, inverting the neoclassical practice which treats the error-term as the residual: 'Before we can explain why people commit mistakes, we must first explain why they should ever be right.' (Hayek, 1949:34). Unknowledge is general and the present behind a veil. Whatever else evolution may be, it will clearly not be the product of an anticipated link between the budgeted means and the planned endstates that individuals expect the economising over time to bring about: 'Evolution cannot be guided by and often will not produce what men demand.' (Hayek, 1988:74).

Chaos is possible where the atoms decide. So, however, is consistency, where the situation itself takes over the leaderly function of constraint: 'A spontaneous order results from the individual elements adapting themselves to circumstances.' (Hayek, 1973:41). Circumstances provide the parameters and limit the individuals' freedom to be fully themselves. Circumstances, on the other hand, are the basis of 'correct expectations' (Hayek, 1973:36) and in that way the source of the background intelligence that unites the actors in their struggle to adapt. The social whole must evidently not be reified into a thing apart: what is called 'society' is in truth no more than 'the intelligible actions of the individuals' (Hayek, 1949:69) who alone can perceive and perform. Nor, however, must it be supposed that each unique individual will necessarily be significantly more event-shaping than is the passive perfect competitor in respect of the mass of persons, perceptions and phenomena to which he is motivated by his survival to orientate his conduct.

The individual proposes. The situation disposes. Purposive action initiates – witness the speculative opportunities that are opened up by an in-depth knowledge of 'local conditions' and a specialist estimation of the 'circumstances of the fleeting moment' (Hayek, 1949:80) that are not yet a public good. The structured whole dovetails the decentralised parts: 'The whole acts as one market, not because any of its members survey the whole field, but because their limited individual fields of vision sufficiently overlap so that through many intermediaries the relevant information is communicated to all.' (Hayek, 1949:86). Chaos is possible where the atoms decide. Chaos is averted where the situation unites.

Hayek states that the 'economic problem of society is mainly one of rapid adaptation to changes in the particular circumstances of time and place' (Hayek, 1949:83). He also believes that the catallactic order successfully meets the challenge of disparate intentions and a multiplicity of ends: 'Exchange is productive; it does increase the satisfaction of human needs from available resources.' (Hayek, 1988:95). Evolution occurs and adaptation takes place; but still there is no single individual who can know the final prices and quantities, the varied qualities and characteristics, in advance of the actual trades which give to the (objective) cost-embodied the economic status of (subjective) value-added. No single mind can anticipate the endstates. The endstates are unintended outcomes. They are not the product of rational choice.

Hayek is evidently a functionalist as well as an individualist, a believer in personal autonomy who also believes that the whole has a logic of its own – a logic which is in no way put at risk by the fact that real-world decision-makers do not know what it is. The duality is shared by Popper, who like Hayek sees it as the key to the human condition: 'The main task of the theoretical social sciences . . . is to trace the unintended social repercussions of intentional human actions.' (Popper, 1963:342). It is at the heart of Adam Smith's celebrated eulogy of the gain-seeking trader, 'led by an invisible hand to promote an end which was no part of his intention': 'The study of his own advantage naturally, or rather necessarily leads him to prefer that employment which is most advantageous to the society.' (Smith, 1776:I, 475, 477). The duality of the part and the whole is the basis of Hayek's theory of economic adaptation. The decentralised process is the best-attainable one. So, therefore, must the market outcome be. No further definition of efficiency is provided. The spontaneous order passes the final judgement upon itself.

Hayek in his discussion of phenomena adopts a forward-looking stance. He shows how phenomena come and go in an uncontrolled process but says little about why they become embodied and when they stay. His theory of market capitalism is in that sense a theory of incremental adaptation rather than a theory of multi-period perseverance.

Even in connection with phenomena, however, Hayek's discussion of evolution would appear to be set against a background of habits and traditions that can contribute to order precisely because their roots are deep: 'Paradoxical as it may appear, it is probably true that a successful free society will always in a large measure be a tradition-bound society.' (Hayek, 1960:61). The courts of law protect the citizen from the State. The market itself is an institution which is presumed to last. Money is expected to retain its acceptability as a medium and its value as a store. Not one of these phenomena has continuously to be renegotiated on an incremental basis. To do so, indeed, would be a threat to their social function. In cases such as these, it is clear, the unintended outcomes of past interactions have a survival status in Hayek's economics that is none the less real for being largely implied.

Menger on money spells out the stages. His analysis of the past in the present clearly documents the reasoning that an incrementalist like Hayek would employ to show that custom can be the tacit complement to choice.

Money, Menger stresses, evolved without direction in response to the perceived deficiencies of barter: 'Money is not the product of an agreement on the part of economizing men nor the product of legislative acts. No one invented it.' (Menger, 1871:262). Money evolved naturally and spontaneously. Like language or common law, it is not the product of conscious design but rather the unexpected consequence of discrete decisions and free-standing interactions: 'The origin of money can truly be brought to our full understanding only by our learning to understand the *social* institution discussed here as the unintended result, as the unplanned outcome of specifically *individual* efforts of members of a society.' (Menger, 1883:155). Members of a society produce an end which was no part of their intention. The legislator, arriving *ex post facto*, does no more than rubber-stamp the *status quo*. His edict will be legally binding, and in that sense a brake on further spontaneity. Even so, it will still be reactive and not pro-active, in its essence no more than 'the acknowledgement of an item which had already become money' (Menger, 1883:153).

The development of an institution is always gradual and not once-for-all. In the case of money, the evolution in the work that the asset was called upon to perform led in the course of time to the phasing-out of the less-efficient currencies (cattle, shells and millet, for example) and the adoption of better-suited intermediaries (notably the monetary metals). Menger gives his own opinion on the objective characteristics of the money-assets that will have the highest income-elasticity: they will be, he says, 'the most easily transported, the most durable, the most easily divisible' (Menger, 1883:154). He also makes clear that money is never more than subjectivity, perception and agreement. Money is not the asset that most people *ought to* use. It is only the asset that they *do* in practice employ.

Looking at the historical record, Menger infers from the evidence that the test of function and that of acceptability both point to the same assets: 'With economic progress . . . we can everywhere observe the phenomenon of a certain number of goods, especially those that are most easily saleable at a given time and place, becoming, under the powerful influence of *custom*, acceptable to everyone in trade, and thus capable of being given in exchange for any other commodity.' (Menger, 1871: 260). Evolution favours tradeability. Tradeability settles into custom. Custom promotes stability. In this way can exchange proceed on a day-to-day basis without the need in-period to re-select the monetary means of payment.

As with Menger, so with Hayek. In-period the businesses compete and the winners survive. Multi-period there is law, market and money that impart to capitalism a conservative character. Even at the level of phenomena, it would appear, there are constants as well as variables in Hayek's economics of discovery.

Hayek in his discussion of things concentrates on the in-period imperative of competition and survival. The emphasis is different when he turns his attention to rules. Hayek writes that 'rules alone can unite an extended order' (Hayek, 1988:19) and that 'general rules must prevail for spontaneity to flourish' (Hayek, 1988:73). Hayek means what he says when he uses phrases like 'rules *alone*' and '*must* prevail' to pick up the multi-period conservatism without which the in-period capitalism in his estimation would lose its capacity to progress: 'The alternative is poverty and famine.' (Hayek, 1988:63).

Hayek is an advocate of individual freedom who is also an advocate of normative constraint: 'The readiness ordinarily to submit to the products of a social process which nobody has designed and the reasons for which nobody may understand is . . . an indispensable condition if it is to be possible to dispense with compulsion.' (Hayek, 1949:23). Hayek is a rational calculator who also argues that the rational calculator must 'accept countless traditions without even thinking about them' (Hayek, 1988:62): 'The individual, in participating in the social processes, must be ready and willing to adjust himself to changes and to submit to conventions which are not the result of intelligent design, whose justification in the particular instance may not be recognizable, and which to him will often appear unintelligible and irrational.' (Hayek, 1949:22). Hayek, in short, is a champion both of present and past, both of comprehension and acceptance, both of liberty and inhibition. Not contradictory but complementary, he would argue, the autonomous and the acquired are in truth the fundamental elements of the mixed economics that alone can sustain continued evolution and protect the community against poverty and famine.

Evolution selects phenomena that are able to adapt well to the contours of the situation. It does the same in the case of the rules: 'Neither all ends pursued, nor all means used, are known or need to be known to anybody, in order for them to be taken account of within a spontaneous order. Such an order forms of itself. That rules become increasingly better adjusted to generate order happened not because men better understood their function, but because those groups prospered who happened to change them in a way that rendered them increasingly adaptive.' (Hayek, 1988:20). Thinking man is self-evidently less the architect than the outcome of his cultural environment in an adaptive process that teaches him the rules: 'Learning how to behave is more the *source* than the *result* of insight, reason and understanding. Man is not born wise, rational and good, but has to be taught to become so. . . . Man became intelligent because there was *tradition*.' (Hayek, 1988:21). Tradition disciplines innate instinct and channels conscious design. Not impulse, not science, not the State, it ensures that the free individual, so easily the victim of 'the fatal conceit that man is able to shape the world around him according to his wishes' (Hayek, 1988:27), does not lose sight of the normative tried-and-tested that, generated without intent and obeyed without assessment, 'can far outstrip plans men consciously contrive' (Hayek, 1988:8): 'Mankind achieved civilisation by developing and learning to follow rules. . . . These constraints selected us: they enabled us to survive.' (Hayek, 1988:12, 14). Any code of conduct that staves off the Hobbesian *bellum* and makes effective cooperation possible must be said to enjoy a very strong recommendation.

The group adapts because the members accept: 'The process of selection that shaped customs and morality could take account of more factual circumstances than individuals could perceive. . . . In consequence tradition is in some respects superior to, or "wiser" than, human reason.' (Hayek, 1988:75). As is the case with the natural selection of phenomena, information is dispersed, individuals lack overview, and outcomes are unintended. What this means in respect of the rules is that those standards will prevail which are the best-adapted to the survival of the group: 'The genetic (and in a great measure also the cultural) *transmission* of rules of conduct takes place *from individual to individual*, while what may be called the natural *selection* of rules will operate on the basis of the greater or lesser efficiency of the resulting *order of the group*.' (Hayek, 1967:67). The invisible hand selects the norms 'on the basis of their human survival-value' (Hayek, 1988:20) and to enable 'those groups practising them to procreate more successfully and to include outsiders' (Hayek, 1988:16). The invisible hand is keen to build upon 'habits and institutions which have proved successful in their own sphere' (Hayek, 1949:88). It has little time for *ought-to-bes* made to order that have not emerged through the self-regulating process of error-correction: 'We have never been able to choose our morals.' (Hayek, 1988:133).

The market for morals, Hayek seems to be saying, enjoys a remarkable similarity to the market for things. In the one case as in the other the outcome of a good process must itself be good. In the one case as in the other the relativism of *de gustibus* must be the last word on the suitability of a choice. Automaticity and physical survival become the selective standards. Precise norms, specific ends are left to 'anonymous and seemingly irrational forces of society' (Hayek, 1949:24) which alone have the range of vision to pick out the functional.

What is legitimate is what has evolved. The capitalist economic system, alone capable of increasing production in step with the rise in population, is an example of an unintended adaptation that has shown itself able to deliver the goods: 'We have never designed our economic system. We were not intelligent enough for that. We have tumbled into it and it has carried us to unforeseen heights.' (Hayek, 1979:164). Capitalism is made legitimate by the superior resource-use which is its contribution to the struggle for existence. So, by extension, must the normative code be legitimate which is at once the consequence of and the precondition for the smooth functioning of the decentralised market. It is in this way that Hayek, theoretically an ethical agnostic, is able to narrow his search from pushpin to poetry, from theft as a pastime to 'the specific moral traditions that do concern me here, such as private property, saving, exchange, honesty, truthfulness, contract' (Hayek, 1988:67). Writing as an evolutionist, Hayek is no more proclaiming those values to be absolutes than he is saying that the capitalist package must be bought uninspected. Hayek's point is simply this, that Hobbes and Malthus are hovering in the wings, that 'Darwin got the basic ideas of evolution from economics' (Hayek, 1988: 24), and that the alternative to a spontaneously evolving ethics is the chaos or the coercion that are so much less conducive to the imperative of material advance.

There is much in Hayek's discussion that recalls the learned rules of a formal religion. There is an inscrutable hand which selects the norms. There is a guarded teleology, stronger on survival than on happiness. There is a resistance to Rousseau-like emancipation from the constraints of external responsibility. There is a role for free will and novelty within the permitted domain of the traditional and the shared. Clearly, there being no hint of a God, a holy book or a church, the parallel should not be pressed too strongly. Nonetheless, Hayek himself is aware of the similarities – and is able to make an informed guess as to the nature of the link: 'Perhaps what many people mean in speaking of God is just a personification of that tradition of morals or values that keeps their community alive.' (Hayek, 1988:140). Communistic religions sink without trace since they are maladapted to the needs of the group. Economical religions flourish since they mobilise resources for the going concern: 'The only religions that have survived are those which support property and the family.' (Hayek, 1988:137). Religions themselves are evidently subject to a process of natural selection.

Religions survive because the community survives. The community survives because capitalism survives. Norms recognisably super-human ought not in the circumstances to be labelled super-natural. Not other-worldly but this-worldly, the rules that evolve are not the will of an extra-economic God but rather the functional prerequisites for economic activity in a resource-constrained community that wants to live well.

It is evolution and not democracy that must be given the last word: 'Most of the rules which do govern existing society are not the result of our deliberate making [but] . . . the product of a process of evolution in the course of which much more experience and knowledge has been precipitated in them than any one person can fully know.' (Hayek, 1967:92). Not reasoning but performance is evidently the guarantor of piecemeal improvement in the quality of the rules: 'Rules of conduct . . . have not developed as the recognized conditions for the achievement of a known purpose, but have evolved because the groups who practised them were more successful and displaced others.' (Hayek, 1973:18). Hayek is clearly putting his faith in a common welfare *ex post* that is not the rational maximand of a common will *ex ante*. He is in that way differentiating his economics of patterns and regularities from the contractarian perspective of James Buchanan, whose libertarianism prevents him from validating any rule to which free individuals have not voluntarily given their assent. The criticism that a Buchanan would make of a Hayek is made up of two inter-connected arguments.

First, there is Buchanan's contention that a rule cannot be called 'good' unless and until it has secured the legitimation of consensual recognition. What this means is that the norm must be identified as superior by the persons involved. The unit agents themselves must define the code that (analogous to the economic exchange – it is what *both* parties *want* – that remains the ideal) may be called 'efficient'. It may be called 'efficient' exclusively because it is perceived as such by the individuals who will be subject to its dominion. Buchanan writes: 'Beyond agreement there is simply no way for the contractarian to go.' (Buchanan, 1977:295). Evolution in the sense of Hayek does not devolve 'the appropriate' to the level of the self that alone knows what are the subjective constraints and where the shoe is felt to pinch.

Second, there is Buchanan's assessment that evolution is no guarantee that the results will in fact be the socially optimal rules: 'History need not be a random walk in sociopolitical space, and I have no faith in the efficacy of social evolutionary process. The institutions that survive and prosper need not be those that maximize man's potential.' (Buchanan, 1975:167). The institutions that survive and prosper need not be those that would be evaluated as 'best' by the people who live under them. The failure of the invisible hand to deliver the most satisfying constraints suggests that conscious action to re-draft the rules might in such circumstances be productive of a more rewarding game. Hayek's invocation of the collective, the group, the organic, the functional has very limited appeal to Buchanan, convinced as he is that dispersed knowledge and methodological individualism will often suggest a constitutional order that is not completely self-regulating.

Buchanan would therefore point with approval to passages in Hayek's writings where even the evolutionary optimist concedes that survival need not be proof positive of efficiency. One such passage would be Hayek's admission that, all rules evolving having some useful purpose, this 'does not mean that in other respects such law may not develop in very undesirable directions and that when this happens correction by deliberate legislation may not be the only practicable way out. ... It therefore does not mean that we cannot altogether dispense with legislation.' (Hayek, 1973:88). Hayek in the last analysis would see some logic in Buchanan's contention that correctives only become self-perpetuating where they satisfy human expectations – and that sometimes the legislator will be necessary to improve on the quasi-biological automaticity of the common law that is good but not good enough.

Viktor Vanberg's comment on the utility of politics is in this context illuminating. Vanberg, for one thing, does not see any reason to expect the best-possible rule automatically to emerge: he notes in particular that Hayek is concerned with the survival of the group whereas the actual winnowing-out is performed by individuals concerned primarily with their own differential advantages. Hayek is a theorist of spontaneous growth and not of intellectual evaluation: 'The present order of society has largely arisen, not by design, but by the prevalence of the more effective institutions in a process of competition.' (Hayek, 1979:154n). Vanberg's reply, following Buchanan, is that he cannot see why the individual, eschewing the temptation to be a free rider, should invest in the behavioural regularities that deliver their real benefits to the *whole*: 'The general notion that social systems with "more successful" systems of rules will eventually win out, seems to be too vague.' (Vanberg, 1986:87).

Vanberg contends that a sub-optimal rule might emerge and might become the focus. He also contends that such a second-best, once adopted, might be resistant to the challenge of a new and even a more attractive social norm: 'Once a co-ordination rule is established in a group, it cannot be assumed that a shift to a more beneficial rule can, in general, be brought about by a spontaneous, invisible-hand process.' (Vanberg, 1986:90). Individuals find it too costly to deviate unilaterally; and there is also the simple impossibility of producing a successful result where the acquired properties are not simultaneously being eroded by others. Large groups, anonymous and amorphous, gravitate easily to the kind of conservatism that gives conservatism a bad name – a state of rest in which all or almost all are under-satisfied, but the homeostatic mechanism simply refuses to get involved: 'The same social conditions that spontaneously enforce a particular convention, may very well rule out a shift to a more beneficial rule to be brought about by an invisible hand process.' (Vanberg, 1986:90). We all want to see a change. None of us in isolation is, however, in a position to bring into being the change that would raise our welfare. Thence the need for a united effort, sponsored by the democratic state and not left to the cumulative feedback of the innumerable and the microscopic.

Buchanan and Vanberg are critical of Hayek because he relies too heavily on unintended outcomes. They argue that he trusts too little to rule-generation by means of agreed-upon governance. Hayek and the Hayekians will nonetheless be unpersuaded that optimality in the normal run of things can better be promoted by democratic intervention than it can by the evolutionary process. A telling argument will relate to the inter-temporal problem which – analogous to the 'one person, one vote – *once*' of new democracies turning authoritarian – recalls the debate on the moral status of marriage without the possibility of divorce, self-enslavement by consent, irrevocable reclusion in a closed convent. Historically, the Hayekians will say, individuals may once have done right to invite the State to institute a given behavioural regularity, not only because *any* norm is preferable to Hobbesian normlessness but because a *specific* norm was regarded then as the best-possible standard. Yet events moved on while statute did not. In the self-regulating order, socio-cultural rules would have stood a chance of adapting to the new situation; and so, arguably, would judge-made law with its facility for flexible response. In the politicised order, on the other hand, it is the task of the police and the prisons to spring to the defence of yesterday's constitution, of yesterday's frame of reference. Democracy, the Hayekians will say, may legitimate in the here-and-now but may also precommit the future to a contract which it did not choose and which it would not want. Just as the advocate of consultation cannot defend the inter-generational transmission of the national debt, so, it would appear, must the true democrat look askance at the inter-generational transmission of a legislated *status quo*. The tyranny of yesterday's consensus is not quite the same as the tyranny of Hitler and Stalin. Even so, the Hayekian would say, it is a station on the road to serfdom and one which does not cover the costs of its short-run benefits.

6.3 EVOLUTION AND CAPITALISM

Alchian and Friedman, writing mainly about phenomena, describe a competitive market which selects the fittest firms and drives high-cost laggards to the wall. Accepting that each individual business will frequently be unaware of its specific supply-and-demand status, acknowledging that the manager on a salary faces a temptation to maximise executive utility at the cost of the profits in which he holds no stake, recognising that many pioneers are actually failed imitators who, trying to copy, stumble into new areas instead, they concentrate their economics on outcomes while leaving to psychology the study of motives and expectations. They say that competitive capitalism can be trusted to allocate the best rewards to those performers who best satisfy the wants of their clients.

Hayek, writing mainly about rules, is concerned with the selection and adoption of culturally determined conventions conducive to the reproduction and improvement of the group. Neither the product of deliberate foresight nor the consequence of random occurrence, social habits are unintended outcomes which evolve spontaneously, like money in the sense of Menger, in response to a systemic need. Hayek recommends that rational beings should conform to the rule-governed order even where thinking individuals are themselves unable to identify the function fulfilled by the custom. The rule has spread – that means that it has defeated other rules in a clearly-defined context. The rule fosters adaptation – that means that it is favourable to wealth-creation through market cooperation. The product of competition, the basis for competition, the norm, Hayek concludes, is validated by evolution. It is capitalist to the core.

Economists like Alchian, Friedman and Hayek are confident about the causal relationships that run from evolution to capitalism, from capitalism to meliorism. Their optimism allows them to treat the new that pushes out the old as in some way a betterment and not just a change. Before it is possible to share their assessment, however, it is necessary to look more critically at two aspects of the developmental process: the social democracy and the institutional constraint.

(a)   The Social Democracy

The first aspect involves the status of the market itself. Evolutionists explain survival in terms of adaptation to circumstance and economists emphasise the efficient use of a limited endowment. The exchange mechanism is believed by market liberals to be the best-attainable means of attaining these closely related objectives. Market liberals are prone, in Hodgson's phrase, 'to assume that the market is itself selected in a market environment', to infer that there exists a real-world 'market for markets' (Hodgson, 1993:176) in which market spontaneity has definitively out-performed any and all of its competitor products. The erosion of feudal-type status by birth, the rejection of central directive in the Gosplan *cul-de-sac*, the constriction of the altruistic commune to the extended family – historical evidence such as this suggests to market liberals that systemic evolution has reached an end and that free enterprise capitalism has for all time been pronounced the victor.

Francis Fukuyama is one of many thinkers who regard the late-twentieth-century transition from the Berlin Wall to Thatcherite privatisation as part of an irrevocable shift from totalitarian statism to personal liberty: 'The twin crises of authoritarianism and socialist central planning have left only one competitor standing in the ring as an ideology of potentially universal validity: liberal democracy, the doctrine of individual freedom and popular sovereignty.' (Fukuyama, 1992:42). Fukuyama rightly decomposes the broad ideology of liberal democracy into the component constructs of the liberal market (bringing in private property-rights and the legitimacy of gain-seeking aspiration) and the democratic State (picking up the freedom of the press, the right of assembly, the secret ballot, opposition parties, regular elections and universal adult suffrage). He also accepts that the component constructs in the real world will not always and everywhere lend each other mutual support: 'The Mechanism underlying our directional history leads equally well to a bureaucratic-authoritarian future as to a liberal one.' (Fukuyama, 1992:125).

What Fukuyama is saying is that the liberal market is not open to challenge (enjoying as it does a popular association with rising living standards) but that the democratic State cannot so confidently be called the consequence and cause of economic evolution: 'There is . . . no *economic* rationale for democracy; if anything, democratic politics is a drag on economic efficiency.' (Fukuyama, 1992:205). Fukuyama is not saying that the fastest-growing countries are likely to be those that have done away altogether with the need to please voters and win elections. What he is saying is that some of the fastest-growing countries have in practice been those in which the State, leaderly and opinionated, has extended social discipline to gum-chewing, gun-ownership and drug-abuse while ensuring that industry, finance and commerce remain fundamentally *laissez-faire*. Fukuyama's examples of political watchfulness are drawn from the dynamic economies of East and South-East Asia. The success of Hong Kong, Taiwan and Malaysia, he is suggesting, demonstrates that the American or the British approach to the political market cannot be regarded as the only approach that is productive of capitalistic advance.

The capitalist market is chosen because there is no better-performing escalator, the bottom-up State because it 'values us at our own sense of self-worth' (Fukuyama, 1992:200). Free enterprise is chosen because it expediently enriches. Participative democracy is chosen because it satisfies a self-expressive need. It is Fukuyama's belief that the selective standards are separate and separable. An alternative perspective would be, however, that they are in essence the same. Modernisation, historically speaking, has most often meant the capitalist market. The capitalist market, historically speaking, has most often meant the bottom-up State. The correlation need not have been an accidental one.

Thus, at the philosophical level, capitalism and democracy are unified by a common perception of the unique person as a moral agent. It is that sense of the autonomous 'self' as deserving of respect that makes legitimate the exercise of consumer sovereignty, the mobility of labour and capital, the devolution of costs and benefits, the tolerance of tastes and preferences. It is that same emphasis upon independence, responsibility, entitlement, search, self-determination, rational choice, that lies at the heart of a participative politics, emancipated from inherited leadership, benevolent despotism and autocratic power. Both capitalism and democracy are demand-led decision-making processes that, acknowledging the plurality of interests and the scarcity of inputs, seek to reconcile revealed preferences without the imposition of a top-down definition of the general will. The endowments are different: the distribution of income is unequal whereas the command over politicians is strictly one person/one vote. The principle is the same: morally, methodologically, both capitalism and democracy are committed to the primacy of factoring down.

Materially as well as ideationally, the capitalist economy and the democratic State would appear once again to be closely linked. Capitalism presupposes not only the normative legitimacy of rights and exchanges but also the framework of safeguards that contains aggression and makes agreements enforceable. Social values legitimate but law and order protects. In so far as the democratic State holds the monopoly of force, it is in a good position to ensure that private individuals will not invade one another's space. Capitalism expands the choice-set. Democracy enables it to do so.

Ultimately accountable to the citizenry at elections, moreover, the State dares not itself invade or abuse in the manner that a dictator might do if spared the rivalry for the mandate. The State, indeed, must satisfy the electorate not merely in respect of the containment of arbitrary power but also in respect of growing material affluence. There is in that way a democracy-based constraint that favours a relatively liberated market and a relatively limited bureaucracy, responsible taxation that does not cut into incentives and a budgetary position that does not crowd up interest-rates. A political culture built around values like obedience, acceptance, hierarchy, theocracy, loyalty, a political system that institutionalises the historical divisions of race, class, tribe, gender, is less likely to deliver the requisite protection and ensure the expected performance than is one which is an embodiment of the will to express and assert oneself, to put one's opinion on record, to be recognised as an equal, to be treated with respect. Such a will is the will that makes capitalism too, and not just democracy, go round. Materially as well as ideationally, it must be suggested, capitalism and democracy are complements that are more likely to be found in a compound than they are to be separate and decomposed.

Writing of East Asia or writing of America and Europe, Fukuyama's point is that the truth is the mix: 'No real-world society can long survive based on rational calculation and desire alone.' (Fukuyama, 1992:215). It is conservatism that legitimates the individualism that sets the capitalist free. It is conservatism that underpins the selfishness that demands a political stake: 'There is no democracy without democrats.' (Fukuyama, 1992:134). Both in terms of the market and in terms of the State, Fukuyama would say, the pre-existent consensus is the *sine qua non*. His contention that ideas have consequences is a useful reminder that there is more to human nature than animal nature alone. Yet it also opens the door to the possibility that social values, ends and not instruments, will be productive of a state of affairs in which the government is invited to limit the freedom of enterprise in order to promote some higher freedom which the citizens for some reason are more eager to advance. What is true of political democracy is, in other words, true of *social* democracy as well. A society that has the courage to choose polit-ical democracy because it is a good thing in itself retains the option to choose the managed market or even the welfare State where freedom of enterprise in its perception is unable to satisfy its wider cultural aspirations. The conservatism in such a case cages the capitalism, making it a far tamer beast than it would have been in the jungles of Alchian, Friedman and Hayek. Some growth will conceivably be lost and some waste will possibly creep in. Shopping is shopping, however; and market liberals would be the last to reject as invalid the choices made even by conservatives.

Culture can stand in the way of political democracy. Culture, import-antly, can just as easily stand in the way of the capitalistic free market. Consider the growing valuation of compassion and generosity which Adam Smith attributed to the wealth of nations: 'Before we can feel much for others, we must in some measure be at ease ourselves. If our misery pinches us very severely, we have no leisure to attend to that of our neighbour: and all savages are too much occupied with their own wants and necessities to give much attention to those of another person.' (Smith, 1759:297). Consider the growing valuation of security and protection which J.K. Galbraith associated with the affluent soci-ety: 'The notion, so sanctified by the conventional wisdom, that the modern concern for security is the reaction to the peculiar hazards of modern economic life could scarcely be more in error. Rather, it is the result of improving fortune – of moving from a world where people had little to one where they had much more to protect. In the first world, misfortune and suffering were endemic and unavoidable. In the second, they have become episodic and avoidable.' (Galbraith, 1958:115). The evolving taste for fraternal solidarity could clearly be accommodated through private charity, the evolving desire for minimax control by means of commercial insurance. Historically, however, it is a matter of record that citizens have frequently politicised their responses and looked elsewhere than to free enterprise for the adaptation that they require.

Capitalist enterprise has on balance reconciled itself to the provision by the State and not the market of the public goods of law and order and of national defence. It has found it more difficult to reconcile its pursuit of private gain with the many other restrictions which the social democracy has imposed upon its operations. The minimum wage com-pels employers to relieve the poor. Unemployment benefits reduce anxiety and prolong search. Safety-regulations impose the cost of goggles, screens, gloves and nurses. Job security gives the employee a property in his work-place. Two-tier corporation tax induces internal reinvestment even where the best returns are to be found outside. Capitalist enterprise has expressed doubts about collective restrictions on business activity such as these. It has been more amenable to the subsidies, the tariffs, the licences, the bail-outs, the guaranteed sales, the fiscal welfare which have been offered by the State in support of the profit-seeking sector. Nor should it be forgotten that firms as well as households derive an economic benefit from social services such as accessible public housing, inexpensive public transport, a national health service to minimise the tax of ill-health, a national school system to maximise the stock of transferable skills. Business can gain as well as lose from regulation and provision, management and welfare. Crucially, however, it must always and everywhere experience a circumscription of its autonomy in consequence of the politicisation and of the shepherding.

Evolution means adaptation. Where gain-seeking is guided, where entrepreneurship is not left free to choose, it is all but true by definition that the adaptation in question will not mean the same state of affairs as would be identified by the free market optimisation of Alchian, Friedman and Hayek. The adaptation will be a different one. Less clear, however, will be the implications for felt satisfaction of moving from an essentially economising to a more broadly-based set of values and codes. Perhaps it is economic nonsense to retain the Scots in Scotland when the jobs that they crave are located in Düsseldorf. Yet people, whether as shoppers or as voters, must be treated as the best judge of their own welfare. People want what they want. If they rank conservatism and habit over a Scotland that has been closed and shipped abroad, then *that* is the adaptation which a tolerant community will wish most assiduously to promote.

Resources might be misallocated and novelty retarded where the fittest are reselected when the game is redefined. It is possible that there will be a loss in economic efficiency – but possible as well that a post-economic consensus will regard the material loss as no real sacrifice. Poverty and hunger are no longer macro-social challenges in the richer countries. Procreation to the limits of consumption is a threat in rabbit society which human society has long since been able to contain. Caring in the view of Smith and security in the view of Galbraith enjoy a high income elasticity of demand. Considerations such as these might lead a post-economic consensus to assign a low weighting to the pressure-groups, the 51 per cent majorities, the Departmental empire-building, the rational ignorance, the misjudged fine-tuning, the public-spending ratchet, the rise in interest rates, the political business cycles that are so often cited by advocates of economic growth when they blame democratic interventionism for material comfort forgone. Valuing productivity but valuing other things too, the post-economic consensus might in an affluent society insist that the capitalism be made subordinate to the conservatism and that evolution be rescued from thinkers who would confine it to the market alone.

(b) The Institutional Constraint

The theory of evolution is a theory of competition. The selection process is visualised as a large-scale filtering mechanism 'that as it were scans the inventory of social patterns and institutions at any given period of time and screens through to the next those of them that are best adapted to their (respective) roles' (Ullmann-Margalit, 1977:282). The 'best' are selected and the maladaptive die out: 'There is no need to assume a rational calculation to identify the best strategy. Instead, the analysis of what is chosen at any specific time is based upon an operationalization of the idea that effective strategies are more likely to be retained than ineffective strategies.' (Axelrod, 1986:1097). The profit-seeking enterprise proved more effective than the producer cooperative. Share-owning democracy saw off the nationalised utility. Private property triumphed over the tribal commons. Yankee ingenuity vanquished the Soviet Gulag. Survival means 'bestness'. 'Bestness' is what survives. The winners win. The losers either emulate the successes or hand over their resources to the efficient.

Simply stated, the theory of evolution is a theory of competition which lends an optimistic purposiveness to the kaleidoscope of mutation. Examined more carefully, the theory of evolution is subject to a number of institutional complexities which have a significant impact upon the actual trajectory that the economy describes. It is the task of this sub-section to draw attention to some of those constraints which can have so telling an impact on the course into which even *free* enterprise will ultimately be streamed.

The economist is by tradition most at home with the image of hungry agencies scrambling for maximal resourcing in a Hobbesian, Malthusian,

Darwinian, Spencerian, Sumnerian struggle to stay alive. It is that image of deprivation and the fear of deprivation that lies behind the common choice to define adaptation as productivity-enhancing change. Economic growth is 'bestness' because it satisfies the anxious infant's fixation with the supply of food. Economic stagnation is not 'bestness' because it condemns real-world men and women to a handful of rice.

Market capitalism being an expansionary system, its evolutionary dynamic will seldom stop short at a handful of rice. Crucially, however, it is also a populist system, dependent upon individuals for the stamp of 'felt well-being'. If consumers and citizens do interpret 'felt well-being' as material living-standards, then their self-sensed hunger will serve as the Archimedean point that makes possible the association of 'bestness' with husbandry. If, however, their welfare-function embraces a multiplicity of objectives, then the theory of adaptation becomes profoundly recalcitrant to empirical tests. It does not become a tautology: we can only say *whatever is, is best* if we can establish that there is no *better* way of procuring the *same* adaptation. What it does become is a minefield of aggregations, weighting-schemes and trade-offs between the material and the ideal which make efficiency and sub-optimality very difficult to establish.

Clarence Ayres pinpointed the tension in the following statement about the mix: 'What happens to any society is determined jointly by the forward urging of its technology and the backward pressure of its ceremonial system.' (Ayres, 1944:ix). On the one hand there is the rational choice that upgrades our know-how and promotes our prosperity. On the other hand there are the values, conventions, opinions, concepts, world-views, religions that satisfy our intellectual needs and not just our biological imperatives. The constraint, in other words, is a mixed one, both resource-economising and fulfilment-diversifying. That is why we regard it as adaptive and efficient to close our shops on religious holidays and – the example considered in the previous subsection – demand a *social* democracy in order to deliver the services of compassion and relief. In each of these ways we are striving to raise our welfare. The welfare that we are raising is not, however, the meals and the snacks alone. The environment is a multi-dimensional one. Adaptation in the circumstances cannot be compressed into the economic determinism of an Alchian – or a Marx.

The motive and the maximand are problematic at the level of the society. No less is intention a cause of complication at the level of the enterprise. Alchian, convinced by the evolutionary logic of rational choice *as if*, predicts *ex post* success without regard to the *ex ante* objectives which conscious action may have identified for itself: 'There may have been no motivated individual adapting but, instead, only environmental adopting.' (Alchian, 1950:214). The methodological individualist is, on the other hand, less prepared to predict efficiency and growth on the authority of the functionalist's invisible hand. A more scientific approach, the individualist will say, would be to collect data on the actual mix of motives that makes the real, existing market discipline what it turns out to be.

In the jungle the more fit devour the less fit. In an industry, nationally or world-wide, different profit-levels are seen to co-exist. No doubt there would be an optimalisation in the sense of Pareto if the disequilibrium disparities could be corrected through gravitation and arbitrage. Yet the business community might in practice be perfectly satisfied with a range of outcomes that reflects a range of aspirations. Where such a dispersion in attitudes is the rule, what is needed is presumably not the profit-equalisation theorem so much as an open-minded model, sensitive to personal constructs alongside objective endowments and the external environment.

Thus Latsis has been critical of textbook economics for its propensity to homogenise the idiosyncrasies of market capitalism into a choice-less 'situational determinism' that 'turns the decision making agent into a cypher' (Latsis, 1972:233). Of particular interest is his contention that the textbook 'free' marketeers, committed as they are to the straitjacket of the standard size, the calculable and the prescribed, are singularly 'unfree' in the convection of choices for which they are in a position to account: 'We have here a rather paradoxical situation: single-exit situations are best explainable in terms of the libertarian-rationalistic model. In multiple-exit situations explanations of actions may require a model where the psychologistic components may well have a more central role in the explanans. To put it crudely, the more "free" the action, the more deterministic the explanans.' (Latsis, 1976:16). The more the action is the product of non-pecuniary ambitions, the more the adaptation is to convention and not to gain, the less will the pure profit-maximising model be able to predict the 'exit' that is selected.

Veblen's engineers aim at serviceability and quality, not saleability and 'opportunism'. Galbraith's 'technostructure' is obsessed with job-satisfaction, security and growth. In neither case is R and D transformed into marketable novelty because of a primary concern with the dividends and share-values of the absentee capitalists. The separation of ownership from control in the modern corporation itself gives the salaried managers the opportunity to pursue business objectives – accelerated expansion, high-profile prestige, idle curiosity, self-expression through work, the opportunity to enjoy on-the-job leisure, the opportunity to release the non-productive emotions of anger and envy – which reveal them to be profit-motivated but nonetheless not profit-maximising. Competitive processes in such a case would only drive out the less efficient where they drove the firms into losses and ultimately into liquidations. Sub-maximal profits and an unattractive opportunity-cost need not be enough to divert the business community from the *mix* of goals which it has made a conscious choice to rank above the survival of the 'bestness' that it perceives as a bore.

Heterogeneity of aspiration stands in the way of the Walrasian global balance. Impeded competition makes a complementary contribution of its own to the downgrading of the survival of the fittest into the second-best survival of the only-reasonably fit.

Product differentiation (including geographical location) gives even the small supplier a monopoly in its own special brand of service. Entry-barriers such as the need to raise start-up capital, to establish a product image, to expand into economies of scale may even in the long run perpetuate abnormal profits and protect business slack. The transaction-costs of information-gathering, contract-making, monitoring, enforcing can lead to the selection of institutions (consider vertical integration to reduce the likelihood of a challenge to dominance even where the take-over boosts the average cost to the consumer) that are technically and economically sub-optimal. Natural selection relies upon competitive pressures to bring about an improved adaptation. Impeded competition in ways such as these means that firms, seldom very interested in the best-*conceivable* adaptation, will not be driven even to search out the best-*attainable* economies relative to substitute suppliers who are mercifully complacent. Capitalism in such circumstances can turn conservative precisely because protected businesses have no real need to rock the boat.

The finite life-cycle of the biological organism does, conceptually speaking, make rivalry once more a source of initiative and breakthrough. The founding-father grows old and tired; the business passes into the hands of an uninspired next generation 'with less energy and less creative genius'; an assault is mounted by 'younger and smaller rivals' with 'elasticity and progressive force' on their side; and in the end the incumbent business 'almost invariably falls to pieces' (Marshall, 1890: 250, 264). Marshall in 1890 put forward a biologically informed vision of the ageing tree in the forest that, 'stiff and inactive', ultimately decays into the soil 'to make room for other and more vigorous life' (Marshall, 1890:269). By 1910 he had changed his mind: 'As with the growth of trees, so *was* it with the growth of businesses as a general rule before the great recent development of vast joint-stock companies, which often stagnate, but do not readily die.' (Marshall, 1890:263, emphasis added). Natural selection, it would appear, is more and more favourable to stagnation and over-development relative to the biological rise-and-fall that once was the safeguard of the consumer's interest.

Even oligopoly, of course, can be associated with price-wars and aggressive under-cutting. Industrial concentration need not mean passivity and accommodation. Yet competition among the few undeniably offers a unique temptation to the uncertain and the inter-dependent to fall back upon price-leadership, cartels and collusive arrangements such as assist the industry to adapt to unknowledge. A conservative capitalism that relies upon past rules to narrow down future choices is entirely functional where the strategist needs to contain his risks if he is to invest long-term. Whether business rules that cut down on choices are equally functional for a wider society that must adapt to scarcity is a great deal more debatable. What is efficient for one group need not be adaptive for another group, nor the gains from impeded trade be spread evenly throughout the nation as a whole. It is easier to be confident that the benefits will be dispersed in the frictionless institutional environment, automatic and impartial, of the powerless perfect competitor.

Power in economics raises serious questions about unequal influence and the redirection of evolution. At the level of phenomena, the imbalance could mean that dynamic small businesses were made the subject of high charges and crowding out on the part of conglomerates and giants in a position to redistribute: 'Much has been made in modern times of the tendency of the powerful industries of the developed countries to exploit, through their control of the terms of trade, the weaker economies of the Third World. More mention might have been made of the ability of modern large-scale industry to exploit within its own country the small enterprise to which it is far more intimately juxtaposed.' (Galbraith, 1973:270). At the level of the norms, moreover, the concentration of economic power could have a significant causal impact on the rules that are called the fittest, the laws that are allowed to survive: 'Only when it is in the interest of those with sufficient bargaining strength to alter the formal rules will there be major changes in the formal institutional framework.' (North, 1990:68). At the level both of things and of the laws, there is, in the view of Galbraith and North, a regressive gain to be reaped as the direct consequence of size and strength.

Neither Galbraith nor North would agree with Marx that class conflict is the universal dynamic of the evolutionary process. Still less would they agree with Veblen that political domination is but another name for economic success: 'Modern governmental policies, looking as they do to the furthering of business interests as their chief care, are of a "mercantile" complexion.... Representative government means, chiefly, representation of business interests. The government commonly works in the interest of the business men.... Constitutional government has, in the main, become a department of the business organization.' (Veblen, 1904:285, 286, 287). What Galbraith and North would both suggest, however, is that the market for commodities and the market for ideas alike is powerfully stamped by the relative endowments of resources and influence. Perfect competition might conceivably mean the natural selection of the rational maximisers best suited to please. Imperfect competition leaves open the possibility that the inefficient will win because they are big enough to throw their weight around.

Power can twist the present-day equilibrium. Power can also become embodied and acculturated. Once upon a time a given phenomenon might have been the most efficient adaptation to a specific situational constraint. Once upon a time, alternatively, a given phenomenon might have secured its supremacy as a result of threats, deceit and an error of judgement. Whatever may have been its origin, the crucial point is that that phenomenon, once in place, might become encoded like a gene and handed on to a new cohort that needs more than a vestigial organ if it is to make its way through a radically transformed reality. Thus does yesterday's fact serve to restrict the scope for today's adaptation. Momentum-driven, situated in time and space, we start from here but, even so, seldom from scratch.

Paid-out costs are an important cause of the perpetuated head-start. The 4′ 8½″ railway gauge may only have triumphed because heavy fixed investment ruled out a superior marginal adjustment. Public transport would perhaps be preferred to the private car had the motorways, once built, not become a sunk cost that delivered a free service. A communication network based around a local language would on economic grounds do well to convert to English were it not for the scrapping and the re-starting that would make the transition to optimality so expensive an option. The ratchet-effect of asset-specificity and network-externality has a similar effect in protecting the telephone despite the development of new, possibly more cost-effective technologies: 'The interdependent web of an institutional matrix produces massive increasing returns.' (North, 1990:95). Paid-out costs in ways such as these clearly reduce the freedom of agents to adapt flexibly in response to present-day feedback and signals. Nominally 'free to choose', 'their behavior, nevertheless, is held fast in the grip of events long forgotten and shaped by circumstances in which neither they nor their interests figured' (David, 1985:333).

History in that sense lives on in the present: 'It is sometimes not possible to uncover the logic (or illogic) of the world around us, except by understanding how it got that way.' (David, 1985:332). The proposition is borne out by the survival of the under-performing QWERTYUIOP sequence. The DSK alternative can raise typing speeds (the figures vary) by up to 40 per cent and the alphabetical ordering has an intuitive plausibility. QWERTY, on the other hand, was the historical accident that was adopted *first*. In the case of QWERTY, it is clear, 'the dynamic process takes on an *essentially historical* character' (David, 1985:332). Rational men and women are today typing uneconomically in essence because of Sholes.

Sholes in 1867 decided on QWERTY because it minimised the frequency of typebar clashes. It did so, admittedly, on a model of typewriter that has long since been superseded. Yet Sholes's layout lived on even after Sholes's model had been abandoned. Secretaries had acquired human capital in the form of the QWERTY sequence: to perform their duties they expected the familiar keyboard. Employers had invested heavily in the monopoly pattern: the high cost of hardware conversion made the standardisation, however premature, a quasi-irreversible overhead. The bandwagon rolled on. Yet it was an under-adaptive bandwagon. Locking-in and bygones clearly have much to answer for.

QWERTY demonstrates that the 'lucky break' that survives need not be the rational maximum that would have been identified by determined profit-seeking *ab initio*. Loss-minimisation subsequent to investment ensures that rigidity and repetition will enjoy some protection from competition, insulated *de facto* by the transaction costs and the unknowable consequences that always deter the new departure. Besides that, there is the incrementalism of path-dependence and the cumulative causation which snowballs an initial choice: 'Path dependence comes from the increasing returns mechanisms that reinforce the direction once on a given path.' (North, 1990:112). However great the differential, an established surgeon (in contrast to a young undergraduate) will require a major shock indeed to discard sector-specific skills in order to retrain himself for the bar. Even if the profit-rate is higher in an unrelated speculation, a firm with overheads, contacts, information and experience (in contrast to a fresh and uncommitted new entrant) will be reluctant to start again from a barrow. The individual and the business will understandably regret their missed opportunities. Recontracting the alternatives, removing into optimality is, however, a different matter.

That said, the theory of obstacles must not be mistaken for a theory of impossibility. The word-processor has replaced the typewriter, the airplane the transatlantic steamer, the horseless carriage the surrey with the fringe. It would clearly be an error to concentrate on the maladaptive that survives while neglecting the withering-away and the upgrading that also take place. Being fair, there is no scientific technique for summing up the failures and the successes in order to calculate the end-product from the anecdotal evidence. A compromise conclusion would be that the outdated will probably come under threat from the innovative, but that existing organisations will feel most comfortable with an adjustment that is incremental, cautious and slow. Only in the long run, as the existing set-up falls due for renewal, can it normally be expected that existing organisations, reconsidering their adaptations, will incur the transformation-costs that will raise them from the good to the best.

Just as sunk costs can perpetuate imperfections in the case of phenomena, so too can the ruling codes be cut off from the cut-and-thrust of continuing rivalry. The accumulation of norms in a country with a past can in that way act as a brake on the evolution that channels the future.

Thus rules can survive which are hallowed by repetition but still not efficiency-maximising. The 'first in, last out' expectation can deprive the contracting business of its most productive staff. The allocation of guns through queues in a war makes no allowance for national need. Selection by lottery for higher education can have a detrimental effect on economic growth. A male-only orchestra threatens music inferior to that which would have been supplied had no beneficial trades been prohibited by convention. Long apprenticeships and professional associations can be a cause of monopolistic standardisation and spontaneity closed off. A fresh settlement written on a malleable lump of wax might well choose to define less-than-economic practices such as these as out of keeping with its consensual standard of excellence. A community with a history is already the product of an ongoing constitution and a structure of roles. Circumscribing its identity, making it what it is, the *always was* is singularly resistant to any form of treason by change. It should surprise no one that competition and imitation have not overcome the dispersion and the legislative plurality in the 50 American states. Different places have different customs. That's the way it is, once learnt procedures have come to inhibit the mould-breaking of re-thought reactions.

The institutions that survive might be the patterns that are the best-suited to the conditions of the present. The conditions of the present might, however, be an envelope that includes the institutions of the past. Optimality in such a scenario would mean that the best brains should scorn a career in 'trade' for precisely the same reason that the King wears a crown, the Albanians smoke in public and our village keeps up its tradition of *vendetta* despite the depopulation that it has cost us. Rules, like phenomena, can clearly survive which are not the best suited to the task of economic efficiency in a complex environment: 'Institutions exist to reduce the uncertainties involved in human interaction. These uncertainties arise as a consequence of both the complexity of the problems to be solved and the problem-solving software (to use a computer analogy) possessed by the individual. There is nothing in the above statement that implies that the institutions are efficient.' (North, 1990:25). Veblen expressed himself even more strongly when he distanced his evolutionary economics from the guarantee of optimality: 'History records more frequent and more spectacular instances of the triumph of imbecile institutions over life and culture than of peoples who have by force of instinctive insight saved themselves alive out of a desperately precarious institutional situation.' (Veblen, 1914:25). The rules can be dysfunctional from the point of view of productivity. Productivity can be dysfunctional from the point of view of the rules. Adaptation to the lagged is no proof that an even better rule could not somewhere be found.

Trial-and-error experimentation in the marketplace for norms has the disadvantage, even where feasible, of being expensive and confusing.

Also, all precedent is functional in itself to the extent that it serves as a focus for search and expectation. In that sense even a second-best beacon might stand the test of time precisely because it is known to coordinate and trusted to guide. Nelson and Winter give the example of the organisational routine that replicates existing patterns and serves as a *de facto* blueprint for the perplexed: 'We claim that organizations *remember by doing.*' (Nelson and Winter, 1982:99). Organisational memory defuses latent conflicts, structures the deployment of skills, and constitutes a conservative alternative to the neoclassicist's maximisation: 'That, of course, is the heart of our theoretical proposal: the behavior of firms can be explained by the routines that they employ. Knowledge of the routines is the heart of understanding behavior.' (Nelson and Winter, 1982:128). The business, the bureaucracy, is best understood as a matrix of rules. The rules, Nelson and Winter say, do well enough. For all that, there is no prediction that they are the best-possible rules that an effortless and costless scan would have succeeded in identifying: 'Nonoptimal rules may survive in selection equilibrium.' (Nelson and Winter, 1982:154). Satisficing casts a giant shadow – and we start from here.

Unknowledge is always a deterrent to initiative. Today's differentials, today's profits, are at best a hint of what the future will bring, and thus at best a heavily-discounted stimulus to evolutionary adaptation. Central to unknowledge is the unpredictability of other people. The surprise of a meteor crashing to earth or a heat-wave that boosts the demand for ice-creams is of far less significance in economics than is the eternal contingency of how others will react. We simply do not know. Because we do not know, our ability to act rationally is severely impaired.

The darkness of interdependence is the cause of market failure in respect of externalities and public goods. Where there is a free-rider problem, a fallacy of composition, a prisoner's dilemma, there the danger is real that automaticity will not supply the phenomenon or the code that would make people feel most satisfied in their own personal estimation. The deficiency is most marked where expectations are mutually conditioning but where the chain of contacts is too loose, the numbers too large, the links too remote to produce the welfare-enhancing tit-for-tat. A would tell the truth if he knew that his unknown others would tell the truth. B would abstain from shoplifting if she knew that her unknown others would abstain from shoplifting. Both A and B believe the cooperative solution to be their preferred option. Yet neither A nor B can have any genuine confidence that the community will converge on it by means of the invisible hand. Guessing guesses and outguessing moves, the only thing that A and B can know for certain is that the satisfaction-level they can attain is inferior to the aspiration-level which a coordinated response would be able to deliver.

There is simply no way of knowing which way the critical mass is likely to swing. Consider the ignorance which always surrounds the choice of a new-style conformity which threatens with the scrap-heap an old-style conservatism: 'It may, for example, be unsafe to walk home in the dark when the streets are empty, so everybody prefers to take a taxi. If safety improves, the number of those who dare to walk will gradually increase. Once a certain security level is reached, the balance is tipped, and the majority will adopt the habit of walking home in the dark.' (Schlicht, 1998:48–9). The majority in their isolation as individuals might privately favour a change in dress-codes, in tipping-habits, in settlement-dates, the introduction of new networks built around the home fax, the e-mail address, the mobile phone. What all can do, however, one cannot. Uncoordinated, uncertain and alone, the demonstration-effect that triggers the mimicry might not in the circumstances be seen by the faces in the crowd as cost-effective enough to warrant the break. Thus does freedom condemn itself to unfreedom, just as a concerned observer had predicted it would when he wrote as follows about the market imperfection of small decisions: 'Hell is other people. So is economics. Economics, therefore, is Hell.' (Reisman, 1990:141).

In decentralised exchange the signals are deficient, a coordinated response unlikely. It is precisely that felt frustration that leads some citizens to turn to the State for a single conscious design policed by an identifiable authority. A groundswell of democratic consensus would in such circumstances decree that leadership is the source of the most-desired rules and rights; and that fortuitous accident cannot be relied upon to impose best-attainable order upon the gambles and the games. Explicit agreement liberates. Enforceable communication assists the society to evolve. As Commons puts it, arguing strongly against the mechanistic atomism of the nineteenth-century individualists that put the felt public interest on starvation rations in the interests of a dogmatic *freedom from* which underestimated the role of rules: 'Collective action means more than mere "control" of individual action. It means liberation and expansion of individual action; thus, collective action is literally the means to liberty. The only way in which "liberty" can be obtained is by imposing duties on others.' (Commons, 1950:34–5).

The State in such a perspective is seen as improving the rationality of choice. It is not the only perspective. It is expensive to set up new interest groups to challenge existing coalitions. It is difficult to break a *status quo* symbiosis between vested interest and its political patrons. Party-political competition is biased towards quick-return solutions rather than the long-horizoned rethink. Today's rent-seekers become tomorrow's rent-recipients. Today's infant industries become tomorrow's lame ducks. Path-dependence protects the embedded and perpetuates the traditional. Considerations such as these remind the reader that political conservatism might repress at least as much adaptation as it releases. Here as elsewhere in this chapter, the evidence speaks with a single voice on the precise relationship that may be said to exist between mutation and optimisation. Evolutionary economics is the study of the historical process. Teleology and meliorism, however, simply cannot be taken on trust.

7 Individual and Interest

Conscious choices are made by calculating individuals. For that reason they are always and everywhere self-regarding choices. Whether to feed the pigeons or to starve the poor, rational individuals will consistently rank the scenario that provides them with more satisfaction above the scenario that yields them less.

Rational individuals will choose what they want. Their choices in the economic market will, however, be subject to a situational constraint. Consumers, budget-limited, can at least make an unrestricted selection in the range that leads up to the financial cut-off. Utility-seekers and not profit-seekers, the simple fact that their self-interest is directed to final values and not to intermediate instrumentalities gives them the freedom to divert to famine-relief the money they had earmarked for a car or a holiday. Producers are not so fortunate. The business must make its choices with one eye on the competition and in line with the strict test of market survival. The firm is condemned by the interdependent nature of competitive rivalry not to serve the down-and-out who cannot pay or to carry a crippled co-worker cut down by a stroke. *Ecclesiasticus* 27:2 is clear on profit: 'As a peg is held fast in the joint between stones, so dishonesty squeezes in between selling and buying.' The capitalist in a competitive environment knows that his membership in the golf-club and his children's school-fees depend on his turning a deaf ear to invocations such as these. As a consumer he retains the freedom to divert to the homeless the money he had earmarked for restaurant meals. As a merchant or a manufacturer his choices are more circumscribed. The *quid pro quo* of market exchange presupposes a gain-seeking orientation. There would be little contracting in the bazaar or at the bargaining table if the buyers and the sellers all loved their neighbours as they loved themselves.

Business is business and the market is cold. It is possible to see in competitive capitalism the quintessential Hobbesian confrontation, the ultimate state of nature in which the struggle to survive means for the individual an insecure existence, forever 'solitary, poore, nasty, brutish, and short' (Hobbes, 1651:186). Karl Marx was quick to impute a connection. Marx found not in the apocryphal past but in the profit-seeking present the clearest evidence of that '*greed* and the war *amongst the greedy – competition*' (Marx, 1844b:107) which in his view lay at the root of 'the consciousness of reciprocal exploitation as the general relationship of individuals to one another': 'I derive benefit for myself by doing harm to someone else.... All this is actually the case with the bourgeois. For him only *one* relation is valid on its own account – the relation of exploitation.' (Marx and Engels, 1845–6:110). Marx contended that the market reduces the value of the person to supply and demand, product and appetite, narrow selfishness and commodity-worth. So, surprisingly, did Hobbes: 'The *Value*, or Worth of a man, is as of all other things, his Price; that is to say, so much as would be given for the use of his Power: and therefore is not absolute; but a thing dependant on the need and judgement of another.' (Hobbes, 1651:151–2).

Hobbes describes the state of nature as a market for might. It is from that socially contingent covenanting only a small step to argue, as C.B. Macpherson has done, that the *Leviathan* is the story not so much of psychological constants as of the nascent possessive individualism which its author had observed in the decreasingly ascriptive Britain of his own times: 'The postulate of innate desire of all men for more power without limit is only apparently tenable about men who are already in a universally competitive society.... He mistakenly attributed the characteristics of market society to all societies, and so claimed a wider validity for his conclusions than they can have.' (Macpherson, 1962:45, 99). Business is business, competition is 'Warre' – 'and therefore if any two men desire the same thing, which nevertheless they cannot both enjoy, they become enemies; and ... endeavour to destroy, or subdue one an other' (Hobbes, 1651:184).

Marx and Macpherson treat market capitalism as the ultimate cause of the Hobbesian *bellum*. Their interpretation of self-seeking as gain-seeking, their vision of the High Street as red in tooth and claw, their perception of freedom of enterprise as *homo homini lupus*, lends a sombre urgency to this chapter on Individual and Interest. It is a window on the world which could easily lead a true Hobbesian, sharing with the socialists a deep distrust of market anarchy, to demand the dictatorship of an absolute autocrat in order that individuals motivated by interest might be compelled to keep the peace. An alternative perspective would, however, be that market capitalism does not so much provoke as resolve the conflicts that for the true Hobbesian call into question the viability of decentralised activity. The basis for collaboration as Adam Smith saw it was the self-interested exchange: 'Give me that which I want, and you shall have this which you want, is the meaning of every such offer.... Nobody but a beggar chuses to depend chiefly upon the benevolence of his fellow-citizens.' (Smith, 1776:I, 18). The Hobbesian *bellum*, the true Smithian would say, is more likely to be associated with the suppression of the negotiating mechanism than it is with the opportunity to bargain, to contract and to agree. Individual and interest in such a perspective is to be welcomed and not to be feared.

Individual and Interest is the subject of the present chapter. Concerned with the micro–macro interface, the chapter attempts to situate purposive action in the collective context of the economic whole. The discussion is divided into three parts. Section 7.1, 'Methodological Individualism', considers the logic of procedural bottom-up in the light of the fact that subjectivity must always be personal, irreducible and unique. Section 7.2, 'Normative Holism', asks in what circumstances it would be desirable to make the citizen team-player the responsible servant of a shared and common consensus. Section 7.3, 'Normative Individualism', deals with individual and interest in the specific setting of the market economy. It suggests that the ethos of capitalism relies on a rigorous separability which, the sole benchmark for 'goodness' and not just a convenient 'let us assume', is more than a matter of methodology alone.

7.1 METHODOLOGICAL INDIVIDUALISM

Methodological individualism is a reductionist approach to the interpretation of social interaction. It factors down the whole and builds upwards from the part. It argues that decomposition is a necessary condition for an understanding of manifested choice: 'All actions are performed by individuals.... A social collective has no existence and reality outside of the individual members' actions.... The way to a cognition of collective wholes is through an analysis of the individuals' actions.... The *We* cannot act otherwise than each of them acting on his own behalf.... No matter what a man was and what he may become later, in the very act of choosing and acting he is an *Ego*.' (Mises, 1949:42, 44). It argues further that decomposition is a sufficient condition for the explanation of revealed preference: 'If we scrutinize the meaning of the various actions performed by individuals we must necessarily learn everything about the actions of collective wholes.... Nobody ever perceived a nation without perceiving its members. In this sense one may say that a social collective comes into being through the actions of individuals.... The hangman, not the state, executes a criminal.' (Mises, 1949:42, 43). Only the individual can think and act. Only a theory that is self-consciously micro-to-macro can in the circumstances provide an account of the aims and choices of the group.

The focus is on action. It is not on origination. The distinction between the immediate and the ultimate is an important one. Methodological individualism does not as such defend the Noble Savage from the trammels of an unwanted superstructure or champion the civil rights of the genius without a precedent against the intolerance and the tyranny of the majority. A methodology and not a social philosophy, the approach does not as such make common cause with the libertarian's ideal of power devolved. What it does is more modest, less ideologically charged. Adopting the position that all subjectivity is quintessentially discrete, methodological individualism begins at the base with the unit mind. Only in the light of that empathetic *Verstehen* does it aggregate upwards to the households, the corporations and the community itself: 'For the subjective interpretation of action in sociological work these collectivities must be treated as *solely* the resultants and modes of organization of the particular acts of particular persons, since these alone can be treated as agents in a course of subjectively understandable action.' (Weber, 1947:101). However established and unified the structure may be, still it cannot be said to have a mind of its own. Only the component individuals can possess the capacity to sense, to perceive, to intend, to believe, to desire, to evaluate and to infer.

The approach is one in which, as Buchanan and Tullock describe it, 'all theorizing, all analysis, is resolved finally into considerations faced by the individual person as decision-maker' (Buchanan and Tullock, 1962:315). In epistemology, it is at the root of 'Know Thyself', the *cogito ergo sum*, the intellectual individualism of the 'windowless monad', the sense-perception that Adam Smith adopted from earlier Enlightenment sceptics like David Hume: 'Every faculty in one man is the measure by which he judges of the like faculty in another. I judge of your sight by my sight, of your ear by my ear. . . . I neither have, nor can have, any other way of judging about them.' (Smith, 1759:18). In economics, it is a warning that inter-personal comparison is fraught with difficulty, that 'value in use cannot be measured by any known standard', that utility is 'differently estimated by different persons' (Ricardo, 1817: 429): 'Every mind is . . . inscrutable to every other mind, and no common denominator of feeling seems to be possible.' (Jevons, 1871:85). Methodological individualism must always appear pale and undernourished when juxtaposed to a philosophy that identifies essences and names absolutes. It is a second-best approach, better suited to Shackle on imagination, Hayek on uncertainty, Keynes on expectation than it is to the confident socio-cultural holism of Hegel and Marx. Top-down makes sense where the metaphysician or the empiricist can find a map.

Where God's filing-cabinet remains closed and locked, however, there may be no other course but to begin with the individual and to learn bottom-up.

The focus is on individual action. It is not on individual origination. Methodological individualism is a mode of interpretation which builds up the aims and interests of the group from the actions and choices of the component members who alone can decide and weight. It is not as such the heir to that nineteenth-century romanticism which argued that all moral worth must be traced back to atomistic self-expression and treated custom and convention as synonymous with frustration and distortion. Methodological individualism is a scientific approach which argues that the collectivity must be analysed on the basis of single persons and unit acts. It is not as such a psychologistic approach which concentrates on the outcomes of mind while denying that mind itself might be the envelope for the conditioning that went before.

Method of analysis is not the same as explanation of cause: 'It is one thing to state explicitly that all individualism is psychologistic and quite another thing to confuse individualism with psychologism.' (Agassi, 1960:187). Mises is especially clear that to factor down to primary units is not to exclude the earlier impact of the social setting: 'This does not mean that the individual is temporally antecedent. It merely means that definite actions of individuals constitute the collective.' (Mises, 1949:43). In fact, Mises continues, free will is normally circumscribed by socialisation and mind in its natural state seldom encountered in an order that has a past: 'Inheritance and environment direct a man's actions. ... He does not himself create his ideas and standards of value; he borrows them from other people.' (Mises, 1949:46). Most people are not genuine innovators, committed to major new departures. Most people are limited by birth and patterned by experience. Methodological individualism is evidently not recalcitrant to the study of social reproduction or the identification of the habituated response – Veblen himself said as much: 'It is, of course, on individuals that the system of institutions imposes those conventional standards, ideals, and canons of conduct that make up the community's scheme of life. Scientific inquiry in this field, therefore, must deal with individual conduct and formulate its theoretical results in terms of individual conduct.' (Veblen, 1919:243). An approach that builds upwards from individual behaviour is evidently not incompatible with the non-ego conditioning and the shared dynamics of an ongoing whole. Simply, the whole in this perspective must be strained through the parts that alone can put meaning into an observable state of affairs: 'A historical event cannot be described without reference to the persons involved and to the place and date of its occurrence.' (Mises, 1949:59).

The whole cannot be described without reference to the parts. Dispensing with infinite regress, setting out unsentimentally from *here*, it is the contention of the methodological individualist that even social pressures carried over from the past must be interpreted through the actions (as a proxy for the thoughts) of the socialised individuals who live subject to the inherited standards. The past acts through the present, the totality through the unit. The compulsion, the power of all over each, must evidently not be reified into the holistic fiction of a structure without a consciousness that somehow addresses problems without the need for human agency. *Homo sociologicus* has an educated nature that has been moulded by interaction and shaped by sharing. It is not the intention of the methodological individualist to deny the reality of a common language or to call into question the standardising force of imitation and guilt that is the essence of Steven Lukes's demand for conscious choices to be interpreted in their inter-personal context: 'Just as facts about social phenomena are contingent upon facts about individuals, the reverse is also true. Thus, we can only speak of soldiers because we can speak of armies: only if certain statements are true of armies are others true of soldiers.' (Lukes, 1973:117). All that is demanded by the methodological individualist is that the sociologist's investigation should commence with the building-block and not with an agglomeration that can have no end, no volition, no existence of its own: 'The individual lives and acts within society. But society is nothing but the combination of individuals for cooperative effort. It exists nowhere else than in the actions of individual men.' (Mises, 1949:143).

Only individuals can experience sensations or formulate plans. It is because of that obvious and fundamental irreducibility that the methodological individualist homes in on the building-block while treating interconnectedness as a dependent and a derivative state: 'The basic building block in the social sciences, the elementary unit of explanation, is the individual action guided by some intention.' (Elster, 1983: 20). Out goes the spurious concreteness of the 'national interest', 'public policy', 'class consciousness'. In comes the individual Briton with an opinion on defence, the individual Sikh who prefers his hair long, the individual worker who resents the white-collar differential. The aggregation that then emerges is not a whole in excess of the sum of the parts but a simple reconciliation of individual differences by means of bargaining, democracy and collective choice.

The methodological individualist views society as a fiction and an abstraction: 'Only individuals have ends, and can act to attain them. There are no such things as ends or of actions by "groups", "collectivities", or "States", which do not take place as actions by various specific individuals.' (Rothbard, 1962:I, 2). The methodological individualist is therefore committed to consulting the individual units and then passively to adding up: 'By the principle of utility is meant that principle which approves or disapproves of every action whatsoever, according to the tendency which it appears to have to augment or diminish the happiness of the party whose interest is in question. . . . The interest of the community then is, what? – the sum of the interests of the several members who compose it.' (Bentham, 1780:2, 3). The methodological holist, needless to say, has little time for the reduction of norms and habits to a sub-topic in the individual psychology which undeniably will be their immediate conduit: 'Society is not a mere sum of individuals. Rather, the system formed by their association represents a specific reality which has its own characteristics. . . . When the individual has been eliminated, society alone remains. We must, then, seek the explanation of social life in the nature of society itself.' (Durkheim, 1895:102, 103). The methodological holist for that reason proceeds inwards from the synthesis – not outwards from the atom – to situate the agent in the matrix of 'the social milieu which tends to fashion him in its own image' (Durkheim, 1895:6). Society is present in the individual because it is present in the group. Society is not present in the group because discrete individuals took it upon themselves to depart from externality, to ignore constraint.

Inter-temporally, Durkheim argues, the repetition of experience constitutes a pattern to which the integrated may be expected to adapt: 'We speak a language that we did not make; we use instruments that we did not invent; we invoke rights that we did not found; a treasury of knowledge is transmitted to each generation that it did not gather itself.' (Durkheim, 1912:212). The individual in his historical setting clearly has access to a stream of representations which are for the user a free gift from past cohorts. The individual in the spot interdependency is no less likely to be confronted with an altered choice-set, to develop 'a psychic individuality of a new sort' (Durkheim, 1895:103), as a direct consequence of his membership in an association that magnifies the sentiments precisely as a compound is known to transform its chemicals: 'The group thinks, feels, and acts quite differently from the way in which its members would were they isolated. If, then, we begin with the individual, we shall be able to understand nothing of what takes place in the group.' (Durkheim, 1895:104). Consider the 'concrete and living reality' of the social whole, the collective pressures that make the individual a believer 'in the existence of a moral power upon which he depends and from which he receives all that is best in himself' (Durkheim, 1912:225). That moral power, neither a hallucination nor a visitation, is none other than the external coercion of all upon each which the individual consciousness understandably takes to be a superior force. Personified as a spirit, the truth is that 'the god is only a figurative expression of the society', that the notion of religion is inseparable from that of the moral community: 'In all history, we do not find a single religion without a Church.' (Durkheim, 1912:44, 226).

As with Joan of Arc (who heard the voice of society and assumed it was the energy of the sacred), so with the suicide bomber, the violent revolutionary, the football hooligan: 'Under the influence of the general exaltation, we see the most mediocre and inoffensive bourgeois become either a hero or a butcher.' (Durkheim, 1912:211). The deeds are performed by individuals, but still the preferences revealed are those of the 'group incarnate and personified' (Durkheim, 1912:211). The truth is the crowd. That being the case, it would make sense to begin the analysis with the group and not with the discrete Joan of Arc, the factored-down 'mediocre and inoffensive bourgeois', through whom the group is observed to think, to feel and to act. The individual tends to be the instrument. The sum of the individuals tends to be the cause. *Sui generis* determines. Individual agency executes. Confronted with the need to choose, Durkheim opts to explain at the level of the whole.

Methodological holism interprets the culture in the mind disproportionately as the inter-temporal, inter-personal interdependencies that make the subjective perceptions what they are. It therefore proposes that individual action be studied in the context of the social relationships which tend to be at the root. Methodological individualism, on the other hand, concentrates on the individual manifestation and not on the concealed cause. It explains human action in terms of individual choice.

It does so because an aggregate of individuals can never have an independent capacity for decision-making and reflection.

The methodological holist does not deny that individuals are the organs through which the organism acts. The methodological individualist does not deny that the constraint of circumstance restricts the individual's opportunity to transform. The methodological holist accepts that some observed actions originate in the idiosyncratic and not in the pre-programmed. The methodological individualist accepts that some revealed preferences copy shared valuations, embedded and common. There is clearly some overlap between the advocates of synthesis and the supporters of reduction.

Top-down situating the behaviour-pattern, bottom-up reconstructing the choice-calculus, there is a sense in which the holism and the individualism may be said to be two sides of a single coin. Methodologically speaking, the intuition is valid that each approach may be regarded as shedding a different light on the same total picture. Philosophy, however, drives a wedge. Holists tend to find support for their holism in the collectivistic values of integration and belonging. Individualists tend to ground their individualism in the libertarian ethos and the right to express. Even if the methodologies could be shown to be complements, still, it is clear, must the world-views separate the proponents into camps. Methodology and world-view tend to come in a single package. It would be easier to reach a firm conclusion on the question of complementarity if the products were not so commonly joint.

Nowhere is the tension more explicit than in the approach of the two teams to the economics of capitalism. Capitalism advances where individuals challenge. Capitalism stagnates where individuals duplicate. Methodological individualism is as well suited to the explanation of statics as it is to dynamism and alteration. Philosophy, however, drives a wedge. Normative individualism is in sympathy with innovation and interest. Normative holism is friendly to repetition and conformity. At the normative level at least, the two approaches are most definitely substitutes and not complements at all.

7.2 NORMATIVE HOLISM

Normative holism scales up. The group has an identity, an interest and an authority of its own that precommit its present-day cohorts, fully aware that individual reason is 'fallible and feeble', to the 'wisdom without reflection' that is the great gift of blood gone by: 'A spirit of innovation is generally the result of a selfish temper and confined views. People will not look forward to posterity, who never look backward to their ancestors.' (Burke, 1790:119, 121). The social contract relates not to the isolated and the evanescent, 'little better than the flies of a summer' of which the gain-seeking is quickly forgotten, but rather to 'the whole chain and continuity of the commonwealth' that is a partnership with the future precisely because it is a bond with the past: 'As the ends of such a partnership cannot be obtained in many generations, it becomes a partnership not only between those who are living, but between those who are living, those who are dead, and those who are to be born.' (Burke, 1790:193, 194–5). Economically speaking, the accumulated and the shared have a higher pay-off than do the current and the factored-down: 'We are afraid to put men to live and trade each on his own private stock of reason; because we suspect that this stock in each man is small, and that the individuals would do better to avail themselves of the general bank and capital of nations, and of ages.' (Burke, 1790:183). Politically speaking, it is prejudice and tradition, not freedom *from* and the Rights of Man, which are 'the faithful guardians, the active monitors of our duty': 'When antient opinions and rules of life are taken away, the loss cannot possibly be estimated. From that moment we have no compass to govern us. . . . Kings will be tyrants from policy when subjects are rebels from principle.' (Burke, 1790:172, 182). The group has an identity, a function and an imperative of its own. It was because of his openness to a whole with a history and a purpose not reducible to the will of the component units that Edmund Burke, rejecting simple aggregation in favour of the social fact, opted for normative holism even in circumstances where methodological individualism was to be selected as the analytical tool.

A contemporary of Adam Smith, a witness to the Industrial Revolution, Burke was far too familiar with the workings of Change Alley to deny any validity to the position of a Popper on the agency that refracts: 'All social phenomena, and especially the functioning of all social institutions, should always be understood as resulting from the decisions, actions, attitudes, etc. of human individuals.' (Popper, 1945:98). Just as Burke could see a role for explanation that began with the external reality of collective pressures, so he would have raised no objection to an investigation of action that built upwards from preferences revealed. At the normative level, however, the interpretation and the recommendation were less open to the pragmatism of experience. Individuals can alter their destiny – but only within the confines of institutions and forces that they did not select. Individuals can modify circumstances –

but should not exercise their creativity in so radical a manner as to threaten their inheritance or abridge their obligations. A contemporary of G.F.W. Hegel, a witness to the French Revolution, Burke was far too familiar with the mobs and the tumbrils to deny the verdict of Durkheim on the organicism that liberates in the very instant that it represses: 'By making man understand by how much the social being is richer, more complex, and more permanent than the individual being, reflection can only reveal to him the intelligible reasons for the subordination demanded of him and for the sentiments of attachment and respect which habit has fixed in his heart.' (Durkheim, 1895:123).

Rousseau saw the group as artificial, the individual as good by nature but crippled by dominance: 'If some men are by nature slaves, the reason is that they have been made slaves *against* nature.... Man is born free, and everywhere he is in chains.' (Rousseau, 1762:240, 242). Rousseau's Noble Savage is the back-to-basics ideal of an Enlightenment optimist in the shadow of the Bastille. Durkheim's reply is that the Enlightenment self-determinists made the mistake of disregarding the solidarity of union and community without which the Noble Savage would be condemned to purposelessness and imprisoned by the unlimited: 'When one is no longer checked, one becomes unable to check one's self.' (Durkheim, 1897:271).

Catholics guided by a structured hierarchy are less likely to take their own lives than are Protestants who delegate authority to the individual conscience: 'The proclivity of Protestantism for suicide must relate to the spirit of free inquiry that animates this religion.' (Durkheim, 1897: 158). Married men despite their burdens and responsibilities have a higher coefficient of self-preservation than do single men without the dense network of children and relatives: 'The family is the essential factor in the immunity of married persons.' (Durkheim, 1897:198). Wars and revolutions reduce the incidence of self-destruction for the reason that patriotism and commitment, rousing collective sentiments and stimulating mutual support, temper individualism with attachment to a common cause that lies outside the self in time and space: 'As they force men to close ranks and confront the common danger, the individual thinks less and less of himself and more of the common cause.... Suicide varies inversely with the degree of integration of political society.' (Durkheim, 1897:208). Master of his own destiny, accountable to no one for his actions, the individual alone, Durkheim says, is more likely to give in to emptiness and disillusionment than is the individual bonded in to the Church, the family, the political group. Holism to Durkheim was clearly something more than an intellectual abstraction. Writing as a methodological holist, Durkheim stated that collective sentiments were not to be derived from individual intentions: 'The determining cause of a social fact should be sought among the social facts preceding it and not among the states of the individual consciousness.' (Durkheim, 1895:110). Writing as a normative holist, Durkheim predicted melancholia on the part of the individual who has lost his base: 'Seeing no goal to which he may attach himself, he feels himself useless and purposeless.' (Durkheim, 1897:225). Writing analysis, Durkheim said that a social force was a non-individual thing. Writing philosophy, Durkheim pointed to Beachy Head.

The Durkheimian perspective of the individual as an originating essence embedded within a socialised persona is re-stated by Etzioni in the following assertion: 'To be free requires individuals that are not socially isolated, cut off from one another; they must be linked to one another and bound into a community, to form a We, and to be able to sustain one another's emotional stability and inner security. It is on these psychological and sociological foundations that people fully develop and freely express their individuality.' (Etzioni, 1988:138). To be free, Etzioni is saying, is to act in unison: 'Indeed, the greatest danger for liberty arises when the social moorings of individuals are cut.' (Etzioni, 1988: 10).

Asch too assigns a high importance to fellowship, participation, companionship, gregariousness, belonging. A social psychologist, Asch contends that human beings have natural tendencies to link themselves with others. The craving, he suggests, is at once economically purposive (the animal-like propensity to seek survival by means of hunting in packs) and affectively non-rational (sociability, empathy, acceptance, affection being a source of emotional well-being). Asch argues that people have a tendency and a need to rise above the childish pursuit of narrow gratification that is for him a sure sign of arrested development. He also suggests that self-interested economic striving is the direct consequence of *Gemeinschaft* frustrated, *Gestalt* torn apart: 'To me it seems that the accentuation of the self is often a response, not to powerful ego-centred tendencies, but to the thwarting and defeat of the need to be a part of one's group, to know that one is respected and liked, to feel that one is playing a part in the lives of others and that there are issues larger than oneself that unite one with others.' (Asch, 1952:320). What Asch is maintaining is in effect this, that normative individualism is an alienated second-best, the random residual that remains behind when the ties of community have become too loose: 'Self-centredness is the revenge that the ego extracts under these conditions.' (Asch, 1952:321). Normative holism protects the community from undisciplined avarice, from short-horizoned greed. Normative individualism acknowledges the inevitable in a void where the family may be a focus for caring but the wider society is no more than an agglomeration of gulls.

Asch, like Etzioni and Durkheim, welcomes the integration and the advance that are the outcome for all of a 'mutually shared field': 'The individual without social experience is not fully a human being.... The environment of others and the products of their labor become a powerful, comprehensive region of forces within which each individual moves and has his being.... Solitary men could not produce the effects we observe in society.' (Asch, 1952:119, 163). Etzioni, like Durkheim and Asch, does not want the individual to obey society's orders as if a soldier in the barracks, any more than he looks with warmth on moral anarchy and the denial of common values: 'Communities constantly need to be pulled toward the center course, where individual rights and social responsibilities are properly balanced.' (Etzioni, 1995:x). Durkheim, like Asch and Etzioni, favours a middle way between the pull of social pressures – 'we feel their resistance when we try to shake them off' (Durkheim, 1895:18) – and the push of individual interest: 'Our nature is double.' (Durkheim, 1912:264). Neither Asch nor Etzioni nor Durkheim is attracted to the idea that the part can only flourish when passive and subordinate to the commands of a whole. A normative holist and not a normative totalitarian, what each does say, however, is that the individual is most likely to do well when rooted in good soil. Normative individualism would unintendedly deprive the individual of the nourishment he requires to unfold and to become.

7.3 NORMATIVE INDIVIDUALISM

The normative individualist builds self-image and self-respect around the scope for self-determination and the opportunity for self-direction. His *credo*, in the words of Isaiah Berlin, begins and ends with 'the freedom which consists in being one's own master': 'I wish to be a subject, not an object; to be moved by reasons, by conscious purposes, which are my own, not by causes which affect me, as it were, from outside.... I wish, above all, to be conscious of myself as a thinking, willing, active being, bearing responsibility for my choices and able to explain them by

references to my own ideas and purposes.' (Berlin, 1958:131). I am I –
an initiator and a doer, not a slave, an animal or a thing which is acted
upon without being asked for a view. I am I – and that is why the normative individualist treats the freedom from external coercion as the
sine qua non for self-expression and self-fulfilment: 'As liberals, we take
freedom of the individual, or perhaps the family, as our ultimate goal in
judging social arrangements. . . . Freedom has nothing to say about what
an individual does with his freedom.' (Friedman, 1962:12). I am I – and
that is why the normative individualist wants the power to decide to be
devolved from society and State to the smallest-feasible unit capable of
understanding the alternatives and of making a purposive choice: 'The
heart of the liberal philosophy is a belief in the dignity of the individual,
in his freedom to make the most of his capacities and opportunities
according to his own lights, subject only to the proviso that he not inter-
fere with the freedom of other individuals to do the same.' (Friedman,
1962:195). The methodological individualist favours factoring down
because, without decentralised consultation, there can be no access to
the subjectivity of the hidden mind. The normative individualist favours
factoring down because respect for persons is an end in itself.

One person wants a red tie. Another person wants a blue tie. One
person finds the utopia in sport and urban living. Another person finds
the utopia in the arts and the countryside. Respect for persons dictates
that differences of opinion on issues such as these should enjoy an
equal freedom of expression: 'The idea that there is one best composite
answer to all of these questions, one best society for *everyone* to live in,
seems to me to be an incredible one.' (Nozick, 1974:311). Struck by the
sheer diversity of the human experience, Robert Nozick reaches the
conclusion that factoring down is indispensable if the preferences
revealed are indeed to parallel the heterogeneities of the population
pool: 'Treating us with respect by respecting our rights, it allows us,
individually or with whom we choose, to choose our life and to realize
our ends and our conception of ourselves, insofar as we can, aided by
the voluntary cooperation of other individuals possessing the same dignity.' (Nozick, 1974:334). The recommendation is clearly not that of
conformity, obedience, public opinion, social pressure that would satisfy the binding conditions of the holistic integrationist. Instead it is the
plea for tolerance and liberty that was entered so eloquently by John
Stuart Mill in his 'one very simple principle' of 1859: 'The only part of
the conduct of anyone, for which he is amenable to society, is that which
concerns others. In the part which merely concerns himself, his independence is, of right, absolute. Over himself, over his own body and

mind, the individual is sovereign.' (Mill, 1859:68–9). Individual freedom is an end in itself. The normative individualist insists that personal autonomy must not be compromised in the pursuit of some goal that the individual has not personally put first. *De gustibus non est disputandum*: 'The individual has to decide which is God for him and which is the devil. And so it goes throughout all the orders of life.' (Weber, 1948:148).

Milton Friedman sees freedom *from* as the ultimate utility that must be maximised. It is on the basis of that value absolute, and not merely in terms of instrumental efficacy, that he seeks to derive his support for enterprise, exchange, property, contract, negotiation – his support, in other words, for the economic arrangements of market capitalism: 'So long as effective freedom of exchange is maintained, the central feature of the market organization of economic activity is that it prevents one person from interfering with another in respect of most of his activities.' (Friedman, 1962:14). Politicisation prescribes. Gain-seeking consults. Competitive capitalism is legitimate and desirable first and foremost because it 'gives people what they want instead of what a particular group thinks they ought to want. Underlying most arguments against the free market is a lack of belief in freedom itself.' (Friedman, 1962:15).

Freedom is an ethic and a value. Yet there is more. An end in itself, freedom is the means to an end as well. Freedom raises felt welfare, in the obvious sense that the trading partners would not exchange if each did not expect an improvement in satisfaction as seen through his own eyes: 'No exchange will take place unless both parties do benefit from it. Cooperation is thereby achieved without coercion.' (Friedman, 1962:13). Freedom, moreover, releases the entrepreneurial drive and the goal-orientated self-seeking that act as a stimulus to allocative and dynamic efficiency. Competition promotes the economical husbandry of scarce resources. It also provides a productive outlet for 'those basic forces of enterprise, ingenuity, invention, hard work, and thrift that are the true springs of economic growth' (Friedman, 1968:102). In the hard currency of the wealth of nations and not just in the warm glow of the moral absolute, the normative individualist will evidently find much to admire in the 'obvious and simple system of natural liberty' (Smith, 1776:II, 208) which Adam Smith in the Age of Reason was able to praise so highly: 'Projectors disturb nature in the course of her operations on human affairs; and it requires no more than to leave her alone and give her fair play in the pursuit of her ends. . . . Little else is required to carry a state to the highest degree of affluence from the lowest barbarism but peace, easy taxes, and a tolerable administration of justice; all the rest being brought about by the natural course of things.' (Smith, 1755, cited in Rae, 1895:62).

The perspective for Smith was a dual one. The first strand in normative individualism was respect for persons: 'Every man, as long as he does not violate the laws of justice, is left perfectly free to pursue his own interest his own way.' (Smith, 1776:II, 208). The second strand in normative individualism was economic progress: 'The natural effort of every individual to better his own condition, when suffered to exert itself with freedom and security, is so powerful a principle, that it is alone, and without any assistance, not only capable of carrying on the society to wealth and prosperity, but of surmounting a hundred impertinent obstructions with which the folly of human laws too often incumbers its operations.' (Smith, 1776:II, 49–50). The first element in normative individualism was protecting without leading. The second element in normative individualism was the wealth of households. The two arguments were closely linked in the joint product identified by Adam Smith. Conceptually speaking, however, they were separate and remain discrete.

Thus the Good Samaritan pursues 'his own interest his own way', but still does little to advance the cause of 'wealth and prosperity'. The reason is that the Good Samaritan, purposive and independent, opts to rank the relief of distress above an equivalent consumable or investment project. A non-materialistic interpretation of individual self-interest undeniably breaks the link between decentralisation and affluence. It was, on the other hand, a value-orientation which the economist Smith believed he could safely treat as the exception and not as the rule: the 'uniform, constant, and uninterrupted effort of every man to better his condition ... comes with us from the womb and never leaves us till we go into the grave' (Smith, 1776:I, 362–3, 364). Individualism, Smith believed, was reliably acquisitive. Economic progress for that reason could reliably be expected from the real-world individuals whose preferences the liberal is self-mandated to respect.

Just as the respect for persons could be at variance with the wealth of nations, so the wealth of nations could be better pursued without recourse to the respect for persons. This has been the contention of planners such as John Strachey and G.D.H. Cole who have looked to the skilled technocrat to supersede individual choice and in that way to speed up the rate of growth. A scientist's appreciation of the bureau-crat's wisdom relative to the entrepreneur's guesstimate calls into question the primacy of exchange. Here as before, however, Adam Smith saw no need to introduce any modification into the joint product that he identified. The managed economy, he said, is in truth exposed to 'innumerable delusions' and tarnished by 'public prodigality and misconduct': 'I have never known much good done by those who affected to trade for the public good.' (Smith, 1776:I, 208, 363, 478). As far as Smith was concerned, the omniscient Chancellor was as unrepresentative in real-world conditions as the Good Samaritan would be.

Self-interest was dependably a material interest. Economic growth was dependably the product of exchange. Respect for persons, in short, was dependably bound up with the advancement of wealth – for those who were in a position to pay. It has always been the objection of Smith's critics that he has too little to say about the dignity and the self-development of those who were not. Where the respect for persons has no obvious link with the wealth of nations, it is understandable that some philosophers should have looked to the State and not the market for the required dose of normative individualism.

Thus Polanyi has written as follows about the freedom to choose of autonomous individuals who live in slums and suffer from the cold: 'Socialism *is* the heir to Individualism. It *is* the economic system under which the substance of Individualism can alone be preserved in the modern world.' (Polanyi, 1935:365). Respect for persons where the persons cannot pay will not mean the High Street shops so much as rent-control, income maintenance, council housing, guaranteed employment, educational opportunities, the National Health. The individualism will be the same as that which imbues the first of the two strands in Adam Smith's double-barrelled perspective. The individualism will be the same; but still the inference that is drawn will be quite a different one. In the words of Steven Lukes: 'The only way to realize the values of individualism is through a humane form of socialism.' (Lukes, 1973: 157). Where this leaves market exchange and the wealth of nations is unclear. The Smithian duality at least promised a rise in living standards – for those who were in a position to pay.

National affluence is the consequence of private interest: 'Every individual is continually exerting himself to find out the most advantageous employment for whatever capital he can command. It is his own advantage, indeed, and not that of the society which he has in view. But the study of his own advantage naturally, or rather necessarily leads him to prefer that employment which is most advantageous to the society.' (Smith, 1776:I, 475). Private vices in a competitive economy are evidently in a position to deliver spillover benefits – as if guided by an invisible hand which guarantees the fulfilment of function even where the micro-rationality of the individual agents fails to extend to the macro-implications. Thus is the evolution and success of the capitalist system an unintended outcome of a skein of small decisions, the wealth of the nation the unexpected result of acquisitive impulses and gain-seeking emulation.

The proposition is a general one, clearly formulated by Adam Ferguson in the following tribute to the power of circumstances that exceeds the wisdom of authorities: 'Mankind, in following the present sense of their minds, in striving to remove inconveniencies, or to gain apparent and contiguous advantages, arrive at ends which even their imagination could not anticipate, and pass on, like other animals, in the track of their nature, without perceiving its end.' (Ferguson, 1767:122). Ferguson's conviction, that individuals in acting fail to anticipate the hidden states that their rational choices will bring about, was shared by Karl Popper when he reached the conclusion that 'only a minority of social institutions are consciously designed': 'Even those which arise as the result of conscious and intentional human actions are, as a rule, *the indirect, the unintended and often the unwanted by-products of such actions.*' (Popper, 1945:93). Adam Smith took the general proposition and applied it quite specifically to the economics of market capitalism. As individuals seek products and profits, so the feudal system gives way to its commercial successor. As individuals labour for utility and status, so the nation grows like Britain and does not stagnate like China. As individuals specialise and concentrate, so mental mutilation sets in as the price of the heightened productivity. The indirect, the unintended, the unwanted – Adam Smith was insistent on all three counts that individual action was the motor but that the destination would not be known until it had become a *fait accompli*.

Much was unknowable *ex ante* and interconnected *ex post*. Smith in the circumstances recognised the need to incorporate the historical and sociological insights of methodological holism into his account of the wealth of nations. Yet individual action was the motor; and that is why Adam Smith as an economist was unprepared to compromise on the philosophy of normative individualism. Other economists have followed his example. Influenced by his economic philosophy, they have absorbed his economic psychology as well as his market capitalism. They have had to do so. Normative individualism is only translated into normative economising where individuals behave in a manner that is conducive to value for money.

Market capitalism depends upon the hedonic calculus that was encapsulated so memorably by Bentham: 'Nature has placed mankind under the governance of two sovereign masters, *pain* and *pleasure*. It is for them alone to point out what we ought to do, as well as to determine what we shall do.' (Bentham, 1780:1). Jevons founded the whole of his market marginalism upon this condition: 'Pleasure and pain are undoubtedly the ultimate objects of the calculus of economics. To satisfy our wants to the utmost with the least effort – to procure the greatest amount of what is desirable at the expense of the least that is undesirable – in other words, *to maximize pleasure*, is the problem of economics.' (Jevons, 1871:101). The condition relates to the subjective estimation of costs and benefits, punishments and rewards. Making a clear distinction between means and ends, inputs and outputs, it implies that the sensory unit will act rationally to minimise his diswelfares, to maximise his satisfactions. The trade-offs and substitutions that then result are at the core of the waste-avoiding, efficiency-boosting society that faces up to the scarcity of its endowments by means of recourse to careful evaluation. Just as an animal will instinctively seek refuge from a storm or a fire, so an economic agent will be led by the desire for comfort to pare down the fallow in the pursuit of utility or profit.

An economic psychology which explains human actions in terms of the push of pain, the pull of pleasure, has no need to disaggregate its categories. Injustice is wrong because it is a cause of pain. Generosity is right because it is a source of pleasure. Truth-telling is good because it makes people feel good. Ugliness is bad because it makes people feel bad. The Good Samaritan does not conform to an unbreakable rule but buys the felicity of an unspoiled conscience. The Bad Samaritan does not live by a moral code but sells non-murder in order to consume non-imprisonment. Learned habits and social values (Durkheim's *conscience collective*) are themselves not a countervailing force but simply a purchase made. Mises is saying just this when he expresses the view that post-medieval man, declining to put passive blending-in above goal-centred initiative, is not prepared to magnify the instrument into an absolute. The representative individual, Mises writes, 'chooses to adopt traditional patterns or patterns adopted by other people because he is convinced that this procedure is best fitted to achieve his own welfare'

(Mises, 1949:46). The representative individual, Mises continues, 'is ready to change his ideology and consequently his mode of action whenever he becomes convinced that this would better serve his interests' (Mises, 1949:46). The representative individual, Mises concludes, will purchase no more conservatism than he can afford because he is led Bentham-like towards the avoidance of felt discomfort, the utility of felt well-being: 'Man becomes a social being not in sacrificing his own concerns for the sake of a mythical Moloch, society, but in aiming at an improvement in his own welfare.' (Mises, 1949:160). The economic psychology that underlies the capitalist system presupposes an alert flexibility in respect of aversion and attraction. It has no need to probe more deeply into the micro-motives that make the trade-off what it is.

The anticipation of the cost–benefit mindset is in no way an assertion that the whole of human life may be reduced to the pig-like pursuit of the fuller trough. The anticipation of a trade-off does not mean that monetary command over material consumables must be taken to be the sole end and purpose of all human endeavour. What it does mean is that competing endstates must be situated within the framework of the economising procedure. The research scientist who answers questions stemming exclusively from 'wonder' in the sense of Smith or 'idle curiosity' in the sense of Veblen must be seen as paying for his peace of mind through the sacrifice of a salary in industry that different investigations would have enabled him to secure. *Homo faber* who unfolds his creative essence by means of careful craftsmanship and pride in a job well done must be seen as satisfying his 'instinct for workmanship' at the expense of the additional income that corner-cutting and throughput would have brought within his reach. The monk who treats prayer as an end in itself and always does his duty must be seen as substituting task-centred fulfilment and the invariant Gospel Truth for the aesthetic, the pecuniary, the sensual opportunities that are his self-perceived next-bests forgone. Normative economising does not deny that human beings have a range of desires, drives, motives and instincts that cannot be reduced to the pig-like pursuit of the fuller trough. What it does assert is, however, that psychological needs are only satisfied at a cost; and that the representative individual has a reasonable awareness of the sacrifices that accompany the selection. Awareness is crucial. The subjective calculation must be the agent's *ex ante* own, not the reconstruction of the statistician who fits in the values in the light of the outcomes. It is the assertion of the normative economiser that even the monk has a workable appreciation of the choices outside his church and demonstrates a reasonable alertness in the shaping of his life.

The cost–benefit mindset is as general as the postulation of purposive action. That said, market capitalism would collapse overnight if all that economising predicted was that monks would buy the services of the Bible and sell the pleasures of the flesh. For Smith's 'wealth and prosperity' to be the consequence of Smith's 'obvious and simple system of natural liberty', it is clear, the normative economiser is bound to rely on the valuation of affluence and not just on the axiom of interest. The fuller trough is back on stream. Thus the consumer must serve the producer through an unceasing acquisitiveness that acts as a deterrent to leisure and saving, through a rapacious ranking of more to less that staves off the stagnation of 'enough'. The producer, similarly, must serve the consumer through a ready alertness to the profitable exploitation of unsatisfied wants, through a narrow selfishness that causes him to cater even to whims which he himself would regard as unworthy. The consumer would not serve the producer by rejecting goods and services in favour of visits to the elderly at the margin. The producer would not serve the consumer by expressing himself in a work of art that no household would want to display. For market capitalism to emerge from normative individualism, what is clear is that consumers must expect utility from exchangeables and that producers must seek profits through sales. The two parties, supplying each other's demands, will in that way end up net contributors not to Bible-reading in the cloister but to 'wealth and prosperity' in an expanding economy.

The two parties to an exchange respond *de facto* to one another's needs. The reciprocity, the mutuality of their interest-based cooperation is the cement that keeps the community one. As Mises writes, explaining why he as both a methodological and a normative individualist nonetheless believes that 'man is a social animal that can thrive only within society', the complementarity of contract is a powerful bond: 'Man serves in order to be served.' (Mises, 1949:184, 194). The outcome is service to others. The intention is not. The ranking of the consequentialism above the deontology is defended by Adam Smith in his famous appeal to the meat, the beer and the bread on offer in the shops: 'It is not from the benevolence of the butcher, the brewer, or the baker, that we expect our dinner, but from their regard to their own interest. We address ourselves, not to their humanity but to their self-love, and never talk to them of our own necessities but of their advantages.' (Smith, 1776:I, 18). Just as healthy crops are the appetising returns to dirt and manure, so, it would seem, are 'wealth and prosperity' the unintended outcomes of greed and covetousness. What this means in terms of economising is that greed is good precisely because it is functional. Sentimental conservatism, retarding growth, prevents the marginal from finding employment. The qualitative in place of the quantitative is a source of under-production, misspecification and bottlenecks. Treating people as means and not as ends puts the workers in a position to afford a house, a car and a holiday abroad.

Not value-free but judgemental and prescriptive, normative economising presupposes a narrow-horizoned self-love that focuses the isolate not on his community but on his shopping. Thus does market capitalism emerge from normative individualism, guided as it must be by instrumental rationality, the cost–benefit posture, materialism and interest that as a composite ethos put the motivation into the mechanism. Methodological individualism and methodological holism are the perspectives and the windows on the world. Normative individualism and normative economising, on the other hand, are the value-orientations that make market capitalism a self-sustaining system.

8 The Ethical Constraint

On the one hand there is Mandeville on the selfishness that succeeds: 'Pride and Vanity have built more hospitals than all the Virtues together.' (Mandeville, 1714:I, 261). On the other hand there is Marx on communism beyond shirking and greed: 'Only then can the narrow horizon of bourgeois right be left fully behind and society inscribe on its banners: from each according to his ability, to each according to his needs.' (Marx, 1875:566). In the middle there is Adam Smith: 'How selfish soever man may be supposed, there are evidently some principles in his nature, which interest him in the fortune of others, and render their happiness necessary to him, though he derives nothing from it, except the pleasure of seeing it.' (Smith, 1759:3). Stranded on the middle ground, what the pragmatic Smith expected from human nature in all its complexity was a balance between self-love and benevolence, a mixed orientation that made modern capitalism other-regarding even as the wealth of nations was dependent upon gain-seeking and competition.

Smith expected from human nature neither the Hobbesian *bellum* nor the Garden of Eden. His prediction of taste in combination with sacrifice, duty blended in with utility, is echoed by other theoreticians of market capitalism whose explanation of external reality goes beyond the wealth-seeking maximand of the materialistic *quid pro quo*. Thus David Collard, pointing to inter-generational transfers, voluntary work for a political party, the gift of money, blood or a kidney, self-policing honesty in public affairs, non-contractual aid to a stranger attacked in the street, concludes that material self-interest cannot account for the whole of resource allocation: 'Human beings are not entirely selfish, even in their economic dealings.' (Collard, 1978:3). Howard Margolis, similarly, has taken the view that individuals who deliberately donate their vote and consciously abstain from theft must be acting on the basis of preference-functions additional to those that are picked up by the shopping paradigm: 'The conventional economic model not only predicts (correctly) the existence of problems with free riders but also predicts (incorrectly) such severe problems that no society we know could function if its members actually behaved as the conventional model implies they will.' (Margolis, 1982:6). The truth is the middle and the mix. The truth even in market capitalism is not the *either/or*: 'We are neither pure saints nor sinners – just human beings. Unfortunately, there aren't many human beings populating the world of economic models.' (Thaler, 1992:3).

There is much in real-world revealed preference that *self*-centred economic models are simply not in a position to predict. The other-regarding orientation is too familiar a social fact for it to be forgotten in the *obiter dictum* of the *ceteris paribus* pound. Not least should the social fact be brought into the analysis where it can be shown to fulfil an economic function such as Edmund Phelps has in mind when he writes as follows in defence of the productive contribution made to market capitalism by the stranger gift: 'The price system would work less well, and would be less widely applied, were it not that the economic agents – portrayed by the Walrasian model of the price system as flint-hearted maximizers – in fact display a decent regard for the interests of those with whom they exchange and for society as a whole.' (Phelps, 1975: 3). In the words of Fred Hirsch: 'Conventional, mutual standards of honesty and trust are public goods that are necessary inputs for much of economic output. . . . The Good Samaritan remedies a market failure.' (Hirsch, 1977:79, 141). Thinkers such as Phelps and Hirsch would understandably be discouraged by the Schumpeterian pessimism evoked by Etzioni when he blames the textbook economics for promoting the amoral, anarchic and nihilistic attitudes that are the enemy of the self-restraint that is the *sine qua non*: 'The market is dependent on normative underpinning (to provide the pre-contractual foundation such as trust, cooperation and honesty) which all contractual relations require: *The more people accept the neoclassical paradigm as a guide for their behavior, the more the ability to sustain a market economy is undermined*.' (Etzioni, 1988:250). Thinkers such as Phelps and Hirsch would be much more favourable to the Christ-like sacrifice demanded by Marshall when he invites the responsible economist to make it a personal crusade to accelerate the evolution of 'economic chivalry': 'No doubt men, even now, are capable of much more unselfish service than they generally render; and the supreme aim of the economist is to discover how this latent social asset can be developed most quickly and turned to account most wisely.' (Marshall, 1890:8). A 'supreme aim' cannot reasonably be buried as a *ceteris paribus*. How selfish soever man may be supposed, there is an other-regarding element in his nature which cannot reasonably be excluded from an account of real-world exchange.

The present chapter is concerned with that other-regarding element. It is divided into three sections. Section 8.1, 'The Nature of the Gift', establishes that altruism is embedded in the social matrix and is a constituent part of the individual's self-definition. Section 8.2, 'The Social

Ethic: Durkheim and Kant', examines the inter-personal origins of the other-regarding sentiments. Section 8.3, 'Ethics and Economics', illustrates wealth-enhancement through moral principles with the specific examples of price and trust.

8.1   THE NATURE OF THE GIFT

Language can make every unilateral transfer into an embodiment of the donor's blinkered selfishness. The suicide-bomber sells his life for peer-group recognition. The parent saves for the future because the child's consumption maximises the parent's utility. The entrepreneur retains a redundant operative because a dismissal would cost him a spoiled conscience. Language can make every gift into a neoclassical exchange. It can make the whole of altruism into a self-regarding swap.

The *quid* without the *quo* can undoubtedly be treated as just another shopping-trolley choice. Blau on dishonesty illustrates the hidden nexus in the following way: 'Men who forgo the advantages made possible by cheating do not act contrary to their self-interest *if* the peace of mind and social approval they obtain for their honesty is more rewarding to them than the gains they could make by cheating.' (Blau, 1964:258). Generosity can undoubtedly be defined to be just another synonym for gain. Intuitively, however, most people would almost certainly reject as facile sophistry any linguistic schema which failed to make a distinction between 'the ingratiating employee who holds a door open for his superior' (Collard, 1978:4) and the devout Buddhist who, unobserved and unthanked, 'makes merit' by releasing a trapped insect. Most people, arguably, would feel more comfortable with a linguistic schema which made a qualitative differentiation between the broad approach to self-interest (an approach which unifies human behaviour with that of non-evaluatory animals by denying the uniqueness of action in line with values and ideals) and the narrow approach which distinguishes clearly between personal pleasures and non-ego prescriptions. The broad approach reduces all choice to the highest-ranked satisfaction, self-perceived: it employs the *zweckrational* postulate to explain the purchase both of spinach and of the Second Commandment, both of care for a retarded child and of a drunken visit to a nightclub. The narrow approach notes that the suicide-bomber is losing his life, the responsible parent sharing his consumables, the sentimental employer sacrificing attainable profit: it recognises that interpersonal transfers such as these are at variance with the common understanding of *self*-interest and insists that most people have in their mind a clear image of two realms, two maximands, 'two major purposes – to advance their well-being *and* to act morally' (Etzioni, 1988:83). The *quid* without the *quo* can undoubtedly be treated as just another shopping-trolley choice. The advocates of the narrow approach nonetheless maintain that it 'feels wrong' to treat murder as if it were a tin of beans.

Some people are attracted by homogeneity and mono-utility, others by mix and balance. There is no way to adjudicate between individuals who see self-interest as ubiquitous and those who see it as a part but not as the whole. There is no accounting for tastes. It is not the task of this section, attempting the impossible, to show that the broader definition is superior or inferior to the narrower approach. Rather, it is the task of this section simply to clarify the gift-relationship and to establish the reasons for the non-paid-for allocation. The discussion is divided into three parts: 'Macro to Micro', 'Micro to Macro' and 'Altruism and Evolution'.

(a) Macro to Micro

The normative holist treats the one-way transfer as a social fact. Born into society, subject to collective control, the individual absorbs the common characteristics and conforms to the ongoing standards: 'We do not have to construct these rules at the moment of action by deducing them from some general principles: they already exist.' (Durkheim, 1925:26). So much for the economist's *de novo* calculation. In place of the *tâtonnement* there is limitation and constraint.

Durkheim emphasised that much of the self comes in fact from outside: 'Our individuality is, therefore, altogether relative.' (Durkheim, 1925:216). Group identity being a source of personal identity, he argued, unremunerated action can be at least as satisfying as selfish action to an individual who is integrated and remains in touch: 'We are vitally hurt by everything that diminishes the vitality of the beings to whom we are attached; being attached to them, it is to a part of ourselves that we are attached.' (Durkheim, 1925:215). Durkheim, concentrating on the sharing of sentiments and the rootedness of solidarity, said that it was hard for him to see precisely where the Ego ended and the Alter began: 'Egoism and altruism are two abstractions that do not exist in a pure state; one always implies the other, at least to some degree.' (Durkheim, 1925:217). The altruistic suicide of the soldier defending his fatherland is a case in point: 'Where the ego is not its own property, where it is blended with something outside itself' (Durkheim, 1897:221), there the individual feels most fulfilled where he does his duty and gifts what he cannot imagine himself to withhold.

The woman who immolates herself on her husband's funeral pyre (like the samurai who commits ritual *hara-kiri* or the devotee who throws himself beneath the wheels of the Juggernaut) is making a gift which has been preordained for her by conservatism and belonging. The same may be said of the taxpayer who rejoices that his money is being taken to raise up his fellows. Aneurin Bevan, as Minister of Health directly responsible for the inauguration of Britain's National Health Service in 1948, praised the new system because it allocated goods and services on the basis of medical need alone: 'A free health service is pure Socialism.... As such it is opposed to the hedonism of capitalist society.' (Bevan, 1952:106). He also said that his early inspiration had been the ideal of mutual aid within the framework of an organic community: 'The redistributive aspect of the scheme was one which attracted me almost as much as the therapeutical.... What more pleasure can a millionaire have than to know that his taxes will help the sick?' (Bevan, 1958:Col. 1389).

Bevan asserted that it was the taxes and not the consumables that would maximise the pleasure. His assessment of the better-buy can be translated into the unsentimental language of cost–benefit capitalism: 'The funding of a welfare state may be an example of Pareto-optimal redistribution. If people care about the welfare of others, everyone may be (subjectively) better off in a state of affairs where some resources have been transferred from the well-endowed to the needy.' (Miller, 1988:163). Socially integrated men and women can 'feel good about themselves' as a direct consequence of providing an unremunerated benefit to others. The improvement in their felt felicity causes them to demand the transfer. Were Bevan's diagnosis to have been an accurate one, egoism and altruism would then have become all but interchangeable names for the same impulse and choice.

Malinowski studied the circular flow of ritual gifts in the Trobriand Islands. He discovered that the ring of Kula was embedded in a network of relationships, in a whole which 'forms one interwoven fabric': 'Sociologically, though transacted between tribes differing in language, culture, and probably even in race, it is based on a fixed and permanent status, on a partnership which binds into couples some thousands of individuals. This partnership is a lifelong relationship, it implies various mutual duties and privileges, and constitutes a type of inter-tribal relationship on an enormous scale.' (Malinowski, 1922:85, 92). Malinowski found that the social teleology was primary and constraining. The individual, he said, neither influences the transactions nor comprehends their interconnectedness: 'Not even the most intelligent native has any clear idea of the Kula as a big, organised social construction, still less of its sociological function and implications.' (Malinowski, 1922:83).

The Kula is a network of gifts and counter-gifts. The objects in themselves are 'meaningless and quite useless' (Malinowski, 1922:86). The ceremonial ornaments of red necklaces (*soulava*) and white shell armbands (*mwali*) must not be confused with utilitarian tradeables (*gimwali*) like yams and fish. Yet their (temporary) ownership and (early) transfer is central to social unification in the Melanesian culture. Kula symbols cement structured relationships. They consolidate the lasting ties of patronage and support. The trophy separated from the return-trophy, Kula-giving is an expression of credit, trust and confidence despite the passage of time. Not subject to haggling or to a commercial bargain, Kula ratios have all the constancy of traditional obligations untainted by short-run venality.

For all that, the Kula remains an exchange relationship, predicated upon equivalence and suffused with expectation. Just as the first round of drinks in England is bought on the assumption of the accustomed future reciprocation, just as today's dinner-party supplied carries with it the implication of tomorrow's dinner-party demanded, so the Kula among the Melanesians is built around the principle (a world away from primitive communism) that each will do his share and will pass on to his collaborator in effect the value that he has received. The Kula, in short, is a circle of overlapping interests bound up with convention, myth and magic which concurrently comes from and reinforces the process of social control. Malinowski found little evidence of individual spontaneity without prescriptive compensation in the gift-giving that he observed in the Trobriand Islands.

Marcel Mauss reached a similar conclusion about the *do ut des* – 'I give so that you may give' – even in pre-monetary, pre-industrial societies: 'The market is a human phenomenon that, in our view, is not foreign to any known society.' (Mauss, 1950:4). The *quid pro quo* is to be found even in less developed, less mercantile societies, Mauss observed. There the material life is less dependent upon gain-seeking negotiation – but the exchange of politeness takes the place of the exchange of goods: 'It is not individuals but collectivities that impose obligations of exchange and contract upon each other.' (Mauss, 1950:5). Exchange of recognition or exchange of property, what is striking, Mauss reflected, is the ubiquity of exchange.

The gift is to be understood as a sub-case in the theory of n-person rights and duties. To give a present is a voluntary act. To refuse to give, however, 'is tantamount to declaring war; it is to reject the bond of allegiance and commonality' (Mauss, 1950:13). The voluntary in that sense verges upon the compulsory as well, precisely because dishonour and rejection are the high price that must be paid whenever the freedom of choice escapes from the tramlines of convention.

The *potlatch* held by the Kwakiutl tribe of North America illustrates the social nature of the gift: 'The obligation to reciprocate constitutes the essence of the potlatch.' (Mauss, 1950:41). The Kwakiutl grasp that they are expected both to provide and to receive hospitality; and that the sequential feasts, banquets and festivals are not wealth-magnifying economic transactions but rather a part of a 'much more general and enduring contract' (Mauss, 1950:5). That contract is a supra-dyadic one, a systemic and a *social* agreement rather than the economically-useful nexus of individuals pursuing satisfactions. It is an acceptance of friendship and solidarity, intercourse and contact. The potlatch is a commitment and a value. Importantly, it is simultaneously an exchange and a price. The individual pays in the gift that is specified. The individual receives in return the reward that is due.

The idea that a commitment can also be an exchange is not an unfamiliar one. The fairy who ought to be invited to the festivities pursues deadly vengeance in *The Sleeping Beauty* when excluded from her agreed-upon involvement. God, loving and benevolent, nonetheless demands a Covenant from the Chosen People and raises no objection to donations, sacrifices and kneeling in support of prayers and invocations. The street beggar sings a tuneless song to symbolise his belief in the work ethic and his fear of charity that shames and stigmatises. The welfare recipient resists the self-perception of the inferior who cannot reciprocate by pointing to a history of taxes paid and a future of self-reliance intended. In familiar instances such as these, the gift and the exchange enjoy a symbiosis which makes it difficult to observe them in isolation.

It is too easy to say that the monk is closer to the gift ideal, the Gradgrind, the Shylock or the Scrooge to all that the traffic will bear. The truth is more of a mix. The hermit trades in self-abnegation but is paid compound interest in Heaven. The usurer maximises money but is remunerated through spoiled status. On the one hand bad food followed by Salvation, on the other hand good food accompanied by loss of face – a thinker like Mauss would argue that the moral and the material life are not so often real-world alternatives as they are social facts bound together in a social bundle. Thus it is that a thinker like Mauss is obliged, methodologically speaking, to situate the notions of interest and generosity in the context of the surrounding ties: 'The principle and the end of sociology is to perceive the whole group and its behaviour in its entirety.' (Mauss, 1950:81). The truth is the whole. The micro follows on from the macro which alone can give sense to the gift.

(b)   Micro to Macro

The previous discussion treated the part as an inference from the whole. The present discussion begins with the unit and scales upwards to the aggregate. Adopting the bottom-up world-view of the methodological reductionist, it accounts for ethics and altruism in terms of three clusters of causal variables: consent, kinship and sympathy.

   Constraint by agreement figured prominently in Chapters 5 and 6. There it was shown that dutiful conformity to a multi-period rule will in certain circumstances be the self-denying means to a gain-maximising end. I will contribute if you contribute: our agreement replaces uncertainty with coordination and makes our inter-dependence somewhat less of a lottery. I will abstain if you abstain: our tit-for-tat brings about conformity without re-negotiation and protects our public good from depletion through free riding. Macro to micro the holy books will be invoked, and so will the cultural meanings that the time-bound altruist has endogenised deep in his personality: 'The development of individual motivation is . . . a process of the internalization of social norms.' (Parsons and Smelser, 1956:32). Micro to macro the conservatism by consent has more of the character of a capitalistic contract. I sign my name because you sign your name. The rules decided upon, we are safe to get on with our lives.

   The ethical and the altruistic can emerge from a normative calculus that cannot be reduced to the consequences of the standard in a single spot situation. They can also emerge from the institution-specific conditions which define the kinship group. Kin means consent: frequency of interaction gives habits and conventions the authority of the co-determined. Kin means sympathy: familiarity and contact buttress the donation even of a kidney with an emotive support. Kin means continuity: an initial gift stands a good chance of being reciprocated at a later date while the offspring (a topic to be discussed in the following sub-section) carry forward more of the common genes than do the children of complete strangers. What all of this suggests is that the family may be seen as the conservative production-unit of a long-lived spillover which spreads outwards into the wider way of life.

Self-denial emanating from kinship is rooted in blood and buttressed by instinct. The archetype is the care and attention even of the wildest predators who perpetuate their species precisely because they 'exert themselves for the benefit of their offspring' (Marshall, 1890:202). As with the animals, so with the capitalists. Alfred Marshall believed that the parental bent, biology's great gift to all living creatures, actually became more pronounced in an affluent and an acquisitive society. Nowadays, Marshall said, 'the ties of family are in many ways stronger than before', 'the obligations of family kindness ... more intense' (Marshall, 1890:5). Man, 'more unselfish', is in a richer nation 'more inclined to work and save to secure a future provision for his family' (Marshall, 1890:566). Thus does the altruism that is the product of prosperity become the cause of still more altruism and still more prosperity in a nation where responsible parents devote progressively more of their effort and capital to a good start for the children in whom they invest so many of their hopes.

Schumpeter too has emphasized the extent to which even *homo economicus* does not go home alone. Historically at least, Schumpeter writes, the achievements of the self-interested entrepreneur can only be explained when proper acknowledgement is made of the wife, the hearth and the progeny: 'The family and the family home used to be the mainspring of the typically bourgeois kind of profit motive. Economists have not always given due weight to this fact. When we look more closely at their idea of the self-interest of entrepreneurs and capitalists we cannot fail to discover that the results it was supposed to produce are really not at all what one would expect from the rational self-interest of the detached individual or the childless couple.' (Schumpeter, 1942: 160). Historically at least, Schumpeter writes, the accumulation of wealth has been inseparable from the multigenerational gift. Burke at the time of Smith had said the same: 'The power of perpetuating our property in our families is one of the most valuable and interesting circumstances belonging to it, and that which tends the most to the perpetuation of society itself. It makes our weakness subservient to our virtue; it grafts benevolence even upon avarice.' (Burke, 1790:140). While the handing-on of the family's home and name is as much an aristocratic as it is a bourgeois ideal, Schumpeter unlike Burke chose to link it not with the ascribed status that is symbolised by the hereditary power of the House of Lords but with the business dynasty that makes each capitalist's sacrifices into a death-defeating investment in an achievement preserved. Schumpeter understandably expressed serious reservations about the rise of the joint-stock company. A financial speculation and not a conservative commitment, the paper share is not conducive to the altruism that would once have prevented the rational capitalist from settling for the quick returns of evanescent short-termism: 'He loses the capitalist ethics that enjoins working for the future irrespective of whether or not one is going to harvest the crop oneself.' (Schumpeter, 1942:160). That loss to Schumpeter was yet another sad step along the road that was leading inexorably to the bureaucratised – the post-*capitalist* – society.

Altruism emanating from kinship is by definition not selfish egoism, not personal pleasure. The break in the spectrum is not always easy to see. Parental investment in a child's education can carry with it an implicit duty for the child to do his best. Parental gift-giving at an early age can be remunerated through parental pride in doctors and lawyers later on. The Schumpeterian capitalist works and saves for his own glory and not simply for the descendant cohorts which will carry on his mission. Social approbation rewards parents who have supplied the customary transfers. A spoiled conscience sanctions parents who have not given the traditional presents. Once again, it is clear, pure altruism is not always easy to observe unalloyed.

The kinship group is a focus for the *quid* without the *quo*. So, if less urgently, are the concentric circles of acquaintances and strangers which lie just beyond the blood and the genes. In the one case as in the other, Adam Smith said, self-restraint and benevolence may be explained in terms of empathy, compassion, the exchange of places 'in fancy' (Smith, 1759:4), the sharing of sentiments in the mind. A man can empathise with a woman in childbirth or with a corpse that is insensible to its condition. A person who is well-fed can imagine what it is like to be hungry. A person who is sane can imagine what he would feel if he were mad. In all of these cases the individual can enter into the distress of the other but in none of them will he directly experience the distress himself. In all of these cases, in other words, the individual will be in a position to distance himself from his own personal situation and to make the following declaration to a fellow being with whose state he has become emotively involved: 'My grief... is entirely upon your account, and not in the least upon my own. It is not, therefore, in the least selfish.' (Smith, 1759:466).

Adam Smith is here insisting that the sympathetic sentiment is 'not in the least' a self-regarding one. He would therefore want further to classify the corrective action that results from the psychic dis-ease as a self-denying choice in the strict sense of Hoffman: 'Altruistic behavior is behavior that promotes the welfare of others without conscious regard for one's own self-interests.' (Hoffman, 1981:124). Sen, however, is unconvinced. Gift-giving in response to sympathy is, admittedly, a warm-hearted and a positive-sum form of self-interested action: B's utility accrues to A *as well as* B when A gives up consumables he could have enjoyed in order to relieve what he regards as B's greater need. Even so, it has a self-interested dimension nonetheless: 'When a person's sense of well-being is psychologically dependent on someone else's welfare, it is a case of sympathy; other things given, the awareness of the increase in the welfare of the other person then makes this person directly better off.' (Sen, 1977:92). Gift-giving in response to duty is closer to the true meaning of the *quid* without the *quo*: 'One way of defining commitment is in terms of a person choosing an act that he believes will yield a lower level of personal welfare to him than an alternative that is also available to him.' (Sen, 1977:92). Choosing duty, the individual is forgoing immediate satisfaction. Choosing sympathy, he is augmenting his utility through the purchase of fellow-feeling that complements and does not compete.

The self may be at the centre; but at least there is a reallocation of assets in consequence of an awareness perturbed. People oppose the burying of nuclear wastes in century-proof containers because they can share the outrage of the as-yet-unborn when confronted with the seepage from the sea-bed of radioactive pollutants. People donate food and clothing to the victims of a foreign earthquake because they can picture to themselves the collapsed buildings and the broken dreams. People are generous with the support they give to health-related charities because they can empathise with the familiar contingencies of illness and death. An openness to others is the cause of the *self*-centred disequilibrium that triggers off the *other*-regarding transfer. Visualisation and internalisation undeniably introduce an egoistic element into the ethical impulsion. Crucially, however, both parties enjoy satisfaction at the same time from the same resources. Egoism though this may be, it is also a thoroughly un-Hobbesian way of looking after oneself.

Sympathy permits but it does not compel. Sympathy will sometimes provide a motive but it can never impose a duty. Emotion can be narrow – as where a person finds it easier to identify with his neighbour or his friend than with the totality of the long-necked tribesmen being persecuted in a country the name of which he cannot spell. Affect can be unreliable – as where love turns to hate, envy to fear in line with the boredom and excitement of fleeting moods and whims that have little of the tenacity of capitalistic gain-seeking in pursuit of pay. Imagination can be short-horizoned – as where the sympathetic taxpayer eagerly funds today's pensions out of today's revenues without demanding an inter-generational guarantee that future cohorts will replicate his concern when he himself grows old. Sympathy, in other words, is necessary but it need not be sufficient. Duty is a longer-lasting craft. Duty is action within the framework of the rules. The game once agreed upon, the individual has then an obligation to give.

(c)   Altruism and Evolution

E.O. Wilson defines altruism as a voluntary choice to sacrifice a part or the whole of the actor's own opportunity-set: 'When a person (or animal) increases the fitness of another at the expense of his own fitness, he can be said to have performed an act of *altruism*.' (Wilson, 1975:117). The operative words are 'at the expense'. Altruism in Wilson's definition means that there is a personal loss of wealth, of life-chances, of life itself. Altruism in Wilson's definition takes on board the economic constraint of limited resources and imputes to the sharing of assets the *de facto* character of a self-destructive tendency. Wilson's perspective is that of sociobiology, of 'the systematic study of the biological basis of all social behavior' (Wilson, 1975:4). Sociobiology since Malthus and Darwin has traditionally been about competition, fitness and survival. Practical and objective, it can only with great difficulty incorporate the notion that starvation would be a self-regarding action where a priest gained more satisfaction from sharing his food than he did from consuming it himself. Hard-line economists would call the starved priest a selfish priest. Sociobiologists like Wilson would be less reluctant to invoke the non-reducible construct of altruism.

As far as Alfred Marshall was concerned, altruism was indispensable and evolution its screen and filter: 'The struggle for existence causes in the long run those races of men to survive in which the individual is most willing to sacrifice himself for the benefit of those around him; and which are consequently the best adapted collectively to make use of their environment.' (Marshall, 1890:202–3). Marshall recognised that the ascent into collective adulthood by means of personal forbearance was not a process that was always and everywhere infallible: 'The struggle for survival may fail to bring into existence organisms that would be highly beneficial.' (Marshall, 1890:201). He also emphasized that *natura non facit saltum* and that the conservative would do well to content himself with only a very gradual improvement: 'That must necessarily be a slow growth, the product of many generations: it must be based on those customs and aptitudes of the great mass of the people which are incapable of quick change.' (Marshall, 1890:203). Marshall accepted that the automaticity was incomplete and that the progress was slow. All things considered, however, Marshall believed that some self-sacrifice was the precondition for sustained capitalist development and that the course of evolution on balance was on its side.

Altruism, Marshall was convinced, enjoyed a high evolution elasticity. What he did not spell out was the logic behind the sift. The soldier who rescues the cowardly at the cost of his life is ensuring that it is the more selfish who will benefit and survive. The watching deer who raises the alarm saves the group but attracts the hunters to himself. The kindly employer who pays over the odds relieves the hungry but makes his business less able to compete. The problem is simply stated: Nice guys finish last. Survival of the survivors could evidently mean the survival of the narrowly egotistical and not the natural selection of the blood-donors, the charity-workers and the Good Samaritans who strengthen the fitness of the *whole* quite explicitly by reducing the fitness of the *self*.

Given enough time, the bias of natural selection could well be in favour not of the self-denial that boycotts cheap footballs manufactured by indentured children but of the self-interest that animates the textbook's Economic Man: 'The first principle of Economics is that every agent is actuated only by self-interest.' (Edgeworth, 1881:16). Yet even the maximising Edgeworth was too much of a realist to mistake an Ideal Type for a sociological prediction: 'The concrete nineteenth century man is for the most part an impure egoist, a mixed utilitarian.' (Edgeworth, 1881:104). Edgeworth's mixed ethos is a valuable corrective to the abstraction of the Economic Man. No less, however, is it of value in assisting the reader to make real-world sense of Wilson's 'at the expense'. What is likely, more specifically, is that the evolution of altruism is most persuasively modelled when it is situated in a context which includes the imperfection of interest as well. Three inter-connected explanations are likely for this purpose to be of especial relevance.

The *first* explanation is one which models social development on the basis of Abraham Maslow's hierarchy of need. At the lower level of physical need a transfer is a deprivation since the donor too is hungry and cold. At the higher level of relatedness and belonging, the zero sum drops away since the self-fulfilment of the donor presupposes good access to a neighbour to love. Thus does yesterday's greedy infant evolve into the caring parent of today.

The beggar needed St Anthony. St Anthony, however, needed the beggar. Their needs, as described by Lutz and Lux, were as complementary as man and woman, not as antagonistic as cat and mouse: 'When those at the higher end of the need hierarchy help those at the lower, they are in fact promoting their own growth. This follows because service and help to others is one of the needs at the top of the hierarchy.... There is a perfect synergy of needs when the higher help the lower. Both gain, and in this mutual benefit it can actually be said that each group gives the other what they need; the rich give the poor enough to take them out of their poverty, and the poor give the rich the opportunity to serve.' (Lutz and Lux, 1979:167). Each gains and neither loses. Maslow makes clear that there is self-interest in the exchange that is implied: 'The dichotomy between selfishness and unselfishness disappears altogether in healthy people because in principle every act is *both* selfish and unselfish.... Duty cannot be contrasted with pleasure, nor work with play when duty *is* pleasure, when work *is* play.' (Maslow, 1954:179). No doubt there is self-interest in the exchange when the rich deny themselves a fourth car in order to pay, Bevan-like, to help the sick. It is, Maslow would say, a remarkably grown-up form of self-interest nonetheless. Once upon a time the self meant the *bellum*. Nowadays the self means the blood-bank. Affluence – and adulthood – is a Kantian thing indeed.

Maslow's psychology, like capitalistic economics, builds in the filter of thought. So perception-ridden an approach to self-denial given interdependence evidently sheds only limited light on the conditioned reflexes of the deer which raises the alarm. It may not always make sense to conflate the animal and the human kingdom to the extent that a Skinnerian behaviourist like Homans would do when he declares that 'the pigeon is thoroughly social' (Homans, 1961:31). In respect of the soldier who sacrifices his life or the employer who pays a supra-competitive wage, however, an evolutionary expansion in altruism may clearly be hypothesised in terms of an expansion, with wealth, in the sympathy of nations. Emulated, embedded, imitated, rewarded, the altruism then becomes self-magnifying for reasons which are none the less functional for being mixed up with interest.

Of course the transfer can be seen as a rational purchase, an investment (as where a lapel badge is made a 'selective incentive') in social esteem. Of course psychic income may be the attractive dividend to the enthusiastic participator who gets involved: 'There is much fulfilment associated with the citizen's exertions for the public happiness.' (Hirschman, 1982:90). Of course the alternative to action might mean the discomfort of guilt which it makes sense to avoid: 'In the majority of cases it is not really the famine in India but my own conscience that I am appeasing.' (Wicksteed, 1910:413). It is obvious as a simple matter of dictionary definition that 'my own conscience' cannot be the same as 'at the expense'. Crucially, however, the famine-victims will receive their food and will not be expected to pay. They will become the object of compassion because, in Maslow's view, social growth and its motivational dynamic makes more comfortable citizens more caring and more concerned.

The *second* explanation, turning from social standing to economic success, continues the theme of mix by relating self-sacrificing actions to self-serving objectives. Thus, as Becker sees it, altruism might be favoured by evolution precisely because it improves the individual's survival-prospects and does not diminish them: 'If altruism, on balance, raises own genetic fitness, then natural selection would operate in its favor.' (Becker, 1976:292). Altruism in such a perspective is a form of enlightened self-interest, a speculative investment made subject to a long-term discount-rate. Credit extended to a retailer who is down might be reciprocated by search forgone when the retailer is up. Compassionate leave for an employee creates an implicit obligation which might be settled by thank-you throughput in excess of the initial loss. An hour devoted to a shopper who is 'just looking' might produce a return in time when the same shopper decides to spend. Every parent – and every child – knows what it means to 'buy affection'. Altruism fulfilling a not dissimilar function in economic life, there is a certain plausibility in the suggestion that evolution will favour the *quid* without the *quo* because the norm is itself the means to an individually valued end.

The *third* explanation, inspired directly by Darwin, relates altruism and evolution with specific reference to the biological imperative and the inter-generational drive. In studying nature, Darwin advised, it would be an error 'to forget that every single organic being around us may be said to be striving to the utmost to increase in numbers' (Darwin, 1859:119). Multiplication is primordial and it is irreducible. Darwin's competition to survive is in that sense about the survival of others and not simply about the survival of the self: 'I use the term Struggle for Existence in a large and metaphorical sense, including dependence of one being on another, and including (which is more important) not only the life of the individual, but success in leaving progeny.' (Darwin, 1859:116). As far as Darwin was concerned, natural selection operated essentially at the level of the offspring-group and only secondarily at the level of the Economic Man.

The peacock employs his ornamental plumage as a counter in the process of sexual selection. Mistletoe competes with other fruit-bearing plants for the privilege of having its seeds disseminated by the birds. In instances such as these it is the reproductive instinct which is at the heart of the biological market. Propagation, however, can prove a costly bid. Bee-stings protect the colony's food-stocks but are fatal to the bee. The female nighthawk distracts intruders from her nest but puts herself at risk from predators. A mother rescues her child from a burning house. A father ventures into a freezing river. In such circumstances a cost can be incurred but still the 'at the expense' is by no means clear-cut: 'Self-sacrifice for the benefit of offspring is altruism in the conventional but not in the strict genetic sense, because individual fitness is measured by the number of surviving offspring.' (Wilson, 1975:117). Bone-marrow donated to help an unknown stranger might reasonably be termed a genuine gift. Mutual defence and cooperative foraging are more ambiguous where it is blood kindred of whom the average survival and fertility are then greater as a result: 'These blood relatives cooperate or bestow altruistic favors on one another in a way that increases the average genetic fitness of the members of the network as a whole, even when this behavior reduces the individual fitnesses of certain members of the group.' (Wilson, 1975:117). The penguin who tests the water for the danger of a seal should therefore dwell not on his own imperilled life-chances but instead on the heightened competitiveness of the affined group that, sharing his genes, will carry his seed into a future that he himself will never glimpse.

Reproduction has a cost. Reproduction has a benefit. Juxtaposing the cost to the benefit, Wilson confesses that offspring create real problems for the 'at the expense': 'The theory of group selection has taken most of the good will out of altruism. When altruism is conceived as the mechanism by which DNA multiplies itself through a network of relatives, spirituality becomes just one more Darwinian enabling device.' (Wilson, 1975:120). Here the altruism comes with interest mixed in; but at least the implicit exchange ensures that the lioness will not devour her cubs. Self-control perpetuates her pride. A lack of parental benevolence, of mother-love, would cause her name to die out forever: 'It must somehow be the case that being generous (at least sometimes, to some beneficiaries) is selectively more advantageous than being selfish!' (Hirshleifer, 1977:20). Evolution in that way raises the average stock of (mixed-motive) altruism over time.

Dawkins, sharing with Wilson the 'at the expense' that defines the entity's altruism – 'It behaves in such a way as to increase another entity's welfare at the expense of its own' (Dawkins, 1989:4) – is hardly so confident about the biological basis even of moderate cooperativeness. The gene and not the person, Dawkins writes, is the prime mover in human history. The gene, he continues, is quintessentially the narrow-minded replicator: 'At the gene level, altruism must be bad and selfishness good. . . . The gene is the basic unit of selfishness.' (Dawkins, 1989:36). Siblings are modelled from a common parentage. Even so, the siblings have no biological need to assign equivalent weighting to the chances of survival of an external competitor: 'I contain 100% of my genes, so I am worth more to me than he is. I am the only individual that any one of my selfish genes can be sure of.' (Dawkins, 1989:106). Evolution in Wilson's view can favour a kind of group-orientated altruism. Evolution in Dawkins's view has a far more self-interested bias.

Dawkins, importantly, is not prepared to abandon altruism merely because he believes it is not the chosen candidate of the evolutionary process. Not a fatalist but an engineer, Dawkins appeals to moral education to lean against the biological winds: 'Our genes may instruct us to be selfish, but we are not necessarily compelled to obey them all our lives. It may just be more difficult to learn altruism than it would be if we were genetically programmed to be altruistic.' (Dawkins, 1989:3). It may be more difficult, but still it is an exercise that must be undertaken: 'Let us try to *teach* generosity and altruism, because we are born selfish.' (Dawkins, 1989:3). Thus does section 8.1, 'The Nature of the Gift', end where section 8.2, 'The Social Ethic: Durkheim and Kant' begins – not with the determinist's inevitabilities but with the Good Society and the legitimation of norms.

8.2   THE SOCIAL ETHIC: DURKHEIM AND KANT

The subject of this section is not the Platonist's quest for universals that cannot be factored down to opinions and preferences. No eternally valid case is made against the sale of military exemptions, human organs, licences to commit adultery, against the deliberate deception of the mentally retarded. Nor is any reason presented why the Bible's 'Thou shalt not kill' is morally superior to the nihilist's 'Thou shalt indeed kill, and kill all the time'. Concerned not with the specificities of the norms but rather with their inter-personal transmission, the subject of this section is the learning mechanism which makes sensitive agents aware of what they may reasonably do and how far they may justifiably go. The subject of this section is thus not ethics *per se* but instead the *social* ethic and its conservative constraint. Two sources of intellectual inspiration are cited as being of especial interest: Durkheim and Kant.

Social values have normative content: individuals ought to be free, opportunity ought to be equal, exchange ought to be just. Moral values too are prescriptive and binding: promises should be honoured, aggression should be avoided, the truth should be told. Comparing the social *ought to* with the moral *should*, Emile Durkheim declared that he could not see the difference: 'The domain of the genuinely moral life only begins where the collective life begins. ... We are moral beings only to the extent that we are social beings.' (Durkheim, 1925:64). The surrounding *sui generis*, Durkheim said, is the sole source of the moral standards: 'There are no genuinely moral ends except collective ones. There is no truly moral force save that involved in attachment to a group.' (Durkheim, 1925:87). Were the socialising band to lose its hold, so then would the moral life, since it would no longer have an object.

The ethical, Durkheim said, is no more than the common, puffed up by consensus: 'If society is the end of morality, it is also the producer.' (Durkheim, 1925:86). Social values are a cause of recurrence, consistency and regularity in the behaviour-patterns of the team-mates. Social values set limits to the self since the source of the discipline is external to the individual. Social values are recognised to be functional and desired because they integrate. Social values evoke voluntary acceptance and do not presuppose the frightened submission of the slave who cannot choose. Social values have intertemporal stability whereas anarchic self-reliance is condemned to come and go. In all of these ways, Durkheim said, social values have a moral character – while moral values have the moral property precisely because their authority is that of the group.

Durkheim's conflation of the moral with the social leads to an uncompromising relativism in time and space: 'Each social type has the morality necessary to it.' (Durkheim, 1925:87). Optimistic about evolution and unconvinced as to absolutes, Durkheim was sharply critical of ethical systems which postulated a universality when they ought to have spotted a social fact. In respect of theology and religion, Durkheim hinted that revelation might be the polite name for other people's customs and warned that the worship of God could actually conceal the social pressures for which the name of God may be said to stand: 'Divinity is the symbolic expression of the collectivity.' (Durkheim, 1925: 105). In respect of natural rights and irreducible essences, Durkheim stated that 'each individual taken separately has no moral worth' (Durkheim, 1925:59) and refused to attach an imperative to a self-serving sequence. Only a supra-individual valuation of individuality, he said, can make the satisfaction of ego or even the alms-giving to alter into an obligation that is more than a whim. Try as he might, Durkheim could not therefore find any source of ethical conduct that could not be reinterpreted as the impersonal power of the social whole.

Durkheim's moral conservatism appears on the surface to have little common ground with the means–ends efficacy of the utilitarian capitalist economy. The distinction between the commandment and the calculation was in his perspective a real one. It would, however, be a mistake to exaggerate the gulf.

Belonging and community, for one thing, give the individual the cosmology of ideas and practices, reinforced by the solidarity and support of the fellow members who share his purposes. The individual, Durkheim said, 'is not truly himself, he does not fully realize his own nature, except on the condition that he is involved in society' (Durkheim, 1925: 68). Alcoholism, dejection, pessimism, anomic suicide tend disproportionately to be the affliction of childless couples, unmarried men and all those who allow the bonds of embeddedness to dissolve: 'Man is the more vulnerable to self-destruction the more he is detached from any collectivity.' (Durkheim, 1925:68). The individual who wishes to survive in composure would in the circumstances do well to buy the discipline of the social in preference to the despair that is the free gift of being alone.

Self-mastery empowers personal development. In that sense there is an affinity between the ethical and the expedient which is as unambiguous *ex post* as it is unintended *ex ante*. On the one hand, moral rules (in contrast to rules legitimated by private consequences like the rules of dental hygiene) have an absolute power which transcends the next-bests, the outcomes and the benefits: 'One must obey a moral precept out of respect for it and for this reason alone.' (Durkheim, 1925:30). On the other hand, moral rules are useful to the individual, constraints that emancipate and do not stunt: 'Liberty is the fruit of regulation.... Man possesses all the less of himself when he possesses only himself.' (Durkheim, 1925:54, 69). No rational person would settle for less if he knew he could contract differently for more. No prudent shopper, it must follow, would do other than to opt for an impersonal governor and for a moral constitution.

The interests are implicit in the absolutes in Durkheim's association of the moral with the inter-personal. The same may be said of Immanuel Kant where he concedes that non-hedonic deontology can turn out to be good consequentialism as well.

Thus Kant, giving the illustration of truth-telling, shows that an ethical norm can be functional for the group without being any the less of a commitment in itself. His reasoning is this: 'I can indeed will to lie, but I can by no means will a universal law of lying; for by such a law there could properly be no promises at all.' (Kant, 1785:71). Liars, Kant said, would in a house of lies live forever in fear that they might receive their payment 'in like coin'. The con-man does not want to be conned and the robber does not want to be robbed. Resistant to chaos and sensitive to interest, each will therefore be attracted by the 'single categorical imperative' which collective survival would seem to endorse: 'Act only on that maxim through which you can at the same time will that it should become a universal law.' (Kant, 1785:88).

Kant's solution is the Golden Rule, the generalisable standard of 'do unto others as you would have others do unto you'. His alternative to the Hobbesian void has clear affinities with Adam Smith on the empathetic imaginings, the Biblical invocation to 'love your neighbour as a man like yourself' (Leviticus, 19:18), Abraham Lincoln on 'all men are created equal', John Locke on the natural law: 'Reason, which is that law, teaches all mankind, who will but consult it, that being all equal and independent, no one ought to harm another in his life, health, liberty, or possessions.' (Locke, 1690:7). It has, on the other hand, little or nothing in common with the utilitarian inclinationism which would reduce rightness to pleasure and subordinate intentions to effects. Even the 'greatest happiness of the greatest number', Kant insisted, could never compensate for the treatment of the self or of another as an input and a thing to be used. Rejecting as amoral the hypothetical imperative of prudential choice, Kant therefore put his authority behind the following rule: 'Act in such a way that you always treat humanity, whether in your own person or in the person of any other, never simply as a means, but always at the same time as an end.' (Kant, 1785:96). Nascent capitalism would possibly have been denied its Industrial Revolution had the mill-owners in Manchester and Bradford taken to the *Metaphysic* with the same enthusiasm that they took to money.

Yet the complete picture is somewhat more complex. Kant enjoins the individual to act on universals and not to trade his principles at the margin. Kant also concedes, however, that the life in common will be more harmonious and less conflictual where self-restraint is practised and obligation prevents disorder. The complete picture, in short, is not just the conformity of the part but also the cordiality of the whole to which the conformity contributes.

The interests are implicit in the absolutes, in Kant's moral theory as they are in the religious scriptures that merchant so graphically the selling-points of Heaven and Hell. The complementarity of the absolutes to the interests is grasped with particular clarity by David Collard. Collard, giving the example of voluntary donations, has this to say about the categorical imperative as a beacon in unknowledge and an answer to the prisoner's dilemma: 'The non-Kantian altruist considers only his own (negligible) contribution to the redistributive fund in deciding whether or not to attempt a free ride. The Kantian altruist, on the other hand, asks what would happen if other A's behaved similarly: were they to do so the B's would get nothing. The non-Kantian altruist fails to co-operate: the Kantian altruist co-operates spontaneously.' (Collard, 1978:15). Alfred Marshall had himself made the point that the universal law can be a precondition for supply. Thus, for instance, 'the normal arrangement of many transactions in retail and wholesale trade, and on Stock and Cotton Exchanges, *rests on the assumption* that verbal contracts, made without witnesses, will be honourably discharged'; while a lack of self-policing rectitude on the part of the salaried managers of the multi-owned joint-stock companies would actually have been enough to *prevent the development* of this democratic form of business' (Marshall, 1890:29, 253, emphasis added). Alfred Marshall, author of the *Principles*, is well known for his pleasure-and-pain approach to the theory of demand and supply. The extent to which he could rely upon interests in his economics precisely because he believed in absolutes in his ethics is less widely appreciated. Marshall learned German in order to read the classics in the original. Once he described Kant as 'my guide...the only man I ever worshipped' (Marshall, cited in Keynes, 1925:10).

Kant's solution is the Golden Rule. It is a mental posture which economists like Collard and Marshall find complementary to supply despite the fact that a strict Kantian must pronounce it an end in itself. Absolutes might not after all be the antithesis of interests. Even so, the contention that the categorical imperative can make a useful contribution to conservative capitalism is the hostage to certain difficulties in the employment of the Kant-inspired tool.

The point of reference, to begin with, is to Kant the thinking self: even the taboo on murder is derived from the question 'How would *I* feel if *I* were treated that way?'. In establishing a duty to come to the aid of a refugee seeking asylum or a needy single parent, to return a wallet found on a bus, to declare untraceable income for purposes of tax, what the individual is doing is not so much adapting to a time-honoured constraint as creating his own constraint based on his own desire to consume the equivalent universals. The obligation is an absolute and not an interest. Still, however, it is an obligation which is confirmed by the same *I* that seeks profits in the factory and utility in the shops. In that sense the establishment of a Kantian duty is every bit as self-centred as the calculative choice made by the Rawlsian risk-averter when he acts *as if* an altruist – 'Social and economic inequalities are to be arranged so that they are...to the greatest benefit of the least advantaged' (Rawls, 1972:302) – for no other reason than the fact that no one stranded behind a hypothesised 'veil of ignorance' can ever know what he personally will gain or lose: 'No one knows his situation in society nor his natural assets, and therefore no one is in a position to tailor principles to his advantage.' (Rawls, 1972:139). Rawls writes that 'the notion of the veil of ignorance is implicit, I think, in Kant's ethics' (Rawls, 1972:140–1). Probably it is; but it also cuts down the high-minded ideals of truth-telling and mutual support to the less generous, more calculative status of insurance purchased to boost the welfare of the reflecting self.

Inter-personal imputations extend still further the dominion of the self. The impurity is in a sense inevitable, given the truism that alter's mind can never be accessible (if at all) save to alter himself. To love your neighbour *as yourself* is not in the circumstances any real guarantee that you will be loving him as *he* would want to be loved – or as he would love you if invited to love first. It is not an easy task to build up a body of universal laws where (ordinal) rankings are undisclosed and (cardinal) strengths are unrecorded. Whereas the free market can pyramid respect for persons on autonomy manifested through exchange, the categorical imperative must in non-capitalist conditions forever be the creature of guesses and inferences that extrapolate outwards from the self. The procedure is not an infallible one. The social contract implicit in the Golden Rule must in the circumstances be vulnerable to the charge that my 'goodness' is made your 'rightness' as if guided by an invisible myopia that treats you as me because that is the best I can do.

Asymmetrical information confuses all the comparisons. Relatives, friends, colleagues have enough conservatism in common to be able to make some projections on the basis of a common past. Complete strangers, on the other hand, find it difficult to make inter-personal imputations that do not threaten a violation of psychological space. The difference is only a matter of degree. Knowledge has a cost, wants are not clear – and alter cannot respect ego's preferences unless he has a good idea of what they are.

Tolerance of diversity introduces a further complication. The social worker loves his neighbour as himself by offering hot soup, benefits in kind and a neatly-folded copy of *The Guardian*. The down-and-out reinterprets the duty to care in terms of alcohol, cocaine, redistribution in cash and the free choice of the road to Hell. A gives B what A would himself want to be given. B replies that such love is meddlesome and self-regarding, that the Embankment's equal humanity cannot equitably be filleted into Kensington's feel-good shepherding. Problems like these would be resolved at a stroke if A's 'dos' were to be the same as B's 'do untos'; or if, at the very least, the As and the Bs were prepared to compromise on a single generalisable norm. It cannot be expected that either of these conditions will necessarily hold in a second-best situation where love resembles regimentation and alter's rights are treated as if ego's externality.

The self is over-weighted in the instances cited above. Yet evenhandedness too can raise problems in the employment of the Kant-inspired tool. The equal valuation of the future with the present makes it unseemly for public investments to be made subject to a discounting process. The equal status of the borrower with the lender makes it impossible for deferred gratification to be remunerated with an interest-rate. Compassion shown to Death Row murderers in the short run can mean even more addicts and criminals in later rounds of the game: 'Unless an equilibrium is established which imposes self-selected limits on samaritan-like behavior, the rush towards species destruction may accelerate rather than diminish.' (Buchanan, 1975:84). Altruism manifested where tit-for-tat is required can erode over time the national stock of Kantianism itself: consider Becker's 'rotten kid' (Becker, 1981:7–9), determined forever to travel free on the generosity of an all-forgiving father. To do as one would be done by creates an 'after-you problem' (Collard, 1978:9) that immobilises action in the indifference of Buridan's ass. Where A acts to please B but B acts to please A, no door is entered first, no price-tag is ever agreed, and both A and B as Kantians are at serious risk of death from starvation. Some self-interest would save their lives. If too little morality can be a cause of the Hobbesian *bellum*, then too much morality can arguably lead to an endstate that is every bit as dismal.

8.3   ETHICS AND ECONOMICS

Durkheim's focus is consensus: people internalise the modal values and perpetuate the continuing conventions. Kant's standard is universality: people treat others as they would like to be treated and look to others for the same generalisable imperative. The constructs both of consensus and of universality are well illustrated by the ethical economics first of price and then of trust.

(a)   Price

It is too easy to say that the market price is the 'right' price, that the 'rightness' of the price can be deduced from multi-firm competition on the side of supply, unmanipulated taste on the side of demand. It is too easy – because behind the equilibrium must be the *validation* of the equilibrium; and public opinion might simply not accept that the Marshallian cross is as equitable as its proponents contend that it is efficient. Clearly, alongside the textbook's curves, 'there are also social norms of fair exchange, and the going rate of exchange in a group is not necessarily, or even typically, identical with what is considered a fair rate of exchange' (Blau, 1964:154). People have preferences, even about prices. That being the case, it would be more convincing – but also more difficult – to build up a picture of 'rightness' through questionnaires and surveys rather than assuming that people will automatically give their stamp of approval to the price that does no more than clear the stock.

One result which has emerged from the experimental evidence is the fundamental attractiveness of the normal and of the expected: 'Psychological studies of adaptation suggest that any stable state of affairs tends to become accepted eventually, at least in the sense that alternatives to it no longer readily come to mind.' (Kahneman, Knetsch and Thaler, 1986:730–1). Conservatism, it would appear, can be perceived as its own legitimation. Market prices are no exception: 'Terms of exchange that are initially seen as unfair may in time acquire the status of a reference transaction. Thus, the gap between the behavior that people consider fair and the behavior that they expect in the marketplace tends to be rather small.' (Kahneman, Knetsch and Thaler, 1986:731). The *status quo* comes over time to be considered fair. It is considered fair because it is the *status quo*.

The 'just price' in the Middle Ages was a cultural fact. A customary standard deeply embedded in an ongoing way of life, the historically determined ratio was a tradition to be perpetuated, a reference-point that carried a moral imperative. The ethical derivation of the stable rule was a dual one, at once Durkheimian (in the sense that it was the common possession of a single self-conscious community) and Kantian (because the buyer and the seller were invited not to take advantage of a fellow-creature's abnormal need). The 'just price' of medieval Catholicism lives on in present-day Zurich and Berlin, where the vast majority of the 1750 households interviewed by Bruno Frey confirmed that they found the *status quo* more equitable than the gravitational shock.

Thus, questioned about bottled water sold to sightseers in an isolated area on a hot day, 78 per cent of the respondents said it would be 'unfair' or (fully 34 per cent of the sample) 'very unfair' to allocate by price despite the excess of demand. Questioned about the rationing of snow-shovels following a heavy snowfall, 83 per cent said it would be 'unfair' or (69 per cent) 'very unfair' to make use of the price-mechanism. (Frey, 1992:159–60). Irrespective of what the economics profession might recommend, the majority of the households would appear to have had serious reservations about flexible prices despite the existence of scarcity.

Frey correctly observes that the negative attitudes must be put in the context of the next-bests forgone: 'The fairness of pricing must be analysed in a *comparative perspective*. No system of decision making is completely fair, or completely unfair. What matters is how prices perform relative to their alternatives.' (Frey, 1992:160). The real must be compared with the real and not with the ideal that does not exist. In the bottled-water case, Frey identified three viable substitutes. The least popular was a randomised selection such as a lottery in which each participant has an equal chance and no one has a guarantee: only 14 per cent of the respondents said this would be 'fair' and (unlike the other alternatives) it scored less well than the market. The intermediate choice was allocation by officials and bureaucrats employing imper-sonal procedures (including, perhaps, the criterion of need) that had received the legitimation of democracy: 43 per cent said that this method would be 'fair'. The most popular option was a traditional rule like 'first come, first served': 76 per cent said the queue was 'fair' des-pite the neglect of the intensity of want. Only where supply was likely to rise as a consequence were Frey's respondents prepared to regard an auction sale as anything other than an illegitimate attempt to exploit a temporary shortage. Their moral standards left resources misallocated, information undiffused, markets uncleared. Perhaps they did not know what their ethics was costing them. Perhaps they knew but were reluctant to compromise.

Just as there can be a reference price, so there can be a reference profit. Respondents in empirical studies tend to relate prices in their mind not to subjective utilities but to paid-out costs. Perceiving the reference-price as a convention, an expectation and a norm, they are prepared nonetheless to countenance a revision in that price where an alteration in cost – and cost-plus – would otherwise mean the unjust treatment of buyer or seller in the sense of Kant. Smith, Ricardo and Marx on the cost-of-production (and/or the labour) theory of value would apparently have a strong intuitive appeal relative to those non-conservative theor-ies of profit which, writing off historic bygones and starting nostalgia-free from here, say that any surplus is a 'fair' one which is the passive residual of supply and demand. One implication might be that theoret-ical economists would well satisfy the majority's requirements if they modelled the distinction between 'reasonable' and 'excessive' profits – and showed how State regulation could eliminate at a stroke the perceived inequity of the market-clearing reward.

Kahneman and his colleagues conducted approximately 100 interviews in Vancouver and Toronto. Their findings confirm that the reference profit has strong popular resonances. Asked about an overnight rise in the price of snow-shovels, 82 per cent called it unfair since the cost incurred had clearly not been affected by the demand-inducing emergency. Asked if shelf-prices could be raised where replacement stock wholesales at a higher cost, 77 per cent said it would be unfair to backdate the enhancement. It was clearly the historic cost and not the opportunity cost that influenced the respondents when they resisted the profit-maximising response to excess demand. (Kahneman, Knetsch and Thaler, 1986:729, 733).

Prices are widely seen as unfair if they are not proportioned to costs. This is why theatres, sensitive about their reputation, do not follow the ticket-touts in charging by supply and demand for the most popular shows: theatregoers want their money's worth, and that to them brings in the cost embodied as well as the intensity of the craving. Thaler found that consumers were willing to pay a median value of $2.65 for a bottle of beer in a resort hotel but preferred not to drink beer at all if asked to pay more than $1.50 in a local supermarket: the resort hotel was assumed to have higher costs and had in that way won the 'right' to charge a higher price. (Thaler, 1985:206). Kahneman and his colleagues found that 91 per cent of their respondents believed it to be inequitable for a landlord to put up the rent merely because the tenant had taken a job in the vicinity of the home: costs being unchanged, it was not judged fair for the landlord (even if the sum of money were not large in itself) to exploit the special circumstances that *de facto* put up demand. (Kahneman, Knetsch and Thaler, 1986:735). Frank concluded that the absence of peak-pricing for Saturday haircuts could be explained in terms of the acknowledged invariance in the hairdresser's costs: 'In the customer's eyes, the cost of producing a haircut on Saturday does not appear different from the cost of producing one on weekdays. Many of the customers who cannot come during the week apparently would prefer to wait in line at a crowded barbershop than to be served promptly in a barbershop that they feel is overcharging them – even though, in the abstract, the time they would save at the latter barbershop would be worth much more to them than the extra cost of the haircut there.' (Frank, 1985:105). Observations such as these suggest that consumers have a view of what is fair. They feel that a norm has been breached when their trading-partner approaches them for more than his reference-point gain.

When the cost of production rises, the consensus will not reject the rise in price as unjust. Kahneman and his associates found that 79 per cent of their sample took it as entirely unobjectionable for a shop-keeper to pass on in prices the whole burden of an increase in cost: 75 per cent reached the same conclusion about a landlord – even if the tenant would then have to move out as a result. (Kahneman, Knetsch and Thaler, 1986:733). Reference-profit fairness must evidently not be equated with a generous and charitable response.

Participants seem to have regarded the reference-profit as the firm's entitlement when the cost of production rises. They were less insistent about the normal mark-up when the cost of production falls. If costs fall by $40 and prices fall by $20, 79 per cent said that this would be accept-able. If costs fall by $20 and prices do not fall at all, as many as 53 per cent of the Canadian respondents – a small majority but a majority nonetheless – was prepared to ignore the new subsidy from the pur-chaser and to say that no injustice would occur. There would appear to be a moderate asymmetry in the popular reaction to the cost-based price: 'The rules of fairness permit a firm not to share in the losses that it imposes on its transactors, without imposing on it an unequivocal duty to share its gains with them.' (Kahneman, Knetsch and Thaler, 1986:734). Mistrustful of rationing by price, unprepared to treat oppor-tunity cost as a genuine sacrifice, the lay public appears also to be quint-essentially itself in respect of the 'just' profit buffeted by the rise or fall in cost. Fairness by agreement need not mean convergence on the invis-ible hand. It is deserving even so of the social democracy's tolerance and support.

The labour market, being a market for persons, is especially sensitive to the community's standards. Consider the reference wage as the worker's right: 83 per cent in the Canadian study said it would be unfair to cut an existing employee's pay when wages fall in the outside market (although 73 per cent believed it correct to offer a newly-hired worker the lower going rate). Consider the cut in nominal wages when profits drop below the conservative base: 68 per cent found the cut acceptable where the firm is actually making losses – but 77 per cent found the cut unac-ceptable so long as the firm is even slightly in the black. Consider the different assessment despite the identical magnitude: 62 per cent said it was unfair to reduce wages by 7 per cent in a recession (although 80 per cent said it would be fair to cancel a bonus of equivalent value) but 78 per cent said it was fair in good times to raise wages by 5 per cent when prices were rising by 12 per cent. (Kahneman, Knetsch and Thaler, 1986:730, 731, 733). Traditional differentials, past precedents, downward rigidity, upward flexibility, the loss of pay perceived differently from the limited gain, the abstention from under-cutting despite the 'reserve army' of unemployment in the trade, the union's role as the guardian of historical demarcations – all of this builds a normative dimension into the labour market which transcends the market-clearing wage without the need to invoke the misapprehension of money illusion.

The labour contract does not lend itself to full and complete specification: the discretionary penumbra that makes possible 'x-inefficiency' in the sense of Leibenstein (Leibenstein, 1976:Chapter 3) is too great for that. Active re-definition being a fact of organisational life, the lump of labour has the opportunity to exert a major influence on the quantity and quality of the effort that he actually provides. The wage is paid for the minimum: 'Above these minimum standards the worker's performance is freely determined.' (Akerlof, 1982:151).

Workers have the option to do the minimum. Perceived duty to workmates and principals can impel them to do something more. Of particular importance in accounting for the surplus that is in effect a gift would appear to be the past-dominated baseline of the reference-assiduity that Elton Mayo identified in his study at the Hawthorne plant: 'The working group as a whole actually determined the output of individual workers by reference to a standard, pre-determined but never clearly stated, that represented the group conception of a fair day's work. This standard was rarely, if ever, in accord with the standards of the efficiency engineers.' (Mayo, 1949:70). Workers at Hawthorne did what they believed to be fair. It was the consensus of their immediate peers that gave them their benchmark and laid down their rhythm.

Absolutes often come with interests attached. Speaking horizontally, the co-workers at Hawthorne repaid conformity with solidarity and taxed free-riding through loss of reputation. Speaking vertically, the same implication of counter-gift in return would seem to be a feature of the nexus of obligation that binds the wage-recipients to their capitalists. The firm donates a supra-competitive wage despite the involuntary unemployment of outsiders to which it contributes. The firm minimises redundancies over the cycle because workers care about co-workers and morale could be threatened by betrayals. The firm keeps down the spread between high pay and low because the employees are known to value a compressed distribution that reflects their mistrust of social distance. It is easy to treat such market-resistant reactions as risk-sharing and implicit contracting, an investment in goodwill and an input in long-run profit. Of course there are interests in the absolutes. Yet there are absolutes as well – and, in the case of the firm, a reference standard of fairness which the individual business has only limited power to reject. To that extent a complex of price controls, employment regulations, monopoly and merger restrictions, minimum wage laws might not be required. Informal pressures can fulfil the same function in securing the perpetuation of strongly held conventions that ends, and not just means, match the better-known budget restraint in the limits that they impose.

(b)   Trust

Trust is 'the expectation that arises within a community of regular, honest, and cooperative behavior, based on commonly shared norms, on the part of other members of that community' (Fukuyama, 1996:26). A person is said to be worthy of trust if he may be relied upon for truth-telling and promise-keeping, dependable performance and contracted execution: examples would be the doctor who does not abuse information-asymmetry for gain or the judge who does not sell biased decisions for bribes. A person is said to be in breach of trust if he is seen to be active in lying, cheating, fraud, deception, default and that 'opportunism' which Oliver Williamson defines as 'self-interest seeking with guile' (Williamson, 1975:9): consider the politician who, once elected, tears up his manifesto-commitments or the manager who conceals facts which call into question the need for his department. Jack believes that he can later call in the favours he has done. Jill believes that her children will respond *as if* an insurance policy when she is old. Jack and Jill in ways such as these are expressing their confidence in a future-dated expectation that the law will not enforce. Jack and Jill, in short, are putting their faith in a self-policing morality capable of delivering unintended outcomes upon which they can build.

Kenneth Arrow sees trust as a background value with a high social pay-off: 'Trust is an important lubricant of the social system. It is extremely efficient; it saves a lot of trouble to have a fair degree of reliance on other people's word.' (Arrow, 1974:23). He also contends that, like all other envelopes of encoded information, it can never be a commodity 'for which trade on the open market is technically possible or even meaningful': 'If you have to buy it, you already have some doubts about what you've bought.' (Arrow, 1974:23). Trust is crucial for the completion of the gain-seeking circuit – in the limiting case, because money and goods only exceptionally change hands at precisely the same time. Trust is not, however, susceptible to merchanting without putting at risk the very nature of its function: 'You can't very easily establish trust on a basis like that. If your basis is rational decision and your underlying motive is self-interest, then you can betray your trust at any point when it is profitable and in your interest to do so. Therefore other people can't trust you.' (Arrow, cited in Swedberg, 1990:137). Trust, in short, is only able to serve as a profitable business asset where it is not supplied as a profitable business asset. Akerlof on lemons and loyalties bears out the logic of Arrow's assertion that there are no close substitutes for the extra-economic and the multi-period.

Imperfect information makes it difficult or impossible for the consumer to assess the quality of a prospective purchase. In some cases – as with new cars – there is a producer's guarantee that *de facto* returns the risk to the seller. In other cases – as with used cars – that guarantee is not on offer. It is in the market for used cars and not for new cars that the consumer is most likely to end up in possession of a 'lemon' that because of his inexperience he did not recognise to be sub-standard until he had been tricked.

Trust, however, is an important lubricant; and the moral convention does come to the aid of the exposed. The model in health insurance would be the Kantian applicant who frustrates adverse selection by declaring truthfully that he is a bad risk who must be asked for a compensatory premium. What this would mean in the market for cars is that the honest vendor would reveal the faults and cut his price in proportion.

Akerlof does not deny that honesty in this way can restore the balance that unequal knowledge would otherwise upset. Yet he also adds the strict condition that honesty if it is to correct a market failure must be universal and across-the-board. Trust, Akerlof warns, must inevitably be crowded out by duplicity in a mixed moral environment where some men are decent and some men are rogues: 'Dishonest dealings tend to drive honest dealings out of the market. There may be potential buyers of good quality products and there may be potential sellers of such products in the appropriate price range; however, the presence of people who wish to pawn bad wares off as good wares tends to drive out the legitimate business. The cost of dishonesty, therefore, lies not only in the amount by which the purchaser is cheated; the cost must also include the loss incurred from driving legitimate business out of existence.' (Akerlof, 1970:15–16). Decent men and rogues can be all but indistinguishable in the marketplace. The result is the dismal scenario that would be predicted by an imaginative extension of 'Gresham's Law'. The consumer behind the veil must discount the claims of the decent men and of the rogues alike. The decent men will have to sell below value or else withdraw altogether from exchange. The rogues will share neither the sense of injustice nor the temptation to quit. Thus in the long run will bad morals drive out good morals and partial trust give way to no trust at all.

Akerlof's message is that honesty, if universal, can redress a market imbalance. He also accepts that capitalism can itself provide the correctives to some at least of its shortcomings. The second doctor gives a second opinion even though the first doctor has put his professional ethic into his diagnosis. The building surveyor makes an impartial assessment even though the vendor of the house has sworn by its soundness. The solicitor writes a will that codifies the beneficiaries' obligations. The used-car dealer markets information (in that he charges a higher price for good cars than he does for inferior ones) and provides protection (as where he uses his expert knowledge to offer a limited warranty). Advisers, intermediaries and entrepreneurs are clearly in a position to supply a market-based alternative to the ethical virtue of trust – and, of course, to claim a market-determined reward in exchange. Conservatism can redress a market imbalance. So too, apparently, can the market itself.

The used-car dealer will himself face a temptation to trade in exaggeration and concealment, duds and 'lemons'. The multi-period nature of his business will, however, be a disincentive for him to seek out short-term gain at the expense of long-term profit. The reason is that reputation is a business asset, and a reputation for honesty (like a 'brand name') the source of an economic rent. Customers and employers pay over the odds to a trading-partner they can trust. Good morals in that sense are a means as well as an end – and a means that is strongly favoured by the process of natural selection itself: 'Why not cheat? The answer is that in an advanced, personalized society, where individuals are identified and the record of their acts is weighed by others, it does not pay to cheat. . . . Selection will discriminate against the individual if cheating has later adverse effects on his life and reproduction that outweigh the momentary advantage gained.' (Wilson, 1975:120). Hawks see well because the hawks with poor eyesight missed out on prey and did not reproduce. Established dealers are trustworthy because the 'lemon'-merchants bent on a 'fast buck' from duds found it impossible to squeeze even a passing trade from clients with the alternative of a reputed house. Iago, student of Machiavelli, said it all: 'Good name in man or woman ... is the immediate jewel of their souls; who steals my purse steals trash.'

Hamlet, fond of play-acting, offers the following advice: 'Assume a virtue, if you have it not.' His appeal to *persona* and presentation recalls Veblen's theory of conspicuous consumption, where the reward-seeking quality is successful precisely because it is put on display: 'There is a return to *appearing* honest, but not to *being* honest.' (Akerlof, 1983: 181). The payoff accrues to the perception and not to the fact. It is an advantage to be thought of as trustworthy. It is even more of an advantage to be thought of as trustworthy while at the same time conducting oneself as a blackguard and a knave. It is evidently the drama-schools and not the business schools that teach the simulation and the concealment that are, if Hamlet's counsel is to be taken on trust, of real value in training the estate agents and the poker-players of the future.

Multi-period contact does, of course, serve to separate the fake from the genuine; and so do the comparisons thrown up by competitors. Yet psychology itself would appear to be on the side of honesty and uncomfortable with a strategy that is built around pretence.

Thus people who know they are betraying a trust very often let themselves down by means of involuntary clues. Tell-tale signs like blushing, blinking, stammering, perspiring, a change in the heart-rate, an inability to maintain eye-contact are all, like Pinocchio's nose, an indication that a false impression is deliberately being projected by a manipulator and a hypocrite who knows he has something to hide. While some imposters can deceive even a lie-detector, for most people body language is not favourable to falsity: 'In order to *appear* honest, it may be necessary, or at least very helpful, to *be* honest.' (Frank, 1988:18). Virtue in that sense is both its own reward and an input into material success.

The nervous system is on the side of the moral sentiments. So is early socialisation. Unconvinced that cheaters normally prosper, Akerlof advises that perception and fact should be treated as two sides of a single coin: 'It pays parents to teach their children to be honest because the individually functional trait of appearing honest is jointly produced with the individually dysfunctional trait of being honest.' (Akerlof, 1983:181). The *appearing* and the *being* are delivered jointly in a compound. An important reason is the conservatism of learning. Traits once acquired are by no means easy to lose: 'In my model of child-rearing, honesty may begin as a means for economic betterment, but then there is a displacement of goals so that the person so trained will refrain from embezzlement where there is no penalty.' (Akerlof, 1983:180). The used-car dealer, if the product of a socialisation into the corporate virtues of reliability, truthfulness and self-restraint, will be much in demand from new business partners precisely because he is known to shape his life by an unbending norm: 'Even if the world were to end at midnight, thus eliminating all possibility of penalty for defection, the genuinely trustworthy person would not be motivated to cheat.' (Frank, 1988:69). His reputation for service will prove a business asset that itself commands a market price.

A good reputation commands a market price. So too, independently, do the perceived causes of the above-average commitment. Education in a military academy in the United States, or an elite public school in Britain, is often taken as an indicator of team-regarding absolutes inculcated at an impressionable age. An upper-class background (as advertised through dress, manners and accent) can signal an identification with a predictable group pattern and an inheritance of *noblesse oblige*. Membership of a religious sect known for its strict moral code can serve as a testimonial for a high-security applicant who happens to dwell in a high-risk slum. Causal variables such as these (Akerlof's 'loyalty filters') are widely used as screening devices. They are conservative proxies which help to single out the trading-partners most likely to grow over time into a good reputation. They reduce the transaction-costs associated with the recognition of trustworthy conduct. Surprises can occur: even the State can default on its bonds, while irresponsible money-issue (through inflation) always robs cash-holders of purchasing power. Still, however, it is the function of stereotyping that it economises on the filtering costs that inevitably arise whenever economics sets out to employ ethics as a complement to supply and demand.

9 Structure as Capital

The economic market is often described as a Walrasian matrix, as an agglomeration of independent parts, each of them anonymous, powerless, faceless, interchangeable and alone. In such a world-view it is automaticity that takes on the task of allocation. The single unit does what it is told.

There is, however, a different way of looking at the faces in the crowd. A sells a used car to B who is linked to him by consanguinity or is a fellow-immigrant from the same small village in Italy or Pakistan. B pays a tip to C who is not just a taxi-driver but a neighbour, a friend, a member of the local golf-club, the leader of the local scout-troop. C takes his car for service to A who is his long-term business contact, the source of regular referrals to his hairdressing salon, the tenor in his church choir, a drinking-partner in his evening institute. Objectively speaking, the garage-owner, the taxi-driver, the hairdresser are close to being textbook perfect competitors, footnote price-takers whose absence or presence would have little or no impact on the final market outcome. Subjectively speaking, the position is different – since each ant in the anthill, as Marshall astutely observed, can face both a 'general demand curve for his commodity in a wide market' and the 'particular demand curve of his own special market' (Marshall, 1890:379n). Even where homogeneity rules at the level of the *genus*, still there can be monopoly and differentiation at the sub-level of the *species*. The faces in the crowd cannot expect to escape unnoticed.

Experiences and contacts can be an important source of perceived uniqueness within lexicographic uniformity. To that extent the inter-personal relationships of A to B, B to C, C to A, may be seen as a valuable capital that is made up not of things but of linkages. The asset is in the *and*. It is because of the inter-personal seamlessness of the A *and* B, the B *and* C, the C *and* A, that James Coleman was able to liken the decentralised process to a single business that is made up of inter-dependent sections: 'The whole market is so infused with relations of the sort just described that it can be seen as an organization, no less so than a department store. Alternatively, the market can be seen as consisting of a set of individual merchants, each having an extensive body of social capital on which to draw, based on the relationships within the market.' (Coleman, 1990:304). The market is a forum for structured replications and conservative affiliations. The market is not merely faces in the crowd united only by a one-off stake in an impersonal exchange.

The subject of this chapter is the structure and affiliation that is the sunk cost. Section 9.1, 'Social Capital', provides a definition of the asset. Section 9.2, 'The Empowerment of the Social', examines channels through which investment takes place. Section 3, 'Unsocial Capital', considers ways in which the asset might actually prove a liability to an economic system that will not move on from the past.

9.1 SOCIAL CAPITAL

The asset is the network: 'Le capital social est l'ensemble des ressources actuelles ou potentielles qui sont liées à la possession d'un *réseau durable de relations* plus ou moins institutionalisées d'interconnaissance et d'inter-reconnaissance.' (Bourdieu, 1980:2). Physical capital is non-human input and human capital is a productivity-differential made possible 'through the imbedding of resources in people' (Becker, 1962: 9). Social capital is the stock of structured interactions that, neither a final utility like a meal nor a consumer durable like a car, has this in common with plant, schooling, vitamins and on-the-job training, that it may rightly be seen as an investment in the nation's future wealth.

The model is the machine. Social capital, like human capital, is only a metaphor. To say that a man is similar to an aardvark is a true statement but not necessarily a helpful one. To say that social capital bears a family resemblance to the inanimate input is not by the same logic a valuable comparison until due allowance has been made for the differences which separate as well as for the overlap which unites.

Social capital, for one thing, is non-appropriable and non-proprietorial: 'Unlike other forms of capital, social capital inheres in the structure of relations between persons and among persons. It is lodged neither in individuals nor in physical implements of production.' (Coleman, 1990: 302). Physical capital can be bought and sold. Social capital, in contrast, cannot be divided or exchanged. Only at home in an inter-personal relationship, it has the unusual characteristic that it is a capital destined never to be the property of a capitalist.

Social capital, again, is non-exclusive and non-restricted: whereas a machine can be patented and its benefits priced, there is no obvious way of fencing non-contributors out of the self-policing honesty that is the gift to market capitalism of a network of watchful co-religionists. The non-commercial spillover is a club-shared externality. That being the case, the public good is therefore exposed to under-supply as a direct consequence of open access at the margin.

Social capital is typically unplanned. Innovation in industry will usually require a decision to invest. The web of contacts, on the other hand, will most frequently be the by-product of a non-wealth-related activity. The individual in respect of social capital only exceptionally makes a significant contribution at the initiation stage. A business calculates and budgets when it computerises its robots. No one, however, installed the family, or national service, or *Mitbestimmung*, or Alcoholics Anonymous in order to bring about a change in economic efficiency.

Social capital is seldom discounted. In common with physical capital, it has a baseline next-best: this is explicit where neighbours recognise that the cost of a voluntary watch-scheme is less than the cost of paid-for security guards, or where confidence that a promise will be honoured is taken to be more economical of scarce resources than would be an enforceable contract. Unlike physical capital, however, it finds it difficult to formalise the trade-off with future opportunity-sets by means of an outside rate of discount. The commodity is a consumable as much as an input: businessmen *enjoy* cocktail-parties at which alliances are celebrated. The commodity, besides that, can expand with use: some links depreciate over time (as where history-conscious immigrants marry out and become absorbed) but others grow with growing confidence (consider the inter-personal expectations in the Antwerp diamond trade, stored-up obligations that function as if 'money in the bank'). These properties clearly differentiate the unexpected riches accruing to Methodists from the intended rate of return of an oil-well that will more meaningfully be the focus of the cost–benefit analysis.

Social capital, finally, is difficult to delimit. A plough has spatial boundaries. Not so the world supply of dentists or of Zulus, capital only to the extent that the components in the kit are able to overcome the division caused by immigration laws, transportation and communication. The capital-ness can change over time: the European Union, air-travel and the mobile phone clearly do much to cancel out the physical separation. One capital-ness can be nested in another: thus A and B are a specific network in themselves *and also* one dyad that forms part of a general and surrounding network. One capital-ness can cut across a competing capital-ness: witness the divided embeddedness of C, born a Zulu and made a dentist. What follows from these difficulties is a warning that the identification of a social capital is itself an *explicandum*. All social capital is interaction. Whether all interaction is also social capital is a good deal less likely.

There are undeniable differences which distinguish social capital from physical capital. For all the differences, there are also the similarities. Social capital is a long-lived asset yielding its benefits in a stream over time. Social capital is a fixed cost. Social capital is subject to uncertainty. Social capital is illiquid. Social capital deserves a risk-premium. In ways such as these social capital clearly shares crucial characteristics with the more traditional investments that facilitate goal-attainment in the time-honoured manner of Böhm-Bawerk.

Social capital is social structure. Social structure is the bedrock upon which social values must stand. Thus it is that ethically-minded economists like Kenneth Arrow, postulating a direct and constructive linkage between network and mindset, have treated a stranger-gift like trustworthiness not as a conscious choice but as an unintended outcome. For Arrow the origins of other-regarding self-denial are to be sought not in the utilitarian calculus but in the social whole which surrounds and shapes the component part: 'For there to be trust, there has to be a social structure which is based on motives different from immediate opportunism. Or perhaps based on something for which your social status is a guarantee and which functions as a kind of commitment.' (Arrow, cited in Swedberg, 1990:137). Social interaction constrains self-seeking conduct. To the extent that ethical absolutes are a productive input, to that extent personal relationships may be said to be a cause of moral capital while at the same time serving as social capital themselves.

Crucially, however, it is the easy identifiability of the named partner that delivers the economic payoff. In that sense the market for moral and social capital optimises in the opposite manner to the black-box *tâtonnement* that is productive of allocative efficiency in the market for machines and skills. In the normal capitalist case, it is impersonal rivalry between closely substituting competitors that sheers prices and profits to their functional minimum. In the moral and social case, on the other hand, it is identity and not anonymity that makes the market perform. Identity is a brand-name that (like a university department or a familiar greengrocer) advertises a standard of service. Identity makes possible face-to-face enforcement like that within the family (compelling inter-generational care) or within the firm (discouraging idleness and discretionary shirking). Identity is the precondition for investment in a continuing relationship, for the implicit contract, for the return-gift deferred because of a past-based confidence that an obligation will be honoured. In all of these ways, identity serves as a source of information and moderates the uncertainty that always accompanies trade. As Ben-Porath observes: 'It is clear why investment in identity is rewarding in these circumstances, why trust is mutually beneficial, why proximity and general involvement create at little expense the information that is lacking among strangers and generate incentives for proper behavior.' (Ben-Porath, 1980:21). If information were perfect and uncertainty nil, there would presumably be no *economic* premium on moral and social capital. We start from here, however; and that is why identification and capitalism must go hand in hand.

Citing examples like future delivery of goods or money, adverse selection in the market for insurance, information-asymmetry in respect of a second-hand car, Ben-Porath reaches the conclusion that much of economic activity would be inconceivable in the absence of background attitudes and inter-personal networks. Schumpeter before him had articulated a similar commitment to ties and values, a similar concern about rights-based individualism. Schumpeter, needless to say, was an evolutionist who had reconciled himself to the withering-away of the very conservatism that he himself had rated so highly. Not capitalism but either disorder or socialism, Schumpeter wrote, was fated to be the inevitable beneficiary of capitalism's historic success: 'The capitalist order not only rests on props made of extra-capitalist material but also derives its energy from extra-capitalist patterns of behavior which at the same time it is bound to destroy.' (Schumpeter, 1942:162). Ben-Porath would argue that a shortfall or a sub-optimality could be made good through renewed investment in the social capital. Schumpeter, more apocalyptically, would declare that capitalism had produced its own gravediggers and that there was nothing more that could be done.

Less pessimistic than Schumpeter but anxious about the future nonetheless is Francis Fukuyama. Fukuyama's argument is in two stages. First, he argues, ethical absolutes are the precondition for success and not just the icing on the cake: 'Law, contract, and economic rationality provide a necessary but not sufficient basis for both the stability and prosperity of postindustrial societies; they must as well be leavened with reciprocity, moral obligation, duty toward community, and trust, which are based in habit rather than rational calculation. The latter are not anachronisms in a modern society but rather the sine qua non of the latter's success.' (Fukuyama, 1996:11). Second, Fukuyama continues, the social capital that is the source of the constraint is being eroded by evolution and is not being replenished: 'Communities of shared values, whose members are willing to subordinate their private interests for the sake of larger goals of the community as such, have become rarer. And it is these moral communities alone that can generate the kind of social trust that is critical to organizational efficiency.' (Fukuyama, 1996:309).

Fukuyama's 'sine qua non', Fukuyama's 'critical', are the language of necessity and not simply of preference: 'If the institutions of democracy and capitalism are to work properly', he says, 'they *must* coexist with certain premodern cultural habits that ensure their proper functioning' (Fukuyama, 1996:11, emphasis added). It is a strong argument indeed to make obligation and association a precondition for success and not merely a matter of taste. It is, however, an imputation that does at least fill an intellectual gap where the optimisation of the invisible hand is consistently held back by the frictions of ignorance and uncertainty. Chapters 2 and 3 may be said in that sense to have made the present chapter as functional as a traffic-light, as utilitarian as the dentist's drill. Even so, the present chapter concludes with a section on Unsocial Capital which reminds the reader how unscientific it is to do other than to consider each case on its own merits alone.

9.2   THE EMPOWERMENT OF THE SOCIAL

In a one-off interaction there is no history and no prediction. An unscrupulous trading-partner might supply fakes and call them diamonds or fail to pay when he had given his word. Alfred Marshall in 1875 (like Tocqueville in 1831) saw clearly what this freedom from information could mean in a rootless democracy that had substituted mobility for status: 'The doctrine that honesty is the best policy is at a disadvantage when it submits itself to the judgement of a man whose associates would continually be changing even were he stationary.' (Marshall, 1875:364). The Americans, Marshall found in 1875, were continually on the move – and 'money is a more portable commodity than a high moral reputation' (Marshall, 1875:364). This mutability, this unknowability, led Marshall to express serious reservations about the countervailing power of the Kantian universals in a non-authoritarian society where, to use Tocqueville's phrase, 'each American appeals to the individual exercise of his own understanding alone' (Tocqueville, 1840:2): 'It cannot, I think, be denied that a short-sighted man is thus exposed to great temptations in America.' (Marshall, 1875:364).

America, Marshall said, was the nation of disembeddedness and the home of immediacy. Britain, on the other hand, was a nation that enjoyed the protection of a thick growth of intermediate associations, of little republics which educate the member in the need 'to bear and forbear: in adversity he will suffer hunger, in prosperity he will decline his own advancement' (Marshall, 1875:365). Marshall saw the intermediate body, grander than the isolated atom but not all-encompassing like the historicists' *Volk*, as a school for moralists that offered a training in ties. Marshall as an economist took an especial interest in the 'far-reaching wisdom which verges on morality' of that admirably Kantian organisation, 'a first class English trades union': 'Unions generally are showing signs of beginning to ask themselves whether any republic can be justified in adopting regulations, the general adoption of which by the surrounding republics would be injurious to all. In asking themselves this question they are giving themselves a great education.' (Marshall, 1875: 364, 366). Tocqueville, as a lapsed parliamentarian, made a similar point about the discipline and the integration that were so expertly fostered by the devolution of political power to the patriotism of the local: 'The native of New England is attached to his township because it is independent and free: his co-operation in its affairs ensures his attachment to its interest; the well-being it affords him secures his affection.' (Tocqueville, 1835:64). On the one hand the *On Liberty* shopper, on the other hand the Hegelian Totality – it was the contention of Marshall the economist and of Tocqueville the political scientist that it is the function of the affiliations in between at best to build up the stock of social capital, at worst to slow down its rate of depletion.

This section, 'The Empowerment of the Social', is concerned with those affiliations in between. The starting-point is the contention of Marshall and Tocqueville that structured groupings and continuing relationships are instrumental in shaping the institutional patterns that reinforce the ethical norms. Granovetter is only one among many to see in the inter-temporal support of social capital a realistic alternative to the Hobbesian dystopia of dissembling, distrust, disorder and deviousness: 'The embeddedness argument stresses instead the role of concrete personal relations and structures (or "networks") of such relations in generating trust and discouraging malfeasance. The widespread preference for transacting with individuals of known reputation implies that few are actually content to rely on either generalized morality or institutional arrangements to guard against trouble.' (Granovetter, 1985: 490). Anxious about the state of nature and reluctant to rely exclusively on preachers and precepts, contracts and lawsuits, Granovetter seeks a solution to the Hobbesian problem in interlinking allegiances and identifiable iterations. This section, joining in his exploration, examines the

complex of institutions which make a contribution of particular importance to the formation and maintenance of the social capital.

(a)   The Family

The family as a group has a past and a future. It socialises children into
cooperative attitudes and transmits the non-ego authority of traditions
and expectations. It conditions reflexes – as where disputes are settled
amicably and tit-for-tat is given time to become a rule. It sets an example
of altruism – as where people work and save for their children and take
their grandchildren's health into account when paying extra to protect
the ozone layer. It is a school for responsibility – as where the dutiful
look after their aged relatives and try to tell the truth when interacting
with blood. The family is a source of *esprit de corps* and mutual support.
It is a focus for belonging and benevolence which acts as a counter-
balance to the ephemeral self-seeking of the capitalism beyond. The family teaches norms and it teaches membership. Should this background
be a necessary complement to the economic market, the family would
then be the cause of a valuable externality.

It is possible to argue that the family carries an economic coupon-
rate. It is also possible to argue the opposite. Banfield, reporting on
the 'amoral familism' – the 'inability to concert activity beyond the
immediate family' (Banfield, 1958:10) – that he found in his fieldwork
in 'Montegrano' (a fictively-named village somewhere in South Italy) came
close to arguing the opposite. The Montegranesi, Banfield observed,
were strongly committed to the welfare of the kinship group. Public-
spirited within its confines, they felt no further need to make a sacrifice
where donations of food were required by the local orphanage, where
voluntary labour was invited for an irrigation scheme, where witnesses
were sought to expose political corruption, even where the collection-
plate was passed round in church.

The Montegranesi were quick to maximise the material advantage of
immediate family. Collaborative and involved within its network, they
showed no interest in organised action pyramided exclusively upon
the accident of geographical contiguity. Laws were disregarded where
prosecution was unlikely. Taxes were evaded, bribes proffered, workers
under-paid. School teachers arrived late or not at all. Interest and not
fellow-feeling was the consideration that regulated mutual aid: 'Even
trivial favors create an obligation and must be repaid.' (Banfield, 1958:
121). Friendship therefore was potentially costly and had to be rationed:
'Friends are luxuries that the Montegranesi feel they cannot afford.'

(Banfield, 1958:121). Bureaucrats lacked any sense of mission, calling or commitment to the collective good: 'In a society of amoral familists, office-holders, feeling no identification with the purposes of the organization, will not work harder than is necessary to keep their places or . . . to earn promotion.' (Banfield, 1958:91). Fascism was just around the corner: 'In a society of amoral familists, the weak will favor a regime which will maintain order with a strong hand.' (Banfield, 1958:96). Economic deprivation was a fact of life: 'The extreme poverty and backwardness . . . is to be explained largely (but not entirely) by the inability of the villagers to act together for their common good or, indeed, for any end transcending the immediate, material interest of the nuclear family.' (Banfield, 1958:10). The Montegranesi had internalised the values of hard work, charity, attachment and trust. Simply, they had shown themselves reluctant to extend the generality of their ethics. Society in Montegrano had not in consequence become more moral because of the family. It had, on the contrary, become less moral, more mercenary – and less productive as well.

The family as an intermediate association clearly did not carry a high coupon-rate in Montegrano taken as a whole. In other settings, however, its contribution will be more pervasive, its spillovers more conducive to economic growth. Where the child is disciplined into punctuality and loyalty, where it is made second nature to take pride in workmanship and not to neglect chores, there the family may be said to be inculcating reactions which will serve as an efficiency-enhancing input in the production-functions of future employers.

Capitalism, arguably, derives a stream of benefits from the non-rational, non-calculative ethos that is diffused through the family. Capitalism, ironically, may also be putting at risk the support that a fundamentally conservative institution is able to provide. Capitalism is dynamic: geographical mobility breaks up the extended family while technological transformation places a premium on youth over experience. Capitalism is pleasure-seeking: extended from the supermarket into the home, the utility-maximising 'whatever you fancy', 'do your own thing', 'the consumer is king' can mean sexual permissiveness, child abuse, emotional stunting, sequential divorce, marital infidelity, unintended pregnancy, the single-parent family, welfare dependency. Capitalism is scientific: strong on merit and achievement (and thus a threat to nepotism and favouritism intended to keep a business family-run), it is embarrassed by the high cost–benefit ratio of filial loyalty (and thus uncomfortable with the Biblical Commandment to 'honour thy father and mother', the Confucian deference to age, seniority and hierarchy). Even if capitalism is dependent on the network of kin, still there are reasons for thinking that economic evolution will work to the detriment of the conservative support.

Here as elsewhere, it would appear, the capitalist system can be a threat to its own stability. Schumpeter's interpretation of modern economic history is a salutary reminder of the social atomisation that remains a danger: 'In breaking down the pre-capitalist framework of society, capitalism thus broke not only the barriers that impeded its progress, but also the flying buttresses that prevented its collapse.' (Schumpeter, 1942:139). The temptation is clearly a real one for the conservative State to come to the aid of the family, made marginal by evolution.

Leaderly *dirigisme* is undoubtedly an option: thence the argument for laws (making clear, say, that crimes committed by children are the responsibility of the parents), for criteria (the denial of public housing to unmarried – least of all to single-sex – couples), for taxes (as where husband and wife are treated fiscally as a single unit), for subsidies (the case of generous child benefits and of State allowances to housewives who make conscientious parenting their sole career). So, perhaps surprisingly, is State intervention to emancipate the family from the external guidance of the social engineers. Negatively speaking, the government can resist vote-winning proposals for social welfare policies lest the bureaucratisation of love absolve the money-minded family from its responsibility for the young, the incapacitated, the out-of-work and the old. Positively speaking, the government can publish school league-tables, expand the power of the PTA, insist upon parent-governors, finance institutions exclusively through fees (parental self-reliance augmented where appropriate by means of earmarked vouchers and performance-related grants) in order more directly to involve the family in the education of a child. Whether through *dirigisme* or through emancipation, it is clear, there is much the State can do to protect the inter-generational capital that is vested in the family.

(b)   Kinship and Ethnicity

Surrounding the nuclear family is the network of kinship. It is a skein of relatedness that makes a contribution of particular significance to the socialisation of volition. Relatives safely facilitate employment-opportunities because they can draw on personal knowledge of assiduity and reliability. Relatives grant trade credit (and make loans in cash) because they are confident that a clansman would be ostracised who stole from his own. Relatives pay over-the-odds for supplies because they believe they will not be dumped a sub-standard quality or given low priority in respect of delivery-dates. In ways such as these the network of kinship can have an impact on the economic market. It is able to have this impact both because of inside information and because of the non-market attitudes which the network at once reinforces and into which it makes an input.

Ethnicity is often perceived as an extension of kinship. The parallel between blood narrow and blood broad is clear enough. So, importantly, is the similarity in the economic thrust that is observed. Thus a self-employed entrepreneur might want to staff his business with co-ethnics who share with him an emotive solidarity; while an enclave shopkeeper might be in a position to put up his prices because fellow-blacks prefer him to an Asian, fellow-Muslims prefer him to a Chinese. New immigrants often go to work for earlier migrants known in their country of origin: the mobility of labour is in that way smoothed, dishonesty deterred by the shame of a scandal. Savings are often shared (commonly through a rotating credit pool) in order to finance business expansion: elaborate legalities are not needed where the community is tightly-knit or where the kin who remain must make restitution for the defaulter who absconds. The economic significance of particularism and exclusivity must evidently not be written off nor ascribed status be made a vestige when compared with achievement. Whether the unassimilated Jews of pre-capitalist society, a displaced bourgeoisie like the Ugandan Asians, the community-based black economy of the Triads, the Yardies and the Mafia, what is clear is that tradition counts and that cultural understanding makes ethnicity a continuing source of social capital.

Ethnicity, interestingly, is the example cited by Loury when, in a workshop at the Massachusetts Institute of Technology in 1974, he was the second (after Jane Jacobs in 1961) to use the term 'social capital'. His subject was the fact that the earnings differentials of black Americans only partially reflect their personal competence and productive capacity. His contention was that a market failure had been brought about by cumulative discrimination and that the social background was a primary predictor: 'An individual's social origin has an obvious and important effect on the amount of resources that is ultimately invested in his or her development. It may thus be useful to employ a concept of "social capital" to represent the consequences of social position in facilitating acquisition of the standard human capital characteristics. ... This idea does have the advantage of forcing the analyst to consider the extent to which individual earnings are accounted for by social forces outside an individual's control.' (Loury, 1977:176).

Loury's point is about grouping, that 'people tend to group them-selves socially along racial lines' (Loury, 1977:159). The life-chances of black parents' offspring are adversely affected as a result. On the one hand the network of kinship and ethnicity offers lower-return contacts to the children of the victims than it does to the children of the pri-vileged. On the other hand the geographical community ghettoises potential meritocrats into the slum schooling to which even the more successful locals will be obliged to condemn their offspring. Past dis-crimination dominates present prospects. A deficit in skill and status is the consequence of the under-investment. Ethnically mixed neighbour-hoods, the busing of children to integrated schools, quotas in the universities, affirmative action at work, might all be the State's quick response to the social capital that never was.

(c)   The Locality

As with the ethnic community, so with the geographical community, the participation is on-going and the policing is face-to-face: 'Communities are social webs of people who know one another as persons and have a moral voice. Communities draw on interpersonal bonds to encourage members to abide by shared rules. . . . Communities gently chastise those who violate shared moral norms and express approbation for those who abide by them. They turn to the state (courts, police) only when all else fails.' (Etzioni, 1995:ix). The neighbourhood can be stifling, restrictive and judgemental, a threat to minorities (as where school prayers are made compulsory) and a licence for busybodies (as where moral suasion stamps out idiosyncratic dress). The neigh-bourhood can also be supportive, socialising and symbolic, a source of trust (as where reciprocation and reputation have been dependably confirmed over time) and an outlet for attachment (as where baby-sitting is regularly volunteered and random mugging is not). It is the conviction of the believer in the local network that moral anarchy is a more immediate threat than domineering repression. Here once again, it is Durkheim on moral education to whom the admirer of unbridled greed must presumably give way.

The local community is Bourdieu's '*réseau durable de relations*', Bourdieu's socialised atoms 'liés par des *liaisons* permanentes et utiles' (Bourdieu, 1980:2). The local community has a structural stability which makes even the gain-seeking present no more than a fleeting moment in a long-term accommodation. Multi-period pay-offs are not a synonym, Dore concludes, for absolute obligations and internalised commitments: 'Benevolence is a duty. Full stop.' (Dore, 1983:470). They are, however, a useful complement, as may be illustrated by the mutual insurance, the risk-sharing, the long-horizoned inter-indebtedness that develop so naturally in the traditional Japanese village: 'It is a calculation, perhaps, which comes naturally to a population which until recently was predominantly living in tightly nucleated hamlet communities in a land ravished by earthquake and typhoon. Traditionally, you set to, to help your neighbour rebuild his house after a fire, even though it might be two or three generations before yours was burnt down and your grandson needed the help returned.' (Dore, 1983:470). Dore writes: 'You could be *sure* that the help *would* be returned.' (Dore, 1983:470). The main reason is generalised dutifulness in the sense of Durkheim. The supporting reason is, however, the economic villager's neoclassical estimation that benevolence in a stable locality – in Burke's 'inns and resting-places' for the 'public affections', the 'unreasoned habits' (Burke:1790:315) – is indeed the highest-paying policy.

The local community imposes limits and prescribes responsibilities. It appeals in so doing to the frequency with which the right of one member will simultaneously be a claim on another. The right of the train-driver to refuse a drink-and-drugs test is the claim that his passengers ought to accept the higher safety-hazard. The right of the free-fall parachutist to take part in dangerous sports is the claim that bystanders can be exposed to injury and the insurance-pool be required to pay for healthcare. The local community, balancing one member's freedom against another member's externality, is clearly providing the sum total of its members with an education in collectivism. A who does not wear a seat-belt recklessly endangers the life of B's child. C who forgets his neighbourhood watch suffers guilt when D's deer are poached. The locality has a drama society, a tennis club, a school run, a hunt meeting, a Christmas raffle. In all of these ways it teaches its members that their day-to-day is shared with their fellows, that all are parts one of another.

Political devolution will presumably make a contribution to the tribal sense of self. So, less obviously, will advances in information technology that (a step in the direction of the decentralised society embedded without compromise in the global economy) are favourable to telecommuting and make possible the practice of working from home. Subsidies and tariffs can be used to prevent foreign competition from breaking down the mutual support of the long-lived *Gemeinschaft*. Bringing work to depressed areas can be more economical of scarce *social* capital than would be the geographical dislocation of labour. Placing public contracts in such a way as to perpetuate stable communities can be more conducive to the wealth of nations than would be the anonymity and isolation of relocation to new towns and high-rise estates. Science and policy, it is clear, can do much to defend the local community against a fragmenting individualism which might, in the long run, work against the efficiencies that accrue to engagement and familiarity.

(d)   The Business Network

There is a temptation to model business life in terms of the context-free unit negotiating the one-off deal. One individual buys one apple and disappears. One firm sells one orange once. No doubt the free-standing exchange does exist: consider the vendor with whom the tourist trades through the window of the train, the ice-cream salesman who will never be seen again. Often, however, there will be a past and a future that situate the relationship in history and make other people the walls of ego's shop. This section is concerned with three kinds of business network that circumscribe the transaction in time and space.

Across the exchanges there is the regular partner. A is known to work to schedule and to maintain acceptable standards. B is believed not to exploit the consumer's ignorance or to misrepresent opportunistically for gain. In cases such as these, repeat business may be expected as the satisficing response to sustained performance.

Competition through price-signalling is undoubtedly undermined by the complacency. Goodwill and habit making each firm a price-maker and a monopolist even in a multi-firm market, the buyer is put at risk of missing out on a cheaper product elsewhere. On the other hand, there are the clear advantages which accrue to a business relationship that (to employ Robert Solow's distinction) is more like a marriage than a one-night stand. A saving is made on the transaction costs of search and renegotiation. Supply (in the boom), demand (in the slump), is more likely to be secure. Planning of investment can proceed with a diminished degree of uncertainty. Information is made available, both on the industry and on the product itself. Trust is built up and serves to engender a not-unwarranted confidence: 'The butcher shows his benevolence by not taking advantage of the fact that the customer doesn't know rump from sirloin.' (Dore, 1983:475). Ronald Dore is convinced that such trustworthiness is essential for quality assurance in a quality-conscious society that experiences a division of expertise: 'You always *know* whether the butcher is charging you sixpence or sevenpence. But if you don't know the difference between sirloin and rump, and you think your guests might, then you *have* to trust your butcher: you have to depend on his benevolence.' (Dore, 1983:477). You *have* to trust your butcher. Competition through price-signalling might in the circumstances be a small enough sacrifice to make at the margin.

Looking to the future, Dore advances the hypothesis that frequent switches (to keep the price down) will give way to long-term relationships (to nurture the standard of service): 'Relational contracting is a phenomenon of affluence, a product, Hobhouse would say, of moral evolution. It is when people become better off and the market-stall haggle gives way to the world of *Which*, where best buys are defined more by quality than by price criteria, that relational contracting comes into its own.' (Dore, 1983:477). The give-and-take of the stable relationship eliminates so much of the organisational slack, the motivational slippage, the 'x-inefficiency', that the gains in the ability to plan, to cooperate, to minimise shrinkage, to maximise attachment might be more than enough to compensate for the allocative inefficiency that the withering away of cut-throat competition might bring in its wake. Besides that, Dore suggests, the movement from the confrontational to the relational might in itself be the satisfaction of a demand for sociability that enjoys a high income elasticity: 'When affluence reduces price pressures, any tendencies to prefer a relationship of friendly stability to the poker-game pleasures of adversarial bargaining – tendencies which might have been formerly suppressed by the anxious concern not to lose a precious penny – are able to assert themselves.' (Dore, 1983:477). Japanese markets are more quality-sensitive, less price-sensitive than are Britain's. Japanese people are less adversarial and less manipulative. In both of these ways, Dore suggests, Japanese long-termism is the harbinger of what in other countries too is very likely to come.

Long-term relationships between the buyer and the seller are complemented by same-side relationships between the buyers and the sellers themselves. Here once again there are settled networks that, transcending the current, the flexible and the spontaneous, coordinate the responses and solidify the coalition. Other-regarding conduct within the alliance is likely to be a consequence of the competitors' collaboration.

Legal contracts are always a problem: incomplete because of imperfect information, exposed because of an uncertain future, they are at best costly to enforce, at worst a mere statement of intent. Social capital has the advantage that, deriving precommitment from embeddedness, it economises on the adjudicator *ex machina* by means of an appeal to a self-enforcing endogeneity. The cartel brings the oligopolists together to harmonise their prices and avoid the deadweight cancelling-out of minus-sum marketing. The trade association diffuses intelligence about innovations and conditions and promotes personal contacts through social gatherings. The professional body makes itself the conservator of tradition and the regulator of standards. The trades union polices the occupational demarcations and stands in the way of Dutch auction under-cutting. Structured networks such as these coordinate same-side responses and do so without the inconvenience or the expense of the recourse to law.

The State can assist the networks to consolidate their hold. Thus it can exempt the cartel from restrictive practices legislation; it can delegate to the profession the control of new entry; it can stabilise through an incomes policy made in consultation with the federations of the unions and of the employers. The State, clearly, is in a position to empower repeated interaction and with it the group pressures that encourage compliance. Importantly, however, even private individuals can do much to embed their business interests in their social networks. One illustration would be the enduring ties that make possible cooperation and sub-contracting based on trustworthiness and dependability put repeatedly to the test. Another illustration would be hostage-taking.

King A is less likely to make war on King B where King A's daughter has been married off to King B's son. Country A is less likely to conduct a bombing raid on country B where country A's citizens are being used as human shields in country B's capital. Criminal A is less likely to expose a shooting committed by criminal B where criminal B has pre-purchased insurance in the form of a knifing committed by criminal A. What the king, the country and the criminal have in common is this, that the daughter, the citizens and the knifing are all being held as hostages against the threat of betrayal. Oliver Williamson is insistent that the pattern is a familiar one in the business life as well: 'Not only are the economic equivalents of hostages widely used to effect credible commitments, but failure to recognize the economic purposes served by hostages has been responsible for repeated policy error.' (Williamson, 1985:168). Exchange of share capital makes predatory pricing a suicidal option. Interlocking directorates ensure that competitors have a say in decision-making. Holding companies unify investments in a number of separate firms. Product-specific investment is a guarantee to franchisees that no competing franchisee will discredit the quality. The outcome is forbearance and transparency, honesty and allegiance. The outcome is ethics – but the reason is interest. The hostages taken, no rational capitalist would bankrupt a business dynasty into which his son or daughter had consented to wed.

The third kind of business network is to be found inside the organisation and not in its external linkages. The Weberian cog executes what the chart dictates. The self-interested employee has causes, preferences, goals and interpretations of his own. The multiple webs of friends and associates are the social resource on which he draws when he seeks to plot a course for himself at work.

Networks will often be the way into the job. Accumulated contacts snowballed through earlier employments are a common source of information on vacancies, opportunities, promotion-prospects, problem supervisors. Much of the information being personalised and impressionistic in character, it is arguably more efficient rather than less efficient for acquaintances to play an active role in the process of publicising and advising. Employers themselves will not be indifferent to the personal recommendation (an extension of which is the written reference or testimonial) of an associate who moves in the same circles, possibly worked with the candidate at an earlier stage in his career, and can certify that the applicant is a good bet. University degrees confirm trained proficiencies. They fail to pick up mendacity, Iscariotism and sheer bloody-mindedness. For that the employer must fall back on 'reputational capital' and the judgement of the peers.

The hiring completed, the new employee will be in a position to utilise his new networks in an attempt to flesh out the nature of the job. No contract is ever detailed enough to incorporate every aspect of every service or to anticipate future developments in the organisation and its work. In place of the *quid pro quo* that can never be fully written down, the contract will sometimes invoke ('such duties as may reasonably be assigned') the discretionary authority of the formal hierarchy. As with the minutes and the documents, however, so with the managers and the supervisors, it remains the prerogative of the networks to have a *de facto* impact on productivity that will be ignored at their peril by the profit-seekers *ex ante*. Zealots refer information upward that confirms their departmental bias while discarding as misleading the data that challenges their traditional filter. Squash partners share confidences across the organisational chart that ground rational choice in the haphazard logic of lunches, bar-sessions and rides home that Herbert Simon calls 'the patterns of who-talks-to-whom-how-often-about-what' (Simon, 1965:xx). Workmates employ diffuse pressures to standardise procedures, protect historic job-descriptions and regulate the pace of work. The new employee will read his 'Terms and Conditions' in the light of the coffee-room. He will be struck by how much the nature of the job is a matter of convention that his confederates even more than his managers will be in a position to explain to him.

Debts of honour, habitual practices and interlocking coteries are reinforced by lifetime tenure and promotion by seniority. Long attach-ment strengthens the intra-organisational network and confirms the conservative nature of its bias. More affectually, the extended commit-ment also provides an outlet for self-motivated cooperation, personal pride in a job well done, a strong sense of community, an identification with the whole which radically differentiates the stable workplace from the revolving-door job-hopping of sequential contracting. The career structure and the perception of job security as a property-right might reduce worker-alienation and class conflict to such an extent that it would make sound economic sense for the State to legislate in favour of continuity (by making redundancies and dismissals more difficult) and against short-termism (by guaranteeing leave for maternity and sick-ness). It is an unaccustomed inference that *lack* of competition might do more for assiduity and quality than would the free-market incentives of short-term gain. It is, however, an inference that no student of cap-italism can afford to neglect merely because it builds in a guarded defence of rigidity. As Ronald Dore writes: 'It might be *because of*, and not *in spite of* relational contracting that Japan has a better growth performance than the rest of us.' (Dore, 1983:473). History has yet to pronounce its final verdict on the Japanese model. If, however, Dore is right, then the low turnover and the shared understandings of the stable organisation would illustrate yet again the economic value of the busi-ness network that is a home in time and space.

(e)   The Property Nexus

Capitalism always depends on the existence of private property. Capit-alism often benefits from the support of social capital. On the one hand there is the private profit-seeking. On the other hand there is the social embeddedness. It is possible that there is a direct trade-off between the two modes of investment. It is possible, more specifically, that the par-tial collectivisation of titles might be a part of the empowerment of the social without which the capitalist market might be condemned to sub-standard performance.

Thus the involvement in the system of the functionless *rentier*, the absentee shareholder, the exploitative surplus-maximiser might reduce the extent to which the private business can appeal to collaboration, loyalty and shop-floor initiative such as transcend the personal stake of the worker in high pay and low exertion. Tawney was especially clear in his own mind that improved *morale* and the professionalisation of industry waited upon the destruction of the magnet that made all the clocks untrue: 'The first condition of enlisting on the side of construct-ive work the professional feeling which is now apathetic, or even hostile to it, is to secure that, when it is given, its results accrue to the public, not to the owner of property in capital, in land, or in other resources.' (Tawney, 1921:146). Tawney was a socialist and a conservative. He believed that a truly integrated society was a theoretical impossibility so long as the nation's capital remained at the disposal of a profit-seeking sub-set that was a class apart.

The State socialist's response to the presumed corrosive of compet-itive acquisitiveness would be purposive planning and public-sector monopolies. Such an administration of assets would deliver the plus of conservatism while at the same time eliminating the minus of capital-ism. The market socialist would, in contrast, wish to retain the gain-seeking while nonetheless suppressing the free riding which, perceived by the labour-force as the capitalists' entitlement to a private tax, can be the focus for resentment and the cause of division. One option would be profit-seeking competition between State-owned businesses, capit-alist in every respect save for the fact that the employees alone have a share in the returns. Another option would be to construct a socialist capitalism of producer-cooperatives, each one a workers' collective that is the sole titulary of its own property-rights. Assuming that the separation of ownership and labour-power is indeed a serious challenge to social unity, market socialism would solve the problem of the class divide without impelling the abandonment of capitalism's core. Market socialism could in that sense be regarded not as an alternative to but as the basis for a capitalism that is also conservative. The same function would, of course, be fulfilled by a wide dispersion of share-ownership in consequence of growing affluence (accelerated, perhaps, by targeted privatisation and investment-income exemptions). It should also be recorded that what the socialists call justifiable resentment would be called low self-esteem, levelling down and self-pity by other intellectual traditions in the community.

The office-worker withdraws behind a novel when the boss is not looking. The ticket-seller makes a secret second income as a tout. Socialists would explain the uneconomic detachment that is shown in cases like these in terms of a property-based contradiction which prevents social capital from doing its best for the capitalist system. A more moderate assessment would concentrate not on profit-seeking but on power. Tawney himself made consultation and responsibility – and not simply the Marxian notion of the surplus from labour unjustly creamed off – an essential characteristic of his hoped-for future: 'It is idle to expect that men will give their best to any system which they do not trust, or that they will trust any system in the control of which they do not share.' (Tawney, 1921:149). It is possible that consultation and responsibility would give the ordinary employee the feeling of involvement that he requires if he is to emancipate himself from the conviction that, cannon-fodder for an uncaring commander, there is no personal incentive for him to abstain from idleness or to eschew undetected theft.

Labour can become involved in business decision-making through works-councils and assemblies, shop-stewards and union-directorships. Labour can also allow its interests to be represented by the State. Minimum-wage laws, health-and-safety acts, on-the-job training provisions, all give the workers countervailing claims *vis-à-vis* their firms. Power-sharing can be a cause of perceived justice and of mutual trust. Where the consequence is a strengthened attachment, the by-product is likely to be an improvement in productivity that testifies to the economic value of the empowerment of the social.

The welfare State too can have a beneficial impact on the development of social capital. Here once again, it can be contended, it is the function of the non-market nexus to make social relationships that much healthier and more welcoming.

Richard Titmuss saw welfare services like health, education, public housing and income maintenance as the practical embodiment of a consensus that cares: 'All collectively provided services are deliberately designed to meet certain socially recognized "needs"; they are manifestations, first, of society's will to survive as an organic whole and, secondly, of the expressed wish of all the people to assist the survival of some people.' (Titmuss, 1963:39). The organicism and the unity are the foundation for the institutions. They are also the consequence – an outcome as well as a cause of the common welfare experience that the preexistent integration had helped so greatly to bring into being. Titmuss believed that welfare policy was different from economic policy precisely because the market dissolves and reduces whereas, in respect of the socio-political gift, 'what unites it with ethical considerations is its focus on integrative systems: on processes, transactions and institutions which promote an individual's sense of identity, participation and community and allow him more freedom of choice for the expression of altruism and which, simultaneously, discourage a sense of individual alienation'. (Titmuss, 1970:253). Titmuss welcomed the welfare services not only because of their explicit charter but because of their hidden curriculum. Sensitising the atom to the stranger, they make possible a generalised spillover from which even the private sector can derive a benefit: 'Altruism in giving to a stranger does not begin and end with blood donations. It may touch every aspect of life and affect the whole fabric of values.' (Titmuss, 1970:223). Capitalists who want their workforce to be reliable and fair would in the circumstances be well advised to give strong support to welfare services that are the effect and cause of a consensus that cares.

The welfare State builds up the moral muscles that make the community something more than the sum of its sales: 'We want to see a health service developing which will not be separate and aloof from the life of the nation but an expression and reinforcement of national unity.' (Titmuss, 1964:214). The atrophy of the welfare State puts at risk the habit-forming role-plays that are the source of ethical externality by virtue of learning by doing: 'It is likely that a decline in the spirit of altruism in one sphere of human activities will be accompanied by similar changes in attitudes, motives and relationships in other spheres.' (Titmuss, 1970:224). It was Titmuss's practice, in common with other macro-sociologists and other social democrats, to treat the whole nation as his structured network. To him, social capital was effectively coterminous with citizenship. He sought to use the welfare State to make the commonalty of nationhood a genuinely *social* capital and not merely a passport legalism.

Sceptics will regard it as an exaggeration to derive market-sector truthfulness from blood donation, purified of conflict of interest; or to expect that boss and worker will necessarily develop a cordial One Nation regard as a consequence of adjacent beds in a National Health hospital. Critics will object that there is more of paternalism than of altruism in merit goods provided by a professional and political elite; that a passive clientele guaranteed a regular feed will lose the habit of hunting for itself; that moral hazard is the inevitable concomitant of dentistry on demand and abortion as a cost-effective morning-after. Opponents will state that taxation is forced whereas true charity must always be a voluntary choice; that the prosperous and successful are obliged to make a supplementary sacrifice at a higher rate even where they cannot share the taste for relief in *combination* with levelling; that welfare is no more than economic self-interest where all classes utilise the schools and the hospitals without a means-test and where even today's rich appreciate that there is little private insurance against tomorrow's ever-possible destitution. Titmuss's contention, that non-commercial welfare was a significant architect of network unification, will clearly not command anything like universal acceptance. It is, on the other hand, a valuable reminder that situations shape relationships and influence social capital.

(f)   Church and School

Karl Marx, in the very year of the *Origin of Species*, expressed a funda-mental lack of faith in free-standing ideas and high-minded precepts. Material reality, Marx said, is the *primum mobile*, while the philosopher can only be the reporter who arrives *post festum* on the scene: 'The mode of production of material life conditions the general process of social, political and intellectual life. It is not the consciousness of men that determines their existence, but their social existence that deter-mines their consciousness.' (Marx, 1859:425). Galbraith at the height of the Cold War was able to say something similar about the convergence in economic systems – 'Much of what happens is inevitable and the same' (Galbraith, 1967:388) – that would, he predicted, be the direct consequence of the momentum inherent in matter: 'The imperatives of technology and organization, not the images of ideology, are what determine the shape of economic society.' (Galbraith, 1967:26). Both Marx and Galbraith believed strongly in the power of perception: it is class *consciousness* in the Marxian model that brings about the prolet-arian revolution, social-democratic *values* in the work of Galbraith that make more and more likely the election of a Kennedy and not the tri-umph of a Thatcher. Neither Marx nor Galbraith, however, was of the opinion that ideas and precepts could ever be strong enough to reverse a major development that had been brought about by economics. Not the cause but the consequence, manifesto-commitments to the one determinist as to the other were little more than actors in a drama that they did not script.

Determinists such as Marx and Galbraith would look askance at a section such as the present one which treats church and school as investing agencies which build up the social capital. Determinists would say that religion and education can indeed disseminate an existing belief-system; but that preaching and teaching simply lack the power to plant a countervailing ideology where the external environment is not a propitious one. The work ethic and deferred gratification, made compulsory by the conditions of survival in *laissez-faire* capitalism, will take root and thrive. Money termed the 'root of all evil' and a revulsion towards profit-seeking will be as out of place as a pig in a drawing-room. It is no surprise in the circumstances that chapels without clients are being converted into flats for stockbrokers while the intellectual is becoming not an opinion-leader and a role-model but a figure of fun.

Determinists are not convinced that church and school can add significantly to the constraint that makes capitalism a *conservative* system even as it is also a dynamic one. Idealists are more hopeful. Arguing that ideas have consequences, they take the view that the lecturing institutions serve to repair and rebuild the nation's scarce stock of normative capital. More hopeful still are the social interactionists. Persuaded that the churches and schools are social networks and not just listening-places, they see in the learning experience the function of community-formation which is a function apart from the content of the sermons and the lessons *per se*. In considering the contribution of church and school to social capital, it would be an error to concentrate with the determinists on the letter of the law while neglecting the replications and affiliations that are its standard support.

Religions are old. Rooted in the past and conservative by nature, they are the recorded response to a pre-capitalist world. That response is often an unfamiliar one to the present-day individualist who has invested greedily in acquisitive self-interest. The Hindu criticises materialism and mortifies the flesh. The Buddhist practises meditation and trusts to his begging-bowl. The Christian derives human equality from the Creator's equal love and makes himself the good steward who carries out the ultimate property-owner's revealed intent. Passivity, fatalism, withdrawal, service – the substitution of responsibility for affluence and self-development for self-indulgence may raise the moral tone of the social ethos but it *prima facie* contributes little to the accelerated expansion of the profit-seeking system.

Wealth-maximisation, Marx indicated, becomes under capitalism a quasi-religious imperative: 'Accumulate, accumulate! That is Moses and the prophets!' (Marx, 1867:595). As 'accumulation for accumulation's sake' becomes the new sacred text, so, it is implied, will 'Moses and the prophets' be guided as if by an invisible hand into the archive of the dysfunctional, the discarded and the out-of-date. Even the Marxians, however, recognise that religion retains a residual role that is both a support to the capitalist system and a measure of its spiritual inadequacies. On the one hand there is the social-control function of a palliative and a comforter that absorbs the pain: 'Religion is the sigh of the oppressed creature, the sentiment of a heartless world, and the soul of soulless conditions. It is the *opium* of the people.' (Marx, 1844a:43–4). On the other hand there is the *memento mori* of the felt incompatibility between the Godliness of the ideal and the spiritual impoverishment of the class-alienated economy: '*Man makes religion*; religion does not make man. . . . The abolition of religion as the *illusory* happiness of men, is a demand for their *real* happiness. The call to abandon their illusions about their condition is a *call to abandon a condition which requires illusions*.' (Marx, 1844a:43, 44). Marxians, although atheists, see in religion both a protective purpose (that of the tranquilliser that pacifies the for-sale self) and a self-transcending function (teaching as it does that the Creator makes a benevolent transfer and that Paradise is a communistic community). The Marxians treat religion both as intellectual support and as countervailing dogma. In the one way as in the other, it is clear, they are expressing the belief that 'Moses and the prophets' continue to be of practical importance in a capitalism that is also conservative.

Religious teachings can inhibit capitalist expansion. One illustration would be Jesus on the prohibition of usury: 'If you lend only where you expect to be repaid, what credit is that to you?. . . . Be compassionate as your Father is compassionate.' (Luke 6:35, 36). Another illustration would be Jesus on the conflict of interest: 'You cannot serve God and Money.' (Luke 16:13). Passages such as these would seem to suggest that capitalism, 'not so much un-Christian as anti-Christian' (Tawney, 1937:170), will be braked into a crawl by the Bible readings and the prayer-meetings. Yet religious teachings, far from inhibiting capitalist expansion, can actually accelerate it. Max Weber's correlation of commercial success with Calvinist Christianity is an important demonstration of the unintended but very real connection. Calvinism as a theological system stressed the value of empiricism (to discover God's will in God's works), rationality (to economise efficiently on the Maker's allocated endowment), diligence (to serve the Divine purpose through this-worldly labour in a calling), thrift (in preference to consumerist self-indulgence, inappropriate to an ascetic in a veil of tears), individualism (in preference to membership and brotherhood, a real risk where a neighbour might be a sinner predestined to be damned). Weber does not say that Calvinism created capitalism. What he does say is that the *Geist* of Calvinism corresponds closely to the *Geist* of capitalism – and that real-world outcomes strongly support the tentative conjectures: 'Business leaders and owners of capital...are overwhelmingly Protestant.' (Weber, 1904–5:35). If Weber is right, then the conclusion must be that the transition from acquisition through piracy to acquisition through book-keeping was very much smoothed by the new intellectual system of the Reformation in Geneva.

Religions teach an intellectual system. They also police the norms. The enforcement alongside the transmission function is captured by Tawney in his demonstration that the sacred can constrain through external discipline and need not wait upon the discretion of the individual conscience: 'Calvin...made Geneva a city of glass, in which every household lived its life under the supervision of a spiritual police.' (Tawney, 1926:125). It was God's will that man should eschew ostentation and luxury, should espouse labour and thrift. It was the community's duty to ensure that the fallen God-fearer should cleave to the path that the Good Shepherd had prescribed. Thus did belonging reinforce ethics and circumscribe the choices of the communicant with a temptation to defect.

Religion can be as monolithic as a monopoly church that takes upon itself the propagation of a single perspective. Religion can also be as heterogeneous as a perfect market in sects, each of them in competition with the others for adherents, none of them large enough to split the nation into an Ulster, an India or a Palestine. David Hume was in favour of a nationalised establishment, Adam Smith of safety in numbers. Laurence Iannaccone, judging between the two, is in no doubt that the evidence lends the stronger support to the proposal for multiple outlets and to the automaticity of the invisible hand: 'Combine the typical sect's comprehensive behavioral guidelines with its members' high levels of commitment and participation; add extensive monitoring and sanctions, both formal and informal; and one arrives at a very effective means of constraining opportunistic behavior and transmitting values to children.' (Iannaccone, 1997:109). The sects may be more effective than the Church, but the functions still share a family resemblance: 'They assist those who suffer financial setbacks and ill health. Their social networks help members form joint business ventures, establish long-term friendships, and find suitable marriage partners.... They also provide information about an individual's reliability and credit-worthiness.' (Iannaccone, 1997:109). Closed denomination or simply local parish, the faith-based community serves to perpetuate traditional standards and to empower embeddedness that keeps selfish maximisation in check.

Religious associations are cultural corporations that teach and police. So are the educational institutions. They too disseminate a custom-bound value-system – and do so within the framework of a sub-group, a network, a face-to-face pool.

At the level of the intellect, the schools typically enjoy the social privilege of distinguishing authoritatively between normalcy and deviance. The schools typically endorse the values of self-reliance and personal responsibility, meritocratic achievement and payment by results, deferred gratification and the telescopic vision, respect for hierarchy and the legitimacy of control. In ways such as these the investment in credentialism may be said to be an investment in the reproduction of *social* capitalism and not just in productive skills (in *human* capital) *per se*. Progressive education, education that concentrates on self-development, education that eulogises the immobility of birth, education that condemns the circulation of elites will probably be that much less functional for a dynamic economy that relies on specific attitudes to ensure its efficient performance. It is likely in addition to be the persons already socialised into the attitudinal capital who will be the most active in investing successfully in the certificates and qualifications that will give them superior access to the higher rungs of the occupational ladder. This order of precedence is one reason why people from bourgeois backgrounds are often disproportionately represented in formal education *and* in the top jobs to which the ambitious, the acquisitive and the materialistic will be especially motivated to aspire.

The schools inculcate attitudes. They also supply structures. The interdependence, reinforcing the ideas, is an important part of the joint product which formal education inputs into the legitimation of the 'We' that limits the freedom of the 'I' to break with the past. At one level there is the lifetime stock of friends and contacts that, old boys bound together by the school-tie and later by the Club, provides a small-group incentive to keep in good repair the profitable reputation for loyalty and reliability that was won (even before the Regiment) on the playing-fields and on the river. At another level there is the shared experience of the schooling itself. Durkheim emphasises that the acceptance of interpenetration is in no small measure a conditioned reflex: 'To appreciate social life to the point where one cannot do without it, one must have developed the habit of acting and thinking in common.' (Durkheim, 1925:233). Durkheim looks to the schools to teach young persons how it feels to live and breathe as a part of a group.

Thus the school should treat as strictly instrumental the mechanistic logic of abstract mathematics that reduces the whole to the sum of the parts. The school, to prevent individual isolation and social *anomie*, should also treat as subordinate and problematic the Rousseauist drawing out of the innate *Emile*, the libertarian *freedom from* that acknowledges no master but the self: 'The theories that celebrate the beneficence of unrestricted liberties are apologies for a diseased state.' (Durkheim, 1925:54). In place of a curriculum that serves as a eulogy for the factored-down, the schools should concentrate on subjects like biology and history which demonstrate the persistence of aggregates and the unity of collectivities. Team sports channel self-interest into collaboration. The class discussion of a novel or poem is favourable both to empathetic understanding and to the common impulse. Punishments and rewards going to the whole and not to the part remind even the meritocrat that 'to a certain extent he is working for everybody and everybody is working for him' (Durkheim, 1925:246). Essays from past years can be put on display. Cohorts of alumni can be invited back to continuing rituals like annual dinners. In ways such as these, Durkheim believed, the school can educate the child in the moderation of desires and the attachment to groups: 'If man is to be a moral being, he must be devoted to something other than himself; he must feel at one with a society, however lowly it may be.' (Durkheim, 1925:79).

Durkheim's proposals can be augmented with others. Peer-group tutoring could make children more supportive. Cross-cultural education could improve sensitivity to alternative modes of expression and self-presentation. Role-play and role-reversal could enrich the network through a first-hand appreciation of what it means for a black to be a pink and a man to be a woman. Non-competitive assessment could break down the barriers that jealousy, anxiety, and fear of failure so often put in the way of spontaneous mixing. Constructive imitation could be fostered through a screening of *The Life of Mother Teresa* and not of *Reservoir Dogs*. A school choir and a social-service society could be organised to facilitate the *collective* use of leisure.

Nor should it be forgotten that the Government too has the opportunity to become involved in network-making through education. The State can legislate for comprehensive education in order to countervail the divisiveness of class. The State can insist on a common curriculum in order to guarantee a common culture. The State can re-house the less-privileged in order to make the school catchments that much more cross-sectional. Accusations there will undoubtedly be of propaganda, repression and brainwashing. Recognising that there will never be a need for the social engineers to produce a state of affairs that the invisible hand would have produced in any case, the charges will not be without foundation. The real point is, however, this. Education is a topic in the empowerment of the social. A nation that wants to expand its stock of social capital has a democratic right to ask its State to contribute to its campaign. What would matter in such a case would be the principal and not the agent. So long as it is the consensus that takes the lead, State intervention need not mean the transcendence of the social rather than the reinforcement of which it is the cause and the effect.

9.3 UNSOCIAL CAPITAL

The preceding chapter, 'The Ethical Constraint', was concerned with the intellectual construct of attitudinal capital. It showed that the altruistic imperative and other moral impulsions could have an economic payoff that made a commandment into the means to an end. The present chapter, 'Structure as Capital', has turned its attention to the inter-personal basis upon which the embedded absolutes must rely for support. It has shown that the thicket of relationships can serve to develop and enforce a range of binding standards which can contribute in their turn to the rate of economic growth. The preceding chapter was about fitting in and self-restraint. The present chapter has been about integration and solidarity. Both chapters have been positive about the wealth of nations. The reader who is favourably disposed to moral limits, to social bonds *and* to economic affluence may in the circumstances be excused if he comes up for breath with a smile on his face.

The case, however, is not open-and-shut, the optimism for that reason premature. Moral philosophy can build with some confidence on the strength of its universals and its generalisations. Market economics, on the other hand, is forever the creature of its relatives, its contingencies and its shifting sands. What this means in practice is that the impartial observer, proceeding empirically, reacting pragmatically, is unlikely to arrive at a single cast-iron eternality either about the guidelines or about the networks. Different situations will suggest different inferences. That which raises economic productivity in ancient Greece might lower economic productivity in modern Rome.

The past puts signposts in the void. The market, on the other hand, is forever the merchant of doubt. Conservative capitalism, a mixed ethos, combines the certainty of one parent with the agnosticism of the other. All that can be predicted about the backward-looking future is that there might well be a wealth-retarding as well as a wealth-enhancing side to its ethics and to its structures. It is the task of this section to examine the three theses in terms of which it would be correct for the theorist of conservative capitalism to speak not of social but of *unsocial* capital.

The *first* thesis is that the content of the conservatism will not always be conducive to the full flowering of capitalism's potential. Consider the monk who, conforming to a régime of berries, roots and books, seeks his contentment in meditation and not in property-expanding hedonism: 'Labor was something which distracted the monk from concentration upon the contemplated value of salvation.' (Weber, 1948:332). Consider the mystic who, ascetic like the Calvinist, channels his self-abnegation into the flight from the world and not into its mastery: 'He proves himself *against* the world, against his action in the world.... The creature must be silent so that God may speak.' (Weber, 1948:326). Consider the mandarin who, scholarly, learned and rounded, is disposed both to put harmonious arrangement above economic control and to stand against the social distance of private maximisation: 'There was the typical aversion against too sharp a social differentiation as determined in a purely economic manner by free exchange in markets.' (Weber, 1948:441). Consider the Hindu who, sensitive to symbol and attracted by *stasis*, accepts without question the hereditary barriers of caste that rule out the adaptiveness of occupational mobility and the concentration of labour in a workshop *de facto* mixed: 'A ritual law in which every change of occupation, every change in work technique, could result in ritual degradation is certainly not capable of giving birth to economic and technical revolutions from within itself, or even of facilitating the first germination of capitalism in its midst.' (Weber, 1948:413). What is demonstrated by these four illustrations from Max Weber is that to be backward-looking will not always be the same as to be capitalistic. In all four of these cases the values and the peers that tribalise the religious community will lend their full support to a world-view which is eminently at variance with goods, gain-seeking and innovation.

As with certain kinds of religion, so with certain kinds of socialism. Thus the classical Marxist will have little sympathy with the law of contract and the labour–capital divide: alienation, exploitation, false consciousness, subsistence pay, must all be the consequence of private ownership and profit, while the minimal State will be seen as the bourgeois class, bent on accumulation and indifferent to justice. The economic planner, again, will trade in an ethos, and with a network, which puts science above *tâtonnement*, tariffs above surprises, directive above competition, incomes policy above supply and demand: attracted by professionals and bureaucrats in possession of future facts, repelled by uncoordinated speculators who duplicate and waste, the wise leader will approximate management to administration and will treat as an investment in predictability the anti-capitalistic conservatism that finds its expression in risk-avoidance, corporatism, knee-jerk reordering, job-protection, the maximisation of the quiet life. The social leveller, finally, will have strong reservations about any commitment to equal liberty which does not, narrowing the relativities and redistributing the prizes, mean an equal *economic* command as well: as prepared to level down the successful as to universalise the best, the egalitarian will want to tax inheritance (thereby weakening the inter-generational conservatism of the self-perpetuating family), above-average earnings (despite the disincentive to market success of near-confiscation and the politics of envy) and academic excellence (despite the under-development of IQ and genes that is deemed the necessary handicap to upgrade the self-esteem and self-confidence of the academically second-rate). Where ownership and profit, competition and search, incentive and achievement are the functional prerequisites for the capitalist future, those kinds of socialism which challenge the system's logic may be said to be incompatible with the full flowering of capitalism's potential.

The ecstasy of the Dervish and the collectivism of the *phalanstère* do not bring out the best in the capitalist system. The same, more surprisingly, may also be true of pure *freedom from*. Market liberty is the world of personal autonomy, economic valuation, voluntary action, inalienable rights, individual choice, rational estimation, consumer sovereignty, meritocratic remuneration. It is a world of pluralism, variety, privacy, mobility, transformation, utility, a world in which the axial principle is the absence of coercion and not the enhancement of the whole. Market liberty is a world in which past traditions legitimate present contracts – but in which the values and structures to be perpetuated are resolutely private, deliberately non-communitarian. The market is itself a conservative construct, an inherited convention and not a creation *ab initio*. The market is itself conservative. Perhaps, however, it must be embedded in thicker conservatism still if it is to maximise its contribution to the capitalist economy. John Gray is only one pro-capitalist among many who has been critical of thin-context *freedom from* for emphasising emancipation without its complement in culture.

Gray is concerned about the neglect of the under-privileged and the indifference to the future. Convinced that well-being depends on community and not just on pleasure, he has written as follows about a one-dimensional libertarianism too fragile to support the weight of real-world free enterprise: 'Though human beings need a sphere of independent action, and so of liberty, if they are to flourish, their deepest need is a home, a network of common practices and inherited traditions that confers on them the blessing of a settled identity. Indeed, without the undergirding support of a framework of common culture, the freedom of the individual so cherished by liberalism is of little value, and will not long survive.' (Gray, 1993:125). Gray is no admirer of the Stalinist Plan, and neither is he an advocate of permissive self-determination. Capitalism, he believes, must be conservative if it is to be stable. The conservatism that it requires must be thicker still than the passive pass-through of blinkered individualism that starts from here.

The first thesis relates to a content that is inappropriate. The *second* thesis concerns a constraint that has become excessive. The second thesis argues that social capital can rust into unsocial capital once the morals and the networks have passed into the range of diminishing returns.

Thus altruism itself can be a two-edged sword. Blood is donated to help unknown strangers and money is spent on food for the vulnerable. Gifts such as these can complement the capitalist market. Other gifts are more of a threat. Parental subsidies, like State subsidies, can lead to an over-production of skilled manpower. Unemployment benefits can prolong the period spent searching wastefully for a reference-wage that has died out with deskilling and liberalisation. Sentimental attachment, emotive and backward-looking, can postpone the modernisation of a low-efficiency supplier. Compulsive hoarding to fund a potlatch might starve the economy of manufacturing capacity. Excessive saving to fund a bequest might cause future legatees to withdraw altogether from productive work. What is illustrated by these examples is that conservatism, clearly, can weaken capitalism and need not reinforce it.

The micro–macro duality is a common cause of the trade-off between duty and performance. Where there is voluntary wage restraint, the unions that most directly serve the interests of their subscription-payers are those that supply the public bad of inflation even at the cost of the pension-cuts, the tax-rises, the slow growth that will be the spin-off consequences of a private contract honourably executed. Where there is a tradition of corporate philanthropy, the managements that least effectively fulfil their obligations to their shareholders are those that fund the arts without the principals' permission or offer supra-competitive pay to the poorest grades out of the profits needed for re-tooling and re-investment. Where there is a convention of 'honour among thieves', the cooperators in a restraint of trade are fiercely loyal to their fellow-conspirators despite the imperfection that their manipulation of price will introduce into the market's automaticity. Talking ethics, there is in these cases a *prima facie* conflict between the micro-duty within and the macro-duty without. Talking economics, there is a threat to performance as well that Hayek attributes to the ultimate in non-functional conservatism: 'I believe that an atavistic longing after the life of the noble savage is the main source of the collectivist tradition.' (Hayek, 1988:19).

In the tribal troop, Hayek writes, it was mutual aid, not private property, that kept the comrades alive: 'An isolated man would soon have been a dead man. The primitive individualism described by Thomas Hobbes is hence a myth. The savage is not solitary.' (Hayek, 1988:12). In the extended order, he continues, it is a different code – '"social" should really be called "anti-social"' (Hayek, 1988:118) – that is the precondition for progress: 'Not only does all evolution rest on competition; continuing competition is necessary even to preserve existing achievements.' (Hayek, 1988:26). Hayek is not saying that self-sacrifice is *ipso facto* a brake on capitalist development. What he is saying is that self-denial grown excessive must impede the discovery process and therewith the rise in living-standards. Cost-pushing unions, philanthropic executives, oligopolistic brotherhoods all illustrate the threat to performance that Hayek identifies in the solidaristic band.

Excessive networking, like excessive obligation, can add a dysfunctional dimension to the capitalist system. Kinship is a case in point. The family, on the positive side, is an institution with a past and a future. It has an expectation of truth-telling; it inculcates mutual trust; it settles disagreements peacefully. Yet there is a negative side as well. Appointment by consanguinity perpetuates the dynasty but can also mean the business leadership of a non-professional management. Blood-exclusiveness can be a constraint on size that prevents small firms from going multinational or even going public. An obsession with the next generation's patrimony can lead to safety-seeking investment that limits the supply of venture capital. Inward-looking familism can put at risk the wider civic commitment: the family that looks after its own might see no need to contribute to charity (or even to avoid the spillover of litter). Intermarried kin groups can plan whole sectors without the State: even where individual companies are legally separate, the families at the top have a common loyalty. Intermarried kin groups can deter predatory raids simply because they monopolise a controlling interest: where (as in the Korean *chaebol* such as Hyundai) the shares are regarded as a family's collective non-tradeable, even competitive under-performance need not put an inefficient management at risk from an outside take-over. What follows from all of this is a message that is as clear as the structuration to which it relates is excessive. Some contextualisation can condition other-regarding reflexes and integrate the wealth-seeker in a multi-generational whole. Too much contextualisation, however, can be the road to the fossilisation of the unimaginative that is not so much the precondition for the capitalist system as its imminent negation.

Fossilisation, indeed, is the greatest threat to be expected from conservatism in over-supply. The tyranny of the sub-standard is brought sharply into focus in Marshall's example of wood-carvers in the Tyrol, tradition-bound forever to 'crude, ill-shaped reproductions of a pattern that has been set to them': 'An inquiry as to such a load evoked the answer – "Before our father died, he taught us to make horses like this, and we cannot venture on anything new". The horses' necks were all bent in the same impossible and ugly curve.' (Marshall, 1919:808). Such a perpetuation of a rubber-stamped *status quo* is at variance with the ethos of experimentation, initiative and improvement that is market capitalism's distinctive and revolutionary characteristic. It is, however, a form of unsocial capital which was not unknown in Marshall's own conventionalism, or in any settled capitalism which takes pride in its inter-temporal identity. Promotion as a long-service reward precommits the business to a skill-stock which only slowly adapts. Reflex-action cronyism builds wasteful inertia into the process of search. Unchanging routines nourish organisational cliques and stifle the free flow of mould-breaking ideas. Loyalty to the family-surrogate corporation reduces the likelihood that strikes and exits will be employed to produce the market-clearing wage. Just as identifiable attitudes and structures can be unsuited to capitalism, so, it is clear, can even *social* capital turn malign and unsocial once it has passed into the range of diminishing returns.

The *third* thesis relates to a capital that is unsocial because it is too costly. Neither inappropriate in itself nor excessive in its quantity supplied, still the asset-stock is here found wanting by the strictest capitalist standard of all. It is more expensive than the commercial alternative that is its next-best forgone.

Trust makes agreements self-enforcing. Completion bonds, pre-nuptial contracts, law-courts, barristers, suits and compensation fulfil a close-substituting function. Honesty is the antidote to crime. So are locks, security-guards, dogs, computerised data-banks (to boost the probability of detection) and longer prison-sentences (to raise the price charged per offence). Ethical self-policing can add value to the capitalist process. Economics itself, however, can buy and sell its own protective binding. Ethics in this perspective does not so much correct a market failure as take the place of a market-sector corrective. No doubt it is economical for it to do so – where the cost–benefit ratio proves it to be the better buy. Where the accountant complains that the morals do not pay, there, of course, it would make financial sense to bind capitalism with capitalism alone while making of conservatism no more than a sentimental recreation.

Within a structure as within a mindset, there is once again a comparison that need not be an obvious one. The network monitors standards (but the cultural discipline may mean organisational slack and a work-rhythm which is uneconomically slow). The market sells supervision (but the countervailing power necessitates a supplementary cost while the salaried enforcers may fall victim to regulatory capture). The network polices truth-telling (but it may do so with reference to outdated schemata and self-perpetuating prejudices). The market polices truth-telling (but the second opinion involves an expense while laboratory-testing builds in a wait). The network, in other words, copes with uncertainty by means of inter-personal pressures – and the market satisfies the same imperative through the recourse to supply and demand. Unknowledge, here as elsewhere, is the primary obstacle to successful economising: 'Opportunism is of no account in the face of unbounded rationality.' (Williamson, 1985:66). That said, there is no reason to think that the structure will deliver the benefits more economically than will the sale. Transaction costs are always specific and never general. The economist in the circumstances would do well to treat each case on its own merits alone.

The model is Coase and Simon on organisation versus bargain. Coase is *ex ante* open-minded about the precise point at which in-house production becomes more profitable than would be successive buying-in at the going market price: 'A firm will tend to expand until the costs of organizing an extra transaction within the firm become equal to the costs of carrying out the same transaction by means of an exchange on the open market or the costs of organizing in another firm.' (Coase, 1937:44). Simon too adopts a look-and-see attitude to bureaucracy, hierarchy and internalisation on the basis of his recognition that the ability of individuals to receive, store, process and retrieve information is itself stranded somewhere on the middle ground: 'It is only because individual human beings are limited in knowledge, foresight, skill, and time that organizations are useful instruments for the achievement of human purpose.' (Simon, 1957:199). As with the organisations *per se*, so with the mindsets and the networks that can contribute so much to economic progress – and can so frequently stand in its way. Pragmatism is the rule. Relative price is all.

Economic institutions, Williamson writes, 'have the main purpose and effect of economizing on transaction costs' (Williamson, 1985:1). Economising is the key. Where the costliness of people rises above the costliness of commerce, at that point does social capital turn into unsocial capital for no other reason than the fact that it has lost its competitive edge. This does not mean that some ethics and some structure should not continue to be purchased, only that conservatism might be a luxury that is paid for out of a successful capitalism for which the market and not the embeddedness will deservedly claim the lion's share of the credit.

10 Conclusion

The subject of this book has been conservative capitalism. It has sought to show that the past is embedded in the present even of history's most future-orientated economic system. Chapters 2 and 3 made much of extrapolation and expectation, Chapters 8 and 9 of acquired mindsets and habitual networks. Chapter 4 argued that economy is anchored in society, Chapter 5 that society is governed by convention, Chapter 6 that both society and convention evolve gradually over time. Chapter 7 suggested that methodological individualism may be the analytical tool but still the choices and the turnings may have been the free gift of culture, socialisation and cumulative causation. Conservative capitalism is the *social* economy. The reader who concludes that suicide or madness remain the only unrestricted options open to the unfettered autonomy would do well to turn to the index to see if statistical probability has placed him in an at-risk category.

Economics is the study of capitalism: 'Economics is the study of a particular form of organization of human want-satisfying activity which has become prevalent in Western nations and spread over the greater part of the field of conduct. It is called free enterprise or the competitive system.' (Knight, 1921:9). What this book has argued is that economics is compelled by the very nature of its subject-matter to be the study of conservatism as well. Much of the technical mainstream deduces simplified propositions from hypothetical assumptions in emulation of the frictionless vacuum of classical mechanics. In so doing, the 'physicists' pushing out the 'sociologists', it has tended to drive the *conservatism* of capitalism into the footnotes if not into the related disciplines of politics, psychology, economic history, law and sociology. As Frank Knight writes: 'The mathematical economists have commonly been mathematicians first and economists afterward, disposed to oversimplify the data and underestimate the divergence between their premises and the facts of life.' (Knight, 1921:49). Such a divergence renders no service to the understanding of the capitalist system. What this book has therefore maintained is that the economy must be studied *as it is* and not modelled in the frictionless vacuum of *as it would be if*.

This book has sought to show that capitalist economies are hedged and marbled with conservative pressures. It has not sought to adjudicate on the implications for the wealth of nations of the common inheritance. On the one hand, conservatism can foster predictability and reliability. On the other hand, it can be a cause of complacency and replication. If knowledge were perfect, the past would not be needed as an indicator of last resort. If exchange were perfect, contracts and monitors would be the paid-for alternative to a parental guideline enunciated half a century before. Yet we start from here. Unable to generalise about information and aware of the kaleidoscopic nature of what the market can provide, the best we can do is to keep an open mind and to proceed strictly case-by-case.

Conservatism may or may not be a complement to capitalism. The uncertainty surrounding the contribution is inevitable given the difference in the orientation. Thus the efficiency of the capitalist market presupposes egotistical acquisitiveness and competitive possessiveness – but the stability of the conservative whole presupposes social peace and collective solidarity. The one maximand profit and utility, the other maximand acceptance and order, the possibility must be recognised that to pursue the capitalistic goal of dynamic gain-seeking can simultaneously be to imperil the conservative goal of contentment through fitting in. Rivalry can be a threat to harmony. Self-aggrandisement can be a threat to role-playing. Diversity can be a threat to establishment. Establishment can be a threat to diversity. In respects such as these, the two orientations may be said to be so different as to make the economic consequences of the mixed ethos all but impossible to forecast in advance.

Perhaps the capitalism will undermine the conservatism – consider the businessman whose competitive strategy involves the murder of his rival's staff. Perhaps the conservatism will impede the capitalism – consider the unimpeachable loyalty which treats the sale of a sinking share as if it were the betrayal of a rat deserting a long-lasting marriage. Perhaps the conservatism will reinforce the capitalism – consider the public good of self-policing honesty or the Keynesian normal value that sets a limit to volatility. Perhaps the capitalism will strengthen the conservatism – consider the One Nation Welfare State, paid for out of rapid growth. Given the differences in the orientation, it would be unscientific to assume that good conservatism will inevitably be the cause of good capitalism. This, however, must be borne in mind: a nation with a mixed goal-function might still be maximising felt welfare even where material efficiency had been traded in order to procure a higher-valued investment in identity, equity and location. Optimisation is a broad church. No one but the obsessively econocentric would take the survival of the fittest to mean the predestined victory of the *economically* fit. It has been some time since the Pope, the Dalai Lama or even the Prime Minister of Great Britain was selected solely on the promise of the Oxford Street sales.

Conservatism, in other words, is more than an instrument for getting goods into the shops. The attraction of conservatism is not just that it enables capitalism to raise living-standards but that it is somehow a desired final product in itself. Interactions are integrated in structured communities. Rules and conventions give the monads a life in common. The perception of external reality is granted a fulcrum in habit and experience. History-to-come is made less of a closed book through the reassuring counsel of history-that-was. Irrespective of their implications for the rate of economic growth, these characteristics are clearly positive features for which a rational shopper could well want to exchange a third annual holiday in the sun or a vintage Burgundy consumed with every meal. This is not to say that the holidays and the Burgundies are not valid choices in their own right, only that social institutions are choices too. In the words of J.M. Clark: 'The worst evil is to deny those incentives which represent what man recognizes as best in him. If selfish incentives cease to work, that is a failure: if unselfish incentives have no opportunity to work, that is a tragedy.' (Clark, 1936: 26). Capitalist capitalism or conservative capitalism, what is crucial is that sovereign consumers should be informed about the options and allowed to buy the bundle that best accords with their personal tastes.

Bibliography

Agassi, J. (1960), 'Methodological Individualism', *British Journal of Sociology*, Vol. 2, in J. O'Neill, ed., *Modes of Individualism and Collectivism* (London: Heinemann, 1973), pp. 185–212.

Akerlof, G.A. (1970), 'The Market for "Lemons"; Quality Uncertainty and the Market Mechanism', *Quarterly Journal of Economics*, Vol. 84, in Akerlof, *An Economic Theorist's Book of Tales*, infra, pp. 7–22.

Akerlof, G.A. (1976), 'The Economics of Caste and of the Rat Race and Other Woeful Tales', *Quarterly Journal of Economics*, Vol. 90, in Akerlof, *An Economic Theorist's Book of Tales*, infra, pp. 23–44.

Akerlof, G.A. (1980), 'A Theory of Social Custom of Which Unemployment May be One Consequence', *Quarterly Journal of Economics*, Vol. 94, in Akerlof, *An Economic Theorist's Book of Tales*, infra, pp. 69–99.

Akerlof, G.A. (1982), 'Labor Contracts as Partial Gift Exchange', *Quarterly Journal of Economics*, Vol. 97, in Akerlof, *An Economic Theorist's Book of Tales*, infra, pp. 145–74.

Akerlof, G.A. (1983), 'Loyalty Filters', *American Economic Review*, Vol. 73, in Akerlof, *An Economic Theorist's Book of Tales*, infra, pp. 175–91.

Akerlof, G.A. (1984), *An Economic Theorist's Book of Tales* (Cambridge: Cambridge University Press).

Akerlof, G.A. and Dickens, W.T. (1982), 'The Economic Consequences of Cognitive Dissonance', *American Economic Review*, Vol. 72, in Akerlof, *An Economic Theorist's Book of Tales*, op. cit., pp. 123–44.

Alchian, A.R. (1950), 'Uncertainty, Evolution, and Economic Theory', *Journal of Political Economy*, Vol. 58, pp. 211–22.

Arrow, K.J. (1962), 'Economic Welfare and the Allocation of Resources for Invention', in National Bureau of Economic Research, *The Rate and Direction of Inventive Activity: Economic and Social Factors*, in D.M. Lamberton, ed., *Economics of Information and Knowledge* (Harmondsworth: Penguin, 1971), pp. 141–59.

Arrow, K.J. (1963), 'Uncertainty and the Welfare Economics of Medical Care', *American Economic Review*, Vol. 53, in M.H. Cooper and A.J. Culyer, eds, *Health Economics* (Harmondsworth: Penguin, 1973), pp. 13–48.

Arrow, K.J. (1974), *The Limits of Organization* (New York: Norton).

Asch, S.E. (1952), *Social Psychology* (Oxford: Oxford University Press, 1987).

Axelrod, R. (1981), 'The Emergence of Cooperation among Egoists', *American Political Science Review*, Vol. 75, pp. 306–18.

Axelrod, R. (1984), *The Evolution of Cooperation* (New York: Basic Books).

Axelrod, R. (1986), 'An Evolutionary Approach to Norms', *American Political Science Review*, Vol. 80, pp. 1095–1111.

Ayres, C.E. (1944), *The Theory of Economic Progress*, 2nd edn (New York: Schocken, 1962).

Bagehot, W. (1873), *Lombard Street*, 9th edn (London: Kegan Paul, Trench, and Co., 1888).

Banfield, E.C. (1958), *The Moral Basis of a Backward Society* (Glencoe, Ill.: The Free Press).

Becker, G.S. (1962), 'Investment in Human Capital: a Theoretical Approach', *Journal of Political Economy*, Vol. 70, Supplement, pp. 9–49.

Becker, G.S. (1976), *The Economic Approach to Human Behavior* (Chicago: University of Chicago Press).

Becker, G.S. (1981), 'Altruism in the Family and Selfishness in the Market Place', *Economica*, Vol. 48, pp. 1–15.

Bell, D. (1976), *The Cultural Contradictions of Capitalism*, 2nd edn (London: Heinemann, 1979).

Ben-Porath, Y. (1980), 'The F-Connection: Families, Friends, and Firms and the Organization of Exchange', *Population and Development Review*, Vol. 6, pp. 1–30.

Bentham, J. (1780), *An Introduction to the Principles of Morals and Legislation* (Oxford: Clarendon Press, 1823).

Berlin, I. (1958), *Two Concepts of Liberty*, in his *Four Essays on Liberty* (Oxford: Oxford University Press, 1969), pp. 118–72.

Bevan, A. (1952), *In Place of Fear*, revised edn (London: MacGibbon and Kee, 1961).

Bevan, A. (1958), Speech in the House of Commons, 30 July, in *Parliamentary Debates* (*Hansard*), Cols 1382–98.

Blau, P.M. (1964), *Exchange and Power in Social Life* (New York: John Wiley and Sons).

Boulding, K.E. (1956), *The Image* (Ann Arbor: University of Michigan Press).

Boulding, K.E. (1966), 'The Economics of Knowledge and the Knowledge of Economics', *American Economic Review*, Vol. 56, in Lamberton, E*conomics of Information and Knowledge*, op. cit., pp. 21–36.

Bourdieu, P. (1980), 'Le Capital Social', *Actes de la Recherche en Sciences Sociales*, 31 janvier, pp. 2–3.

Brennan, H.G. and Buchanan, J.M. (1985), *The Reason of Rules* (Cambridge: Cambridge University Press).

Buchanan, J.M. (1975), 'The Samaritan's Dilemma', in E.S. Phelps, ed., *Altruism, Morality, and Economic Theory* (New York: Russell Sage Foundation), pp. 71–85.

Buchanan, J.M. (1977), *Freedom in Constitutional Contract* (College Station: Texas A and M Press).

Buchanan, J.M. (1979), *What Should Economists Do?* (Indianapolis: Liberty Press).

Buchanan, J.M. (1986), *Liberty, Market and State* (Brighton: Wheatsheaf).

Buchanan, J.M. and Tullock, G. (1962), *The Calculus of Consent* (Ann Arbor: University of Michigan Press).

Burke, E. (1790), *Reflections on the Revolution in France*, ed. by C.C. O'Brien (Harmondsworth: Penguin, 1968).

Burke, E. (1791), *Letter to a Member of the National Assembly*, in *Works and Correspondence of the Rt. Hon. Edmund Burke* (London: Rivington, 1852), Vol. IV, pp. 357–92.

Choi, Young Back (1993), *Paradigms and Conventions* (Ann Arbor: University of Michigan Press).

Clark, J.M. (1936), *Preface to Social Economics* (New York: Augustus M. Kelley, 1967).

Coase, R.H. (1937), 'The Nature of the Firm', *Economica*, n.s., Vol. 4, in his *The Firm, the Market and the Law*, infra, pp. 35–55.

Coase, R.H. (1988), *The Firm, the Market and the Law* (Chicago: University of Chicago Press).

Coleman, J.S. (1990), *Foundations of Social Theory* (Cambridge, Mass.: Belknap Press).

Collard, D. (1978), *Altruism and Economy* (Oxford: Martin Robertson).

Commons, J.R. (1934), *Institutional Economics* (New York: Macmillan).

Commons, J.R. (1950), *The Economics of Collective Action* (New York: Macmillan).

Darwin, C. (1859), *The Origin of Species*, ed. by J.W. Burrow (Harmondsworth: Penguin, 1968).

David, P.A. (1985), 'Clio and the Economics of QWERTY', *American Economic Review*, Vol. 75, pp. 332–7.

Dawkins, R. (1989), *The Selfish Gene*, 2nd edn (Oxford: Oxford University Press).

Dore, R. (1983), 'Goodwill and the Spirit of Market Capitalism', *British Journal of Sociology*, Vol. 34, pp. 459–82.

Douglas, M. (1987), *How Institutions Think* (London: Routledge and Kegan Paul).

Downs, A. (1957), *An Economic Theory of Democracy* (New York: Harper and Row).

Durkheim, E. (1893), *The Division of Labor in Society*, tr. by G. Simpson (New York: The Free Press, 1964).

Durkheim, E. (1895), *The Rules of Sociological Method*, tr. by S.A. Solovay and J.H. Mueller (New York: The Free Press, 1938).

Durkheim, E. (1897), *Suicide*, tr. by J.A. Spaulding and G. Simpson (London: Routledge and Kegan Paul, 1952).

Durkheim, E. (1912), *The Elementary Forms of the Religious Life*, tr. by J.W. Swain (London: George Allen and Unwin, 1915).

Durkheim, E. (1925), *Moral Education* tr. by E.K. Wilson and H. Schnurer (New York: The Free Press, 1961).

Earl, P. (1986), *Lifestyle Economics* (Brighton: Wheatsheaf Books).

Edgeworth, F.Y. (1881), *Mathematical Psychics* (London: C. Kegan Paul).

Einhorn, H.J. (1980), 'Learning from Experience and Suboptimal Rules in Decision Making', in T.S. Wallstein, ed. *Cognitive Processes in Choice and Decision Behavior*, in Kahneman, Slovic and Tversky, *Judgement under Uncertainty*, infra, pp. 268–83.

Elster, J. (1983), *Explaining Technical Change* (Cambridge: Cambridge University Press).

Elster, J. (1989), *The Cement of Society: a Study of Social Order* (Cambridge: Cambridge University Press).

Ely, R.T. (1893), *Outlines of Economics*, 4th edn (New York: Macmillan, 1928).

Etzioni, A. (1988), *The Moral Dimension* (New York: The Free Press).

Etzioni, A. (1995), *The Spirit of Community* (London: Fontana).

Ferguson, A. (1767), *An Essay on the History of Civil Society*, ed. by D. Forbes (Edinburgh: Edinburgh University Press, 1966).

Festinger, L. (1954), 'A Theory of Social Comparison Processes', *Human Relations*, Vol. 7, in H.H. Hyman and E. Singer, eds, *Readings in Reference Group Theory and Research* (New York: The Free Press, 1968), pp. 123–46.

Festinger, L. (1957), *A Theory of Cognitive Dissonance* (London: Tavistock, 1962).

Frank, R.H. (1985), *Choosing the Right Pond* (Oxford: Oxford University Press).

Frank, R.H. (1988), *Passions within Reason* (New York: Norton).

Freud, S. (1930), 'Civilization and its Discontents', in *The Complete Psychological Works of Sigmund Freud*, Vol. XXI (London: Hogarth Press, 1961), pp. 64–145.

Frey, B.S. (1992), *Economics as a Science of Human Behaviour* (Boston: Kluwer).

Friedman, M. (1953), 'The Methodology of Positive Economics', in his *Essays in Positive Economics* (Chicago: University of Chicago Press), pp. 3–43.

Friedman, M. (1962), *Capitalism and Freedom* (Chicago: University of Chicago Press).

Friedman, M. (1968), 'The Role of Monetary Policy', *American Economic Review*, Vol. 58, in P.G. Korliras and R.S. Thorn, eds, *Modern Macroeconomics* (New York: Harper and Row, 1979), pp. 91–102.

Fukuyama, F. (1992), *The End of History and the Last Man* (London: Hamish Hamilton).

Fukuyama, F. (1996), *Trust* (Harmondsworth: Penguin).

Galbraith, J.K. (1958), *The Affluent Society*, 2nd edn (Harmondsworth: Penguin, 1970).

Galbraith, J.K. (1965), *Economic Development* (Cambridge, Mass.: Harvard University Press).

Galbraith, J.K. (1967), *The New Industrial State*, 2nd edn (Harmondsworth: Penguin, 1974).

Galbraith, J.K. (1973), *Economics and the Public Purpose* (Harmondsworth: Penguin, 1975).

Gauthier, D. (1986), *Morals by Agreement* (Oxford: Clarendon Press).

Granovetter, M. (1985), 'Economic Action and Social Structure: a Theory of Embeddedness', *American Journal of Sociology*, Vol. 91, pp. 481–510.

Gray, J. (1993), *Beyond the New Right* (London: Routledge).

Gray, J. (1995), *Liberalism*, 2nd edn (Buckingham: Open University Press).

Hall, R.L. and Hitch, C.J. (1939), 'Price Theory and Business Behaviour', *Oxford Economic Papers*, Vol. 2, in T. Wilson and P.W.S. Andrews, eds, *Oxford Studies in the Price Mechanism* (Oxford: Clarendon Press, 1951), pp. 107–38.

Hargreaves Heap, S. (1989), *Rationality in Economics* (Oxford: Basil Blackwell).

Hayek, F.A. (1949), *Individualism and Economic Order* (London: Routledge and Kegan Paul).

Hayek, F.A. (1960), *The Constitution of Liberty* (London: Routledge and Kegan Paul).

Hayek, F.A. (1967), *Studies in Philosophy, Politics and Economics* (London: Routledge and Kegan Paul).

Hayek, F.A. (1973), *Law, Legislation and Liberty*, Vol. I: *Rules and Order* (London: Routledge and Kegan Paul).

Hayek, F.A. (1979), *Law, Legislation and Liberty*, Vol. III: *The Political Order of a Free People* (London: Routledge and Kegan Paul).

Hayek, F.A. (1988), *The Fatal Conceit* (London: Routledge and Kegan Paul).

Heiner, R.A. (1983), 'The Origin of Predictable Behavior', *American Economic Review*, Vol. 73, pp. 560–95.

Hirsch, F. (1977), *Social Limits to Growth* (London: Routledge and Kegan Paul).

Hirschman, A.O. (1982), *Shifting Involvements* (Oxford: Basil Blackwell).

Hirshleifer, J. (1977), 'Economics from a Biological Viewpoint', *Journal of Law and Economics*, Vol. 20, pp. 1–52.

Hobbes, T. (1651), *Leviathan*, ed. by C.B. Macpherson (Harmondsworth: Penguin, 1968).

Hodgson, G.M. (1988), *Economics and Institutions* (Cambridge: Polity Press).

Hodgson, G.M. (1993), *Economics and Evolution* (Ann Arbor: University of Michigan Press).

Hoffman, M.L. (1981), 'Is Altruism Part of Human Nature?', *Journal of Personality and Social Psychology*, Vol. 40, pp. 121–37.

Homans, G.C. (1961), *Social Behaviour: Its Elementary Forms* (London: Routledge and Kegan Paul).

Iannaccone, L.R. (1997), 'Toward an Economic Theory of "Fundamentalism"', *Journal of Institutional and Theoretical Economics*, Vol. 153, pp. 100–21.

Jevons, W.S. (1871), *The Theory of Political Economy*, ed. by R.D.C. Black (Harmondsworth: Penguin, 1970).

Kahneman, D. and Tversky, A. (1973), 'On the Psychology of Prediction', *Psychological Review*, Vol. 80, in D. Kahneman, P. Slovic and A. Tversky, eds, *Judgement under Uncertainty: Heuristics and Biases* (Cambridge: Cambridge University Press, 1982), pp. 48–68.

Kahneman, D. and Tversky, A. (1979), 'Prospect Theory: an Analysis of Decision under Risk', *Econometrica*, Vol. 47, pp. 263–91.

Kahneman, D., Knetsch, J.L. and Thaler, R.H. (1986), 'Fairness as a Constraint on Profit Seeking: Entitlements in the Market', *American Economic Review*, Vol. 76, pp. 728–41.

Kant, I. (1785), *Groundwork of the Metaphysic of Morals*, tr. by H.J. Paton, in H.J. Paton, ed., *The Moral Law* (London: Hutchinson, 1961).

Keynes, J.M. (1925), 'Alfred Marshall, 1842–1924', in A.C. Pigou, ed., *Memorials of Alfred Marshall* (New York: Augustus M. Kelley, 1966), pp. 1–65.

Keynes, J.M. (1936), *The General Theory of Employment, Interest and Money*, in *The Collected Writings of John Maynard Keynes*, Vol. VIII (London: Macmillan, 1973).

Keynes, J.M. (1937), 'The General Theory of Employment', *Quarterly Journal of Economics*, Vol. 51, in *The Collected Writings of John Maynard Keynes*, Vol. XIV (London: Macmillan, 1973), pp. 109–23.

Knetsch, J.L. and Sinden, J.A. (1984), 'Willingness to Pay and Compensation Demanded: Experimental Evidence of an Unexpected Disparity in Measures of Value', *Quarterly Journal of Economics*, Vol. 99, pp. 507–21.

Knight, F.H. (1921), *Risk, Uncertainty and Profit* (Boston: Houghton Mifflin).

Knight, F.H. (1922), 'Ethics and the Economic Interpretation', *Quarterly Journal of Economics*, Vol. 36, in his *The Ethics of Competition and Other Essays* (Freeport: Books for Libraries Press, 1969), pp. 19–40.

Kuran, T. (1995), *Private Truths, Public Lies* (Cambridge, Mass.: Harvard University Press).

Lamberton, D.M. (1971), 'Introduction', in his *Economics of Information and Knowledge*, op. cit., pp. 7–17.

Latsis, S.J. (1972), 'Situational Determinism in Economics', *British Journal for the Philosophy of Science*, Vol. 25, pp. 207–45.

Latsis, S.J. (1976), 'A Research Programme in Economics', in Latsis, ed., *Method and Appraisal in Economics* (Cambridge: Cambridge University Press), pp. 1–41.

Leibenstein, H. (1976), *Beyond Economic Man* (Cambridge, Mass.: Harvard University Press).

Leijonhufvud, A. (1971), *Keynes and the Classics* (London: Institute of Economic Affairs).

Lewis, D.K. (1969), *Convention: a Philosophical Study* (Cambridge, Mass.: Harvard University Press).

Loasby, B.J. (1976), *Choice, Complexity and Ignorance* (Cambridge: Cambridge University Press).

Loasby, B.J. (1991), *Equilibrium and Evolution* (Manchester: Manchester University Press).

Locke, J. (1690), *An Essay Concerning the True Original, Extent and End of Civil Government (Second Treatise on Civil Government)*, in E. Barker, ed., *Social Contract: Essays by Locke, Hume and Rousseau* (London: Oxford University Press, 1947), pp. 1–206.

Loury, G.C. (1977), 'A Dynamic Theory of Racial Income Differences', in P.A. Wallace and A.M. LaMond, eds, *Women, Minorities and Employment Discrimination* (Lexington, Mass.: D.C. Heath), pp. 153–86.

Luce, R.D. and Raiffa, H. (1957), *Games and Decisions* (New York: Wiley).

Lukes, S. (1973), *Individualism* (Oxford: Basil Blackwell).

Lutz, M.A. and Lux, K. (1979), *The Challenge of Humanistic Economics* (Menlo Park: Benjamin/Cummings).

Macpherson, C.B. (1962), *The Political Theory of Possessive Individualism* (Oxford: Oxford University Press).

Malinowski, B. (1922), *Argonauts of the Western Pacific* (London: Routledge and Kegan Paul).

Mandeville, B. (1714), *The Fable of the Bees*, ed. by F.B. Kaye (Oxford: Clarendon Press, 1924).

Margolis, H. (1982), *Selfishness, Altruism and Rationality* (Cambridge: Cambridge University Press).

Margolis, H. (1987), *Patterns, Thinking, and Cognition* (Chicago: University of Chicago Press).

Marshall, A. (1873), 'The Future of the Working Classes', in Pigou, *Memorials of Alfred Marshall*, op. cit., pp. 101–18.

Marshall, A. (1875), 'Some Features of American Industry', in J.K. Whitaker, ed., *The Early Economic Writings of Alfred Marshall 1867–1890*, Vol. II (London: Macmillan, 1975), pp. 352–77.

Marshall, A. (1879) (with M.P. Marshall), *The Economics of Industry*, 2nd edn (London: Macmillan, 1881).

Marshall, A. (1885), 'The Present Position of Economics', in Pigou, *Memorials of Alfred Marshall*, op. cit., pp. 152–74.

Marshall, A. (1890), *Principles of Economics*, 8th edn (1920) (London: Macmillan, 1949).

Marshall, A. (1919), *Industry and Trade*, 4th edn (London: Macmillan, 1923).

Marx, K. (1844a), 'Contribution to the Critique of Hegel's Philosophy of Right. Introduction', in *Karl Marx: Early Writings*, ed. by T.B. Bottomore (London: G.A. Watts, 1963).

Marx, K. (1844b). *Economic and Philosophic Manuscripts of 1844*, tr. by M. Milligan (London: Lawrence and Wishart, 1973).

Marx, K. (1852), *The Eighteenth Brumaire of Louis Bonaparte*, in *Karl Marx: Selected Works*, Vol. II (London: Lawrence and Wishart, 1942), pp. 311–426.

Marx, K. (1859), Preface to *A Contribution to the Critique of Political Economy*, in *Karl Marx: Early Writings*, ed. by L. Colletti (Harmondsworth: Penguin, 1975).

Marx, K. (1867), *Capital*, Vol. I (Moscow: Foreign Languages Publishing House, 1961).

Marx, K. (1875), *Critique of the Gotha Programme*, in *Karl Marx: Selected Works*, op. cit., Vol. II, pp. 505–601.

Marx, K. and Engels, F. (1845–6), *The German Ideology*, ed. by C.J. Arthur (London: Lawrence and Wishart, 1970).

Marx, K. and Engels, F. (1848), *Manifesto of the Communist Party*, in *Karl Marx: Selected Works*, op. cit., Vol. I, pp. 189–241.

Maslow, A. (1954), *Motivation and Personality*, 2nd edn (New York: Harper and Row, 1970).

Mauss, M. (1950), *The Gift*, tr. by W.D. Halls (London: Routledge, 1990).

Mayo, E. (1949), *The Social Problems of an Industrial Civilization* (London: Routledge and Kegan Paul).

Menger, C. (1871), *Principles of Economics* tr. by J. Dingwall and B.F. Hoselitz (New York: New York University Press, 1976).

Menger, C. (1883), *Investigations into the Method of the Social Sciences with Special Reference to Economics*, tr. by F.J. Nock (New York: New York University Press, 1985).

Mill, J.S. (1844), *Essays on Some Unsettled Questions of Political Economy* (London: John W. Parker).

Mill, J.S. (1848), *Principles of Political Economy*, 7th edn, ed. by W.J. Ashley (London: Longmans, Green, 1909).

Mill, J.S. (1859), *On Liberty*, ed. by G. Himmelfarb (Harmondsworth: Penguin, 1974).

Miller, D. (1988), 'Altruism and the Welfare State', in J.D. Moon, ed., *Responsibility, Rights and Welfare: the Theory of the Welfare State* (Boulder: Westview Press), pp. 163–88.

Mises, Ludwig von (1949), *Human Action*, 3rd edn (Chicago: Contemporary Books, 1966).

Mises, Ludwig von (1962), *The Ultimate Foundation of Economic Science*, 2nd edn (Kansas City: Sheed Andrews and McMeel, 1978).

Muth, J.F. (1961), 'Rational Expectations and the Theory of Price Movements', *Econometrica*, Vol. 29, pp. 315–35.

Nelson, R.R. and Winter, S.G. (1982), *An Evolutionary Theory of Economic Change* (Cambridge, Mass.: Harvard University Press).

North, D.C. (1981), *Structure and Change in Economic History* (New York: Norton).

North, D.C. (1990), *Institutions, Institutional Change and Economic Performance* (Cambridge: Cambridge University Press).

Novak, M. (1982), *The Spirit of Democratic Capitalism* (London: The IEA Health and Welfare Unit, 1991).

Nozick, R. (1974), *Anarchy, State and Utopia* (New York: Basic Books).

Oakeshott, M. (1962), *Rationalism in Politics* (London: Methuen).

Olson, M. (1965), *The Logic of Collective Action* (Cambridge, Mass.: Harvard University Press).

Olson, M. (1969), 'The Relationship Between Economics and the Other Social Sciences', in S.M. Lipset, ed., *Politics and the Social Sciences* (New York: Oxford University Press), pp. 137–62.

Olson, M. (1982), *The Rise and Decline of Nations* (New Haven: Yale University Press).

Ormerod, P. (1995), *The Death of Economics* (London: Faber and Faber).

Parsons, T. and Smelser, N.J. (1956), *Economy and Society* (London: Routledge and Kegan Paul).

Phelps, E.S. (1975), 'Introduction' to Phelps, *Altruism, Morality, and Economic Theory*, op. cit., pp. 1–9.

Pigou, A.C. (1920), *The Economics of Welfare*, 4th edn (1932) (London: Macmillan, 1960).

Polanyi, K. (1935), 'The Essence of Fascism', in J. Lewis, K. Polanyi and D.K. Kitchin, eds, *Christianity and the Social Revolution* (London: Victor Gollancz), pp. 359–94.

Polanyi, K. (1944), *The Great Transformation* (Boston: Beacon Press, 1957).

Polanyi, K. (1947), 'Our Obsolete Market Mentality', *Commentary*, Vol. 3, pp. 109–17.

Polanyi, K. (1957a), 'Aristotle Discovers the Economy', in K. Polanyi, C.M. Arensberg and H.W. Pearson, eds, *Trade and Market in the Early Empires* (New York: The Free Press), pp. 64–94.

Polanyi, K. (1957b), 'The Economy as Instituted Process', in *Trade and Market in the Early Empires*, op. cit., pp. 243–70.

Polanyi, K. (1977), *The Livelihood of Man*, ed. by H.W. Pearson (New York: Academic Press).

Polanyi, M. (1958), *Personal Knowledge* (London: Routledge and Kegan Paul).

Polanyi, M. (1967), *The Tacit Dimension* (London: Routledge and Kegan Paul).

Popper, K. (1945), *The Open Society and Its Enemies*, Vol. 2: *Hegel and Marx*, 5th edn (London: Routledge and Kegan Paul, 1966).

Popper, K. (1963), *Conjectures and Refutations*, 2nd edn (London: Routledge and Kegan Paul).

Popper, K. (1972), *Objective Knowledge* (Oxford: Clarendon Press).

Quattrone, G.A. and Tversky, A. (1988), 'Contrasting Rational and Psychological Analysis of Political Choice', *American Political Science Review*, Vol. 82, pp. 719–36.

Rae, J. (1895), *Life of Adam Smith* (New York: Augustus M. Kelley, 1965).

Rawls, J. (1972), *A Theory of Justice* (Oxford: Oxford University Press).

Reisman, D.A. (1990), *Theories of Collective Action: Downs, Olson and Hirsch* (London: Macmillan).

Ricardo, D. (1817), *On the Principles of Political Economy and Taxation*, 3rd edn, ed. by P. Sraffa and M.H. Dobb (Cambridge: Cambridge University Press, 1951).

Riesman, D. (1954), *Individualism Reconsidered* (New York: The Free Press, 1964).

Robbins, L. (1933), *An Essay on the Nature and Significance of Economic Science*, 2nd edn (London: Macmillan, 1935).

Robertson, D.K. (1956), *Economic Commentaries* (London: Staples Press).

Röpke, W. (1944), *The Moral Foundations of Civil Society*, tr. by C.S. Fox (New Brunswick: Transaction, 1996).

Rothbard, M.N. (1962), *Man, Economy, and State: a Treatise on Economic Principles* (Princeton: Van Nostrand).

Rousseau, J.-J. (1762), *The Social Contract*, in Barker, ed., *Social Contract*, op. cit., pp. 237–440.

Russell, T. and Thaler, R.H. (1985), 'The Relevance of Quasi Rationality in Competitive Markets', *American Economic Review*, Vol. 75, pp. 1071–82.

Sahlins, M.D. (1972), *Stone Age Economics* (London: Tavistock).

Sahlins, M.D. (1976), *Culture and Practical Reason* (Chicago: University of Chicago Press).

Schlicht, E. (1998), *On Custom in the Economy* (Oxford: Clarendon Press).

Schotter, A. (1981), *The Economic Theory of Social Institutions* (Cambridge: Cambridge University Press).

Schumpeter, J.A. (1942), *Capitalism, Socialism and Democracy*, 5th edn (London: George Allen and Unwin, 1976).

Sen, A. (1977), 'Rational Fools: a Critique of the Behavioural Foundations of Economic Theory', *Philosophy and Public Affairs*, Vol. 6, in his *Choice, Welfare and Measurement* (Oxford: Basil Blackwell, 1982), pp. 84–106.

Shackle, G.L.S. (1967), *The Years of High Theory* (Cambridge: Cambridge University Press).

Shackle, G.L.S. (1972), *Epistemics and Economics* (Cambridge: Cambridge University Press).

Simon, H.A. (1955), 'A Behavioral Model of Rational Choice', *Quarterly Journal of Economics*, Vol. 69, in his *Models of Man*, infra, pp. 241–60.

Simon, H.A. (1956), 'Rational Choice and the Structure of the Environment', *Psychological Review*, Vol. 63, in his *Models of Man*, infra, pp. 261–73.

Simon, H.A. (1957), *Models of Man* (New York: Wiley).

Simon, H.A. (1959), 'Theories of Decision-Making in Economics and Behavioral Science', *American Economic Review*, Vol. 49, pp. 253–83.

Simon, H.A. (1965), *Administrative Behavior*, 2nd edn (Glencoe: The Free Press).

Simon, H.A. (1976), 'From Substantive to Procedural Rationality', in Latsis, *Method and Appraisal in Economics*, op. cit., pp. 129–48.

Simon, H.A. (1978), 'Rationality as Process and as Product of Thought', *American Economic Review (Papers and Proceedings)*, Vol. 68, pp. 1–16.

Simon, H.A. (1979), 'Rational Decision Making in Business Organizations', *American Economic Review*, Vol. 69, pp. 493–513.

Simon, H.A. (1986), 'Rationality in Psychology and Economics', in R.M. Hogarth and M. Reder, eds, *Rational Choice: the Contrast Between Economics and Psychology* (Chicago: University of Chicago Press), pp. 25–40.

Smith, A. (1759), *The Theory of Moral Sentiments*, 6th edn (New York: Augustus M. Kelley, 1966).

Smith, A. (1776), *The Wealth of Nations*, ed. by E. Cannan (London: Methuen, 1961).

Stanfield, J.R. (1986), *The Economic Thought of Karl Polanyi* (London: Macmillan).

Stigler, G.J. (1961), 'The Economics of Information', *Journal of Political Economy*, Vol. 69, in Lamberton, *Economics of Information and Knowledge*, op. cit., pp. 61–82.

Swedberg, R. (1990), *Economics and Sociology* (Princeton: Princeton University Press).

Tawney, R.H. (1921), *The Acquisitive Society* (London: Fontana Books, 1961).

Tawney, R.H. (1926), *Religion and the Rise of Capitalism* (Harmondsworth: Penguin, 1938).

Tawney, R.H. (1937), 'A Note on Christianity and the Social Order', in his *The Attack and Other Papers* (London: George Allen and Unwin, 1953), pp. 167–92.

Thaler, R.H. (1985), 'Mental Accounting and Consumer Choice', *Marketing Science*, Vol. 4, pp. 199–214.

Thaler, R.H. (1992), *The Winner's Curse: Paradoxes and Anomalies of Economic Life* (New York: The Free Press).

Thurow, L.C. (1983), *Dangerous Currents* (New York: Random House).

Titmuss, R.M. (1963), *Essays on 'The Welfare State'*, 2nd edn (London: George Allen and Unwin).

Titmuss, R.M. (1964), *The Health Services of Tanganyika* (London: Pitman Medical).

Titmuss, R.M. (1970), *The Gift Relationship* (Harmondsworth: Penguin, 1973).

Tocqueville, Alexis de (1835, Vol. I; 1840, Vol. II), *Democracy in America*, tr. by H. Reeve (New York: Schocken, 1961).

Tversky, A. and Kahneman, D. (1973), 'Availability: a Heuristic for Judging Frequency and Probability', *Cognitive Psychology*, Vol. 4, in Kahneman, Slovic and Tversky, *Judgement under Uncertainty: Heuristics and Biases*, op. cit., pp. 163–78.

Tversky, A. and Kahneman, D. (1974), 'Judgement under Uncertainty: Heuristics and Biases', *Science*, Vol. 185, in Kahneman, Slovic and Tversky, *Judgement under Uncertainty: Heuristics and Biases*, op. cit., pp. 3–20.

Tversky, A. and Kahneman, D. (1981), 'The Framing of Decisions and the Psychology of Choice', *Science*, Vol. 211, pp. 453–8.

Ullmann-Margalit, E. (1977), *The Emergence of Norms* (Oxford: Clarendon Press).

Vanberg, V.J. (1986), 'Spontaneous Market Order and Social Rules: a Critical Examination of F.A. Hayek's Theory of Cultural Evolution', *Economics and Philosophy*, Vol. 2, in his *Rules and Choice in Economics* (London: Routledge, 1994), pp. 77–94.

Vanberg, V.J. (1988), 'Rules and Choice in Economics and Sociology', *Jahrbuch für Neue Politische Ökonomie*, Vol. 7, in his *Rules and Choice in Economics*, op. cit., pp. 11–24.

Veblen, T.B. (1899), *The Theory of the Leisure Class* (London: George Allen and Unwin, 1970).

Veblen, T.B. (1904), *The Theory of Business Enterprise* (Clifton, N.J.: Augustus M. Kelley, 1975).

Veblen, T.B. (1914), *The Instinct of Workmanship* (New York: Augustus M. Kelley, 1964).

Veblen, T.B. (1919), *The Place of Science in Modern Civilisation and Other Essays* (London: Routledge/Thoemmes Press, 1994).

Veblen, T.B. (1943) *Essays in Our Changing Order*, ed. by L. Ardzrooni (New York: The Viking Press).

Weber, M. (1904–5), *The Protestant Ethic and the Spirit of Capitalism*, tr. by T. Parsons (London: Unwin, 1930).

Weber, M. (1947), *The Theory of Social and Economic Organization*, tr. by A.M. Henderson and T. Parsons (New York: The Free Press).

Weber, M. (1948), *From Max Weber*, ed. by H.H. Gerth and C.W. Mills (London: Routledge and Kegan Paul).

Weinstein, N.D. (1980), 'Unrealistic Optimism about Future Life Events', *Journal of Personality and Social Psychology*, Vol. 39, pp. 806–20.

White, H.C. (1981), 'Where Do Markets Come From?', *American Journal of Sociology*, Vol. 87, pp. 517–47.

Wicksteed, P.H. (1910), *The Common Sense of Political Economy*, ed. by L. Robbins (London: Routledge and Kegan Paul, 1933).

Williamson, O.E. (1975), *Markets and Hierarchies* (New York: The Free Press).

Williamson, O.E. (1985), *The Economic Institutions of Capitalism* (New York: The Free Press).

Wilson, E.O. (1975), *Sociobiology: the New Synthesis* (Cambridge, Mass.: Belknap Press).

Index